We Used to Own

THE BRONX

DEUS AMICI ET NOS

excelsior editions

AN IMPRINT OF STATE UNIVERSITY OF NEW YORK PRESS

We Used to Own

THE BRONX

Memoirs of a Former Debutante

EVE PELL

PUBLISHED BY STATE UNIVERSITY OF NEW YORK PRESS, ALBANY

© 2009 State University of New York

For information, contact State University of New York Press,
www.sunypress.edu

Production and book design, Laurie Searl
Marketing, Susan M. Petrie

Library of Congress Cataloging-in-Publication Data

Pell, Eve.
  We used to own the Bronx : memoirs of a former debutante / Eve Pell.
    p. cm.
  ISBN 978-1-4384-2497-2 (hardcover : alk. paper)
  1. Pell, Eve. 2. Pell family. 3. Middle Atlantic States—Biography.
I. Title.

  CT275.P5224A3 2009
  974.092—dc22

  [B]   2008024274

10 9 8 7 6 5 4 3 2 1

this book is for Cooky

Contents

Acknowledgments

A lthough I have used the correct names for most people, I have changed a few to avoid undue embarrassment.

During the decade it took to finish this book, many people gave generously of their time and attention. Some helped me gather information, others read and criticized, some held my hand. I could never have done this without them. In any family, people have different perceptions. Responsibility for any errors or omissions, of course, is mine. This memoir reflects my own recollections and experiences.

Among the family members, I thank Senator Claiborne Pell, Anthony Pell, Christopher Hartford Pell, Nancy Pell Hayden, Mary Leigh Pell Whitmer, Robert Pell De Chame, Stephanie Pell De Chame, James Hazard, Cathe Rosenberg, as well as the late Katharine Mortimer Blaine and the late Robert Livingston Pell.

For historical material: Nicholas Westbrook and the staff at Fort Ticonderoga, Sue Swanson, former Pelham historian and Blake Bell of

Pelham, Robert Engel and the staff at the Bartow Pell Mansion Museum, the late Alfred England, Cass Shaw, the New York Genealogical and Biographical Society, and David Le Beau of Chevron.

Readers and critics include: Eleanor Bertino, Jonathan Dann, Charles Farnsworth, Elizabeth Farnsworth, Michael Castleman, Michael Hoy, Valerie Miner, Sherry Reson, Susan Leon, the Sewing Circle, Susan Trott and the Saloonistas, and the incomparable Peter Shaplen.

For encouragement: Adam Hochschild, Honor Moore, John D. Soutter, Howard Junker of ZZYZZVA, my office-mates in North Beach, my stubbornly loyal agent Ellen Levine, and the late authors Jessica Mitford and Don Carpenter. Special thanks to the people at SUNY Press. Blue Mountain Center awarded me a residency and never complained about how long the book took to get finished.

Prologue

In 1654, my forefather Thomas Pell, surgeon and fur trader, bought a large tract of wilderness from a council of Native American sachems. When, later on, as proprietor of this chunk of what is now the Bronx and Westchester County, he was granted the Manor of Pelham by the British crown, the seed was planted that set my family apart from ordinary people and bestowed upon me a birthright that included a silver spoon and the Pell pearls.

Pell Street in New York City is named for us, and we have the right to be buried in Manhattan's Marble Cemetery. When we ask for it, the city of New Rochelle honors an old contract by presenting us with a feudal tribute of one "fatt" calf. Besides a family tree dating back to the thirteenth century, we Pells owned our private piece of American history, Fort Ticonderoga. I was related by marriage to the family of Lord Curzon, last Viceroy of India, as well as Harrimans, Fishes, and Stuyvesants. Modern-day relatives are prominent in politics, society columns, and obscure racquets sports played only in private clubs.

It's not all aristocratic fluff: Pell grants, advocated by my cousin Claiborne when he was senator from Rhode Island, make it possible for people with low incomes to attend college. His father, my great-uncle Bertie, played an important role in the post–World War II campaign to have genocide recognized as a crime against humanity.

Because of this ancestry and my family's position in New York's elite Four Hundred, I was raised as American nobility, part of the nation's crème de la crème. For a long time, I cheerfully accepted this: It never occurred to me that my family's tastes, attitudes, and ways of doing things weren't what everyone would want, if only they could have it. My mother, the most beautiful debutante of 1935, always was served breakfast in bed. President Franklin D. Roosevelt, my stepfather's godfather, sent us peanuts at Christmas time.

A major source of our money was the oldest tobacco business in the United States, the P. Lorillard Company, founded in 1760. (The other source was wedlock: since Thomas Pell, men in the family have married rich women.) As you might imagine, we are critical of almost everybody, including our own relatives when they are perceived not to measure up.

But our upper-classness, which one might think liberated us through wealth and privilege, brought with it a very closed-minded ethos. Certain things were "not done" just because they were "not done," no further explanation necessary. We who happened to be born white and upper-class on America's East Coast were raised in a culture that is extremely private, that worships "family," and does not tolerate criticism. We grow up feeling entitled and more deserving than others.

My mother, who suffered much of her life from a series of ailments from arthritis to migraine headaches to colitis, considered herself a very finely tuned machine—so sensitive that she deserves the best possible medical attention. She was a Ferrari, an exquisite racing engine. The lower classes, in her view neither so sensitive nor so finely tuned—were mere Chevys and Fords.

But for all that we were an old family, our values were curiously un-American. Horatio Alger, for example, would not have been welcome in our circle, since we looked down on people who actually made their own money (after we did) as "latecomers." When I discovered that a great-grandfather had succeeded as a hustling entrepreneur in the early days of the California oil business, my Aunt Goody refused to believe it. She insisted that Standard Oil, where he was an executive, had falsified company history.

We took for granted a system antithetical to the American dream: instead of sons outdoing fathers through better education and diligent endeavor, fathers lived better than their children. Instead of ascending steadily into wealth and status, families like ours gently declined. Once-huge fortunes were divided among offspring who had progressively less money, fewer servants, smaller houses, and, by the time my generation came along, not even their own trust funds—we had to depend on our parents for handouts.

To maintain their extraordinary veneer of privilege, my family modeled itself on the British upper crust, with all its Bertie Wooster and Jeeves absurdity, including the callousness that earned us WASPs the nickname "God's Frozen People."

A boarding school classmate of mine told me about the childhood game called "Club" that she played at private school in first grade. "The point of Club was that two or three girls would belong and gather under the sliding board at recess. Then another one would ask, 'Can I belong?' The girls would say 'No.' The rejected child would have to go away. That game of Club was a metaphor for the way we lived our whole upper-class lives."

I grew up nicknamed Topsy in a family that included cousins and aunts called Pookie, Chuckie, Goody, and Tinkie. My mother named me Eve after herself, but I needed to be called something else since otherwise she would likely be known as Big Eve while I was Little Eve. And, for a woman who prided herself on being slender and beautiful, that would not have done. So, since I had dark skin and curly hair, my father, whom I called Clarry, decided to name me after the "pickaninny" in *Uncle Tom's Cabin*.

Following the family pattern, I grew into a snobbish foxhunting debutante who went to private schools, had maids to make my bed and do my laundry. But while I delighted in whirling around ballrooms in a beautiful long dress and galloping across the countryside on my thoroughbred, as I grew older, the silver spoon to which I was born began to taste bad. I began to see that privilege can have corrosive effects on human relations. In addition to well-mannered gentlemen and ladies, the basic training for membership in our caste caused considerable collateral damage—alcoholism and suicide.

As I ventured into the world outside the walls within which I had been raised, I began to see ways of life, quite different from mine, that looked appealing and far more humane than what I had grown up with. Gradually, as the 1950s turned into the 1960s (I graduated from college in 1958) and I moved from the East Coast to San Francisco, my attitudes began to change. Inch by inch, and then all at once, I broke out of the role for which I had been trained.

With zero political experience, by chance and inclination, I joined with leftist revolutionaries and wannabes intent on overturning capitalist society— my people. Doors opened before me, providing opportunities to escape the comfortable but unsatisfying world of my young married set. Heedless of consequences and, I thought, headed for freedom and self-realization, I was soon out of my depth and confused by the violence and death I encountered. Finally, I began to realize that, as a person, I could be more than the demands of those around me. I needed to find something of my own.

But the more I came into my own and thought for myself, the less my father liked me. I had violated his comfort zone of private men's clubs and Harvard reunions, which infuriated him. He threatened to disinherit me if I wrote about him and the family. I had become a black sheep.

Throughout my life, I have found social class to be a confusing and prickly issue. I have been proud of my background and mortified by it; I have run from it and embraced it, conformed and rebelled. My relatives include bigots, humanitarians, eccentrics, athletes, and ordinary people, most of them infused with a strong sense that they are aristocrats. Like them, I love it that our family used to own a manor in colonial America. There is something solid in knowing that we were here at our nation's beginning and in tracing the ups and downs of the family through different periods of U.S. history. But while the family forms a sort of bulwark against time, a base of permanence in a world of flux, it exacts a terrible price.

As I was growing up in the tradition-bound East Coast in the 1940s and 50s, "out West" was a semi-mythical place where people were free and class distinctions didn't count. I remember once, during a period of fighting with my mother, absent-mindedly scribbling, on the inside page of the phone book in her bedroom, places where I had lived up till that point.

Old Westbury, West Hills Road, West Grove, Pembroke West.

Underneath, I jotted, *"Very West Person."*

My mother evidently noticed my doodling, and, as I saw when I picked up the phone book some time later, added her own observation: *"Maybe that's the trouble."*

We Used to Own

THE BRONX

DEUS AMICI ET NOS

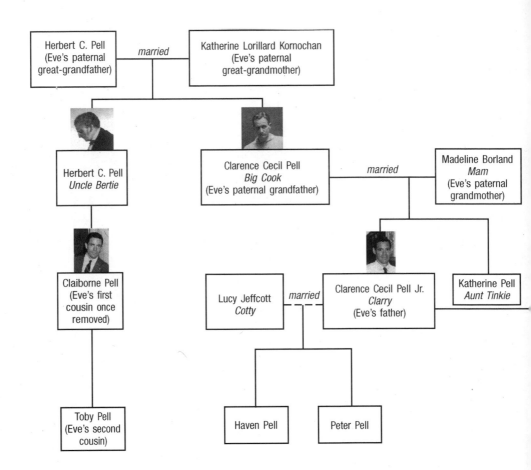

Herbert C. Pell
(Eve's paternal
great-grandfather)

married

Katherine Lorillard Kornochan
(Eve's paternal
great-grandmother)

Herbert C. Pell
Uncle Bertie

Clarence Cecil Pell
Big Cook
(Eve's paternal grandfather)

married

Madeline Borland
Mam
(Eve's paternal
grandmother)

Claiborne Pell
(Eve's first
cousin once
removed)

Lucy Jeffcott
Cotty

married

Clarence Cecil Pell Jr.
Clarry
(Eve's father)

Katherine Pell
Aunt Tinkie

Toby Pell
(Eve's second
cousin)

Haven Pell

Peter Pell

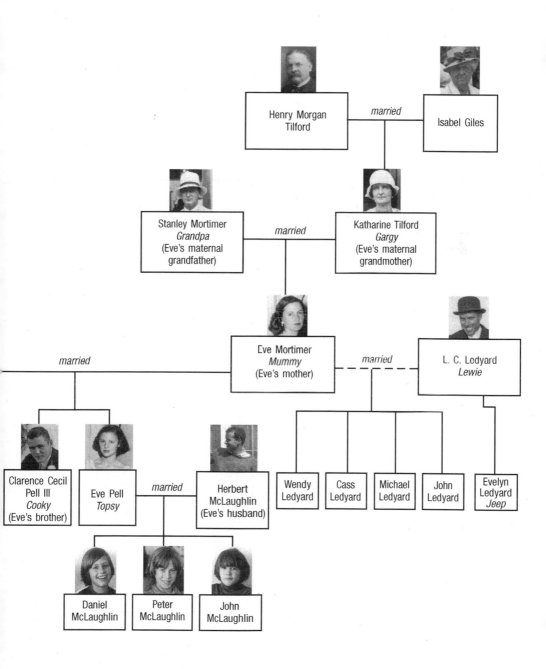

CHAPTER ONE

Deus, Amici, et Nos

GOD, OUR FRIENDS, AND OURSELVES

[W]e are of the very small group of people who are by birth and not by possessions at the social head of the greatest and most important city in the greatest and most important country in the world. We are raised above our fellows as is an English nobleman. . . . People look to us, we represent more—much more—than we are. We cannot avoid responsibility; we can only carry it well or badly.

—Great-uncle Bertie Pell

I come from a family in love with itself. My cousin Claiborne Pell, son of my great-uncle Bertie and now retired after thirty-six years as a U.S. Senator, inherited his father's passion for our family history and our name. When I was just out of college in 1959 and still single, Claiborne reminded me that Pells have a tradition of distant cousins marrying each other. In those prefeminist days, a wife always took the husband's surname. "If you married one of your cousins," he suggested brightly, "you wouldn't ever have to lose the name."

I grew up knowing some of the beliefs, facts, and historical oddities that make up the family creed. When I was in third grade, I could tell the class that our scholarly mathematician forefather in England, Dr. John Pell, invented the division sign in 1659. His younger brother, Thomas, an enterprising soldier and doctor who arrived in the New World about 1635, became a prominent citizen of Fairfield, Connecticut. He amassed a small fortune by trading furs, often with an Indian chieftain named Wampage, and marrying a rich widow. Later, he bought an immense tract of land along

Long Island Sound from a council of local Indians. (The price, I learned later: "2 gunns, 2 kettles, 2 coats, two adzes, 2 shirts, 1 barrel of cider and 6 bitts of money.") Because he staunchly fended off Dutch claims to his property and subsequently was helpful to New York's colonial governors, the Duke of York conferred upon Thomas Pell the "Lordship and Manner" of Pelham. The grant confirmed his title to the property "forever, firmly, freely and clearly . . . as if he held the same from his Majesty the King of England." In return for near-absolute power over the inhabitants of his manor, Pell had to provide the duke with one lamb each year on the first of May.

We even have a family fortress. In 1820, our ancestor William Ferris Pell bought Fort Ticonderoga, then a historic ruin that had played a strategic role in the French and Indian Wars and in the Revolution: It was there that Ethan Allen surprised the British soldiers, giving America its first victory in the fight for independence. Pells restored the fort, which is now a historic landmark.

We Pells consider ourselves the only American colonial family whose landholdings stem from grants by both Indians and the British Crown.

The New York colonial families reproduced the English feudal system in the New World, complete with a rigid social hierarchy that ensconced the elite at the top. They intermarried, took the choice government positions, and blithely assumed the prerogatives of a ruling class: "They were the gentry of the country, to whom the country, without a rebellious thought, took off its hat."

Even now, in the twenty-first century, some of my family still behave like gentry to whom the country should take off its hat. Newspaper writers call us "the ancestral Pells," who have always been "in society." My cousin Toby, son of the senator, is a tall, handsome, gray-haired man with a wide smile and dashing white forelock who ran the Newport Preservation Society, a multimillion-dollar complex of museums and colonial homes. Its main office is in a mansion on Bellevue Avenue once owned by his grandfather, a residence that, because of its orange tile roof, is referred to in Newport as "Taco Pell."

Toby defined the family's sense of its own aristocracy. "As children, we were taught that, had America been more feudal, we would be a noble family," he said. "We were told over the dinner table that we were the creme de la creme."

Like Toby, I went through gates into private clubs and private schools that excluded those who weren't rich enough, or white enough, or maybe their money wasn't old enough. One grandmother lived in Tuxedo Park, New York, a guarded enclave with a small fortress at its gate; a grandfather lived on an estate hidden behind a thick, green wall on Long Island's North Shore. No stranger could enter the private clubs where my relatives relaxed and played games or the Upper East Side buildings where they lived while they were in Manhattan. Uniformed doormen protected them from unwanted intrusions; servants and tradesmen entered by the back door; everyone executed their orders. It never occurred to me to question the rightness of my own inclusion or the exclusion of others; everyone around me simply took their status for granted.

The trappings of the Pell name have continued on into the modern era, and some of the family take these things extremely seriously. In 1988, there were two particularly interesting family celebrations that symbolized conflicting aspects of our heritage. I was lucky enough to attend them both.

The East Coast Gathering

The first was a family reunion in June on the occasion of the three hundredth anniversary of New Rochelle, New York, a town built on land that had once belonged to the family's manor.

In 1688, Sir John Pell, Thomas's nephew and heir, sold the acreage that is now New Rochelle to the Huguenots, French Protestants who had fled to the New World to escape religious persecution. They paid 1,675 pounds and, in addition to the money, they were obligated to provide one "Fatt calfe every fouer and twentyeth day of June yearly & Every Year forever, if demanded" for Sir John's heirs.

In the colonial era, the presentation of the "fatt" calf was a holiday marked with feasting and fun. Then, for nearly two hundred years after the American Revolution, the Pells, who had been dispossessed of their manor, did not request a calf. But sixty years ago a distant cousin reminded city leaders of the old deed and demanded the tribute. The city paid up. Irregularly since then, the demand has been made and fulfilled with a range of ceremonies that have featured colonial costumes, flags, speeches, and, occasionally, a local beauty queen.

In 1955, a New Rochelle mayor refused to honor the old contract. Tongue in cheek, the family responded. There were skilled Wall Street lawyers in the family, a Pell spokesman said, who would take legal action to get our city back if a calf was not forthcoming. Instead of seizing farmers' cottages and plows, the family would confiscate tennis courts and three-car garages. The city backed down. And for its tricentennial observation, the city was paying up in style, inviting all Sir John's descendants to attend and receive their tribute.

New Rochelle treated us as though we were prized historical relics, like spinning wheels, horse-drawn carriages, or oil lamps. City officials had planned a series of events for our entertainment over the weekend. So, on a summer morning, about fifty Pells gathered in a sterile hotel lobby, including my son Peter and me. We stood around in small groups of cousins ranging from very young to old, looking uncomfortable. Those who had never met shook hands formally upon being introduced, while those who were more closely related gave each other little air kisses (women) or handshakes with smiles (men). Not a shriek, not a tear, not a bear hug occurred as the family reunion convened.

The first event was a bus tour of our manor. As we drove, a local historian told us of the Treaty Oak that marked the place where our ancestor Thomas Pell had signed the deed with the Indians. One in-law, apparently irked by Pellishness, explained loudly to no one in particular that *her* family descended directly from Napoleon Bonaparte. Evidently considering herself ahead on points, she kept quiet from then on.

Our first stop was the Bartow-Pell mansion, built on a section of the old land grant. The local garden club had carefully restored the grounds; we walked past a tidy herb garden and through a gate in the wrought iron fence to a wide expanse of lawn. There we sat on the grass, admiring the formal garden, its symmetrically arranged ewe bushes and beds of flowers laid out around a square pool with a winged bronze cherub at the center.

The historian continued: The first people to live here were Siwanoy Indians, who claimed all the land along the shore from New York City north to the Connecticut River. She told the story of Thomas in 1654 buying the vaguely defined two hundred thousand acres—then a wilderness where wolves and bears roamed—including the Bronx and the land along the shore of Long Island Sound north to Mamaroneck. As years went by, however, it became clear that the Indians had sold various sections of this land several times over, and, as other settlers moved in, Thomas's acreage shrank.

Thomas, who died rich and childless in 1669, left the manor to his nephew John, a courtier to Charles II "in ould England."

When word arrived in London that the young man had inherited vast lands in the New World, the historian went on, King Charles knighted him on the spot. Sir John promptly left for America, married into a rich family, and began selling off pieces of his manor until all that remained were about seven square miles, including what is now Pelham. As Commissioner of Indian Affairs, he continued his uncle's policy of befriending and protecting local Indians, including old Wampage and his family who lived on an island across the water from the manor house. A Justice of the Peace, Sir John was elected to New York's first colonial General Assembly. His son, Thomas II, married Anna, a local Indian princess who, according to family lore, was Wampage's granddaughter. (According to our family journal *Pelliana*, Sir John, a canny old fellow, considered the union a way to consolidate the Pells' position as landowners.)

The historian ended her lecture with the fifth Lord of the Manor, Joseph II, a British sympathizer at the time of the Revolution. He was imprisoned by the patriots and beaten so badly that he died shortly afterward. In fact, most of the Pells, knowing on which side their bread was buttered, had sided with King George, and thus did not fare well after the Revolution; they were attainted and their property was confiscated. The manor house was burned. Most of the family fled to Canada for refuge.

But they did not stay long. Political passions in the new United States cooled, and the Pells returned to live in New York City; one of them, William Ferris Pell, made a large fortune on Wall Street importing marble and fine wood for the growing city. No one seemed to care any more that the family had supported the king, and they took a prominent place in New York society.

My relatives beamed as the historian acknowledged the special place of their ancestors in colonial history. Her words bathed the family in an aura of aristocracy—they were indeed extraordinary, and she was giving them their due.

After her talk, we walked over to inspect the ancient graves that remain on the property—of Joseph, the fourth lord, his wife, Phoebe, and two others, all enclosed in a small square plot marked off by concrete posts linked with a metal railing. The weather-beaten graves were weedy and overgrown. "I paid to have pachysandra planted in there," grumbled my elderly, heavyset cousin Rodman Pell, a fishmonger who arrived years before bearing a family Bible that, much to the distress of the assembled family, confirmed his descent from the lords of the manor. His clothing, voice, and demeanor betrayed his working-class status, and he stood out from the others, any of whom could have stepped from the pages of *Town and Country Magazine*. Some of his elegantly clad cousins joked about his jacket, whose fabric, they said, looked like the test pattern on an old TV.

Later, we returned to the hotel to change for the formal dinner, which was to be held at the Bartow-Pell mansion. I sat next to one of my favorite cousins, one with the formidable name of Anthony Douglas Stephen Mordaunt Pell, known to all as Tony. A handsome, stout, jovial fellow, he began telling me stories about one of our most eccentric relatives: Claiborne's father, my great-uncle Bertie, a friend of FDR's from Harvard, a New Dealer and diplomat, and Bertie's wife Olive, an artist who edited her own version of the Bible. It was a rather unwieldy volume, Olive felt, so she cut out the boring parts of the Old Testament, excluded references to eating meat since she was a vegetarian, and condensed the four Gospels into one. She sold some family diamonds to finance the 1952 publication of her handy, compact result, which she named *The Olive Pell Bible*. It had quite a success.

When Uncle Bertie was FDR's Minister to Portugal at the start of World War II, Tony told me, Lisbon was a center of intrigue. Olive was planning a dinner for the diplomatic corps to liven up the wartime social scene; she decided to serve ice cream for dessert. But delicacies were scarce, and no ice cream was to be had. Olive heard that the U.S. Navy, stationed on watch offshore, had a supply on board for the sailors. She asked Uncle Bertie to get some for her party. Oblivious to the wartime emergency and concerned for the success of Olive's social event, he had an urgent message dispatched through the military communications system to the fleet commander at sea, ordering him ashore immediately. The admiral, undoubtedly expecting that a crisis was brewing, encountered Bertie, who had had himself ferried out to the anchored ship in a naval launch, flags flying. Bertie explained he'd heard that the admiral had ice cream aboard; could he have some for his wife's party? "ICE CREAM? ICE CREAM!!" bellowed the apoplectic admiral, muttering furiously as he steamed back to his ship.

As the family dinner went on, there were several speeches. Claiborne gave one about the family spirit and invoked our motto, *Deus, Amici et Nos*, or "God, our friends, and ourselves." He told of one young Pell student who was too poor to buy a tail coat. A rich relative gave him one, and in later years the charity was returned: the recipient gave a tail coat to the son of his benefactor.

The senator told of his father's dedication to the family. As World War II drew closer, Claiborne said, Uncle Bertie began to worry about the fifteenth-century gravestones of our ancestors in Dersingham, England, and the possibility that the Germans might destroy them in the Blitz. He arranged for workmen to protect the monuments with sandbags so that they would not be damaged if bombs should fall into the ancient cemetery. "I wonder how the people who lived there then felt about that," my son Peter mused afterward. "Their houses weren't protected, but those old graves were."

Only one cousin expressed a divergent view: a Congregational minister who reminded the gathering that some aspects of the Pell spirit were obnoxious and selfish—and he urged the family to expand its spirit to include the whole family of mankind.

The next morning threatened rain. We drove to the neighboring town of Pelham, named for the old family manor, to attend the ceremonial raising of a flag newly designed for the occasion. The senator chatted in his courtly manner with town officials and acted as our patriarch. Bagpipes played, VFW officers in uniform surrounded the flagpole. I stood next to him under lowering skies as he pulled the ropes raising the white and blue Pelham flag.

The day turned sunny for the main event.

In New Rochelle, a small crowd waited in front of a makeshift stage in a grassy park near Long Island Sound. A Black Angus calf balked at a ramp leading onto the stage but a burly man roughly twisted up its tail while two others linked arms around its rear end, pushing and tugging the panicked beast up and into position. Once there, its legs splayed out and it collapsed in a miserable heap. Dignitaries on the platform looked down with sympathy on the poor creature, which later struggled to its feet and stood, head hung low, as the ceremony went forward.

The audience quieted. The deputy mayor spoke: "Pells, Huguenots, and humble citizens of New Rochelle who are neither Pells nor Huguenots," he began with a wry smile. "I welcome you. We thank you, Pells and Huguenots. Because of you we can live here and raise our families here." He took the free end of the calf's rope and presented it to Cousin Rodman. "See what we are giving away instead of the city!" crowed the mayor.

Rodman responded: "I accept this fat calf on behalf of all Pells around the world, near and far. And I thank the city for paying the rent on time."

Most Pells were turned out as if for the Harvard-Yale crew races or a boarding school graduation—the men were in blazers and ties, the women in prints and linen dresses. Debonair, white-haired cousin Eddie, a lawyer from

Philadelphia, sported a wide-brimmed straw hat, impeccable white trousers and jacket, along with a cigar and a pretty wife with a charming European accent. Many of the men wore Pell Family Association ties, black, with a discreet pattern of tiny pelicans like the one on the family crest.

That night, I had a melancholy dream. I saw a railway car filled with drunken, older men, one of them riding a horse, making it go faster and faster into a dead end.

The West Coast Gathering

Five months later, however, I experienced a very different aspect of our history at a Jewish gathering in my home city of San Francisco.

Some family background here: To my immediate family, Uncle Bertie was ridiculous. My father, Clarence Cecil Pell Jr., and his father, Clarence Cecil Pell, the grandfather whom I called Big Cook, mainly organized their lives around exclusive private clubs and arcane racquet sports. But Big Cook's brother Bertie and Bertie's son Claiborne plunged into the real world of politics. My side of the family made fun of them: they could not hit a ball very well, they did not care much about sports, they read history and went to museums and were considered to be stuffy and boring. "I was always told that Uncle Bertie was a horse's ass," one cousin told me.

Having read Bertie's 1972 biography, *Brahmin in Revolt*, I knew a little about him. Born in 1884 at the height of the Gilded Age, he was a gentleman who lived off family money. An unusually independent thinker, he was educated at Pomfret, a boys' boarding school in Connecticut, where he was the only person in the entire school to subscribe to a daily newspaper. He went on to Harvard, but after a year or two he left because he felt there was nothing more for him to learn there. He traveled and read history in Europe as a young man and, unlike most of his social class, developed a philosophy based on the European sense of noblesse oblige. A devotee of art, music, and literature, he disdained the profit motive as unworthy of a cultivated person. "Even those of us who shared in the good things must realize that the boom times benefited too few people, that the distribution of profits was unfair," he wrote. To the horror of his friends, he recoiled at the spectacle of unbridled capitalism and later became a lifelong Democrat.

In 1912, he moved back to Tuxedo Park after years of living in Europe. Immediately, he pitched in to support the Progressive campaign for Theodore

Roosevelt, who advocated breaking up the powerful industrial trusts and prosecuting corruption in government. Bertie, whose social status protected him from retaliation by the unforgiving Republicans who ran Tuxedo, was the front man. He organized small businessmen and working people, among them the servants who would have been summarily fired had such activity been known to their employers. "No county committeeman has ever done as much work as was credited to me in that campaign," he reflected years later.

Despite his progressive politics, however, Bertie was hardly a man of the people. He went about in a knickerbocker suit, plus-fours, and a wide cravat, sometimes of swirling dotted swiss. Old-fashioned pince-nez perched on his nose. In winter, he sometimes wore a long, flowing cape, and in summer he was resplendent in grand white suits, always with a waistcoat.

Private clubs were a great part of his life, and his stuffiness about them was legendary. In a letter to a cousin, Bertie wrote: "The successful election of Plummer, Duncan and Creighton Webb at the Union certainly shows that the standard has gone down. . . . It would not be very well to say that none of these men would have been admitted into the backdoor of the old Union as it is highly probable that at least one of them delivered imported biscuits and other delicacies at the kitchen entrance." He continued, "One goes to a club not because of whom one will see but because of whom one will not see."

Hardly words that one would expect from a liberal Democrat, but Bertie was filled with contradictions. His long friendship with Franklin Roosevelt began when they were students at Harvard. Years later, as governor of New York, FDR gave Bertie a position in the state Democratic Party, and, despite the objections of regular Tammany Hall pols, continued to boost his political career. Bertie served a term in Congress representing New York's Silk Stocking District on the Upper East Side. As World War II was breaking out, FDR appointed him Minister to Portugal, and then, in 1941, to Hungary, a fascist state then under Nazi domination. Bertie insisted on being driven through Europe to his new post in a large Buick station wagon. On the way, he saw starving prisoners of war and heard frightening accounts of Nazi atrocities. When he arrived, Bertie joined the best club in Budapest and rented a suite of rooms at the Ritz. Well-liked by the Hungarian people, he openly disrespected German officials. Using his diplomatic status, he helped smuggle Jews out of Europe.

In December 1941, after the Japanese attack on Pearl Harbor, Hungary declared war on the United States and Bertie had to burn the U.S. Embassy codes before his departure. Despite the Germans' efforts to isolate him, five thousand Hungarians showed up at the train station to see him off when he left the country.

Over the opposition of State Department career officers, Roosevelt appointed Bertie to the War Crimes Commission, the international body set up to decide the fate of the Nazis once the Allies had defeated the Axis powers. To those career officers, Bertie, who had not come up through regular bureaucratic channels, was known to be an independent thinker and the president's friend, even something of a loose cannon.

Horrified by what he knew had happened in the Holocaust and what he had seen of Nazi behavior in Europe, Bertie was determined that perpetrators of war crimes should be punished. He wanted to see the guilty—from privates to generals—swing. He had no tolerance for the international law of the day that provided no way to punish a government for crimes against its own people. The political and military leaders of the Third Reich, for instance, could not be tried in an international court for genocide against the Jews of Germany. But his views were opposed by the higher-ups in the anti-Semitic State Department, which had refused to take in Jewish refugees in the 1930s. However, the career officials could not publicly disagree with Bertie on this issue, since revulsion against Nazi atrocities ran high in the nation. So they proceeded quietly to undermine Bertie's work. Behind his back, they cut off his access to the president. They saddled him with a disloyal assistant. Though Bertie worked desperately to get our government to recognize atrocities committed by the Nazis against their own citizens as war crimes, he did not succeed. In fact, with Roosevelt's connivance, he was fired from his post.

The accepted routine for an official who had been sacked was to maintain silence. But Bertie, who did not care if he ever got another post, did not go quietly and he did not give up. He spoke freely to reporters and Jewish groups, telling them that the State Department was soft on Nazis and that he had been fired because he sought to punish war criminals.

By going public, he and others put pressure on the State Department, which ultimately had to reverse its stance. In defeat, he won. After that, Bertie left public life.

As a child, I didn't see much of him. But many years later, when I became engaged to Herbert McLaughlin, who after all was a Yale-educated architect from the swanky Chicago suburb of Lake Forest, he sent me a letter. Herb, like all men his age in 1959, had to perform some sort of military service and upon graduation was going into the Air Force as a lieutenant. Evidently Uncle Bertie did not consider that the McLaughlins were suitable matches for our family—perhaps because their forebears had been immigrant Irish who parlayed a small grocery business into a highly profitable coffee company. His letter went something like this:

> My dear Eve, I have heard that you are to be engaged to a Catholic who is entering the armed forces. It pains me to think of you hanging out your wash in a back yard with other military wives. And I must tell you that, as a Democrat, I have had a great deal more contact with Catholics than most people have. I must assure you that the person who passes the plate in a Catholic church is nothing like an Episcopal vestryman. Give up these plans, my dear Eve, and come travel with me in Europe. . . .

At the time, I howled with laughter at my great-uncle's snobbery, quoted his admonition to all my friends, and married Herb McLaughlin anyway.

In November 1988, a Jewish friend called me. "Why do you joke about your Uncle Bertie?" he asked rather crossly. "His memory is being honored at a dinner by the Northern California Holocaust Center because of his work at the end of World War II. The senator is going to be there."

So, very surprised, I went to the dinner. When a few guests complimented me on my "illustrious" family, I felt false because I had such mixed feelings about being part of it.

The ceremonies began with frightening black and white films of Nazis torching Jewish businesses and places of worship on *Kristallnacht* in 1938. Next, a Holocaust survivor spoke of his experiences at Dachau. Then, in the silent banquet room, Dr. Charles Sydnor, a history professor who had served with the Office of Special Investigations tracking down Nazis after the war, rose to speak. "Herbert C. Pell was as close to an aristocrat as it is possible for an American to be," he began. "But values were more important to him than being rich or well connected." He went on at some length about Bertie's "noble origins," his Yankee matter-of-fact demeanor and, most of all, his relentless crusade to make genocide a crime. "Had Ambassador Pell not shamed his government, there would have been at best only watered-down versions of Nuremberg. His legacy made it possible to track down, denaturalize and deport war criminals." Dr. Sydnor concluded like a rabbi: "In the Name of the Almighty, Blessed be he."

Tears ran down my cheeks. Although I had read about this in Bertie's biography, I had not felt or understood the power of what he did until that moment. Claiborne rose. "My father had trouble sleeping for two years because of his memories of the Holocaust," he said in his soft voice. He deplored the tacit prewar understanding between the United States and Great Britain not to give asylum to the Jews of Europe, to leave them to Hitler. He accepted his father's award.

I left that evening with an altered sense of my family. On the one hand, I felt glad to have moved away from the East Coast and to have made a different life for myself on the other side of the country. On the other, here was something to be truly proud of. Yet as I considered some of the contradictions that make up the peculiar Pellish stance toward the world, I wondered how the snobbish clubman and the stalwart defender of the Jews managed to exist together in the same skin. And I wondered how my side of the family could have written Bertie off as a boring "horse's ass" or cared that Claiborne, a distinguished senator, wasn't a better tennis player.

The two family events, the "fatt" calf presentation and the dinner honoring Uncle Bertie, roiled my conflicted feelings about being a Pell. Apart from a love of sport, our sense of superiority and familial tendencies toward eccentricity and public service, what were we Pells about? It's not money that sets us apart—after all, there are far grander fortunes around. It's our history, dating back so many centuries, our ancestors' role in the colonies and unusual closeness to the Siwanoy Indians, the nineteenth-century prominence of the merchant Pells on Wall Street, our purchase and restoration of Fort Ticonderoga, and what we see as our place in the country's ruling class carried on in the twentieth century by Bertie and Claiborne.

Tony Pell, my dinner partner in New Rochelle and the cousin of whom I am so fond, is a cheerful Boston investment banker who was in his fifties and president of Fort Ticonderoga when I talked to him about the family. Most of the Fort's board of directors are relatives whom Tony worked with. He has thought about the issue of social class in our family and its effect on us. "There are certainly down sides. One of those is this sense of isolation," he told me. "I don't know that we are comfortable with ourselves. There is this sense of being above the hoi polloi when in fact by any American standard we are not at all. But there is a holding on to that idea of being above, and when you can't afford it that's a terrible thing to have. We have paid a dear price, many people have, for that sense of privilege."

CHAPTER TWO

Upstairs/Downstairs

The Victorians believed that the wealthy had better values, or a more powerful God.

—Cynthia Tucker

N ot every family can be the subject of a trivia question. A few years ago, as I was listening to country music on the radio, the disk jockey's voice blared: "Listen up, folks! Griswold Lorillard was the first man in the United States to do something. What was it?"

I knew.

Griswold Lorillard was a long-dead cousin. I had been researching the lives of my great-grandparents and grandparents, in particular those who lived cosseted behind the gates of Tuxedo Park, a little-known country retreat for Manhattan's old Knickerbocker descendants and its more refined robber barons. From the Gilded Age to World War II, these elite families inhabited their mansions in the Park for a few weeks in spring and fall, passing the time between the winter season in New York City and the summer season in Newport.

Well before the turn of the twentieth century, my great-great-great grandfather, tobacco magnate Pierre Lorillard, sold his Newport mansion, "The Breakers." On a whim, he plunged the proceeds into creating a new "colony" as such resorts were then called. Through a mix of inheritance, foreclosures, and poker winnings from his brothers, he acquired seven thousand acres of wilderness just forty miles northwest of New York City; his first move was to have it fenced in. His overseers hired 1,800 Slovak and Italian laborers straight from Ellis Island and set them to work on a luxurious clubhouse, roads, and a sewer system, all to be completed in just eight months. He ordered up forty-room "cottages," it was said, the way other men ordered a brandy and soda. Outside the gates, workers erected a village where the white-collar employees and tradesmen lived, along with a railroad station and shops. Still farther away were their own shanties and tenements, the Italian and Slovak villages.

Newspapers reported that "Prince Pierre" prided himself on being America's most lavish spender. He had the fastest horses, most elegant carriages, finest chefs, wines, and cigars. At his entertainments, footmen served champagne from great glass pitchers along with duck and terrapin specially raised for his tables. Iroquois, his great thoroughbred, was the first American horse to win the English Derby. Tuxedo would be the finest colony for the best people.

Griswold, his son, gave rise to an urban legend. On a grand tour of Europe while a young man, it was said, young Griswold attended a party for the Prince of Wales. Standard dress for dinner at the time was the tail coat and stiff collar—no gentleman would venture out in any other costume. But Grizzy was so taken with a novel, tailless jacket he saw the Prince of Wales wearing that evening that he had his tailor reproduce it. He wore this sartorial innovation at the first Tuxedo Autumn Ball, and, though he was first ridiculed as looking like a "royal footman," the jacket caught on and took the name of the place where it first was seen.

I called in; the DJ answered. "I know what he did and where he did it," I said, and told her. "We have a winner!" she yelled and dropped off the line.

Griswold Lorillard was the first American to wear a Tuxedo.

My father's grandparents, Katherine Lorillard Kernochan Pell and Herbert Claiborne Pell Sr., were among the first members of the colony. My mother's grandparents, Tilfords and Mortimers, followed soon after.

Like the others whom Pierre Lorillard selected to join the Tuxedo Club and build houses there, they were considered "Who was especially Who in the Four Hundred." A magazine article referred to the never-equaled blend of "vintage money, congenial habits, and impeccable social antecedents" behind the massive gates. *Town Topics*, a gossip sheet at the turn of the century, described the place:

> With nearly a hundred modern palaces studding its hills . . . Tuxedo Park has become an important factor in the life of New York society. It is undoubtedly the most exclusive retreat on the American continent. [Social] Climbers have scaled the Newport cliffs only to find the hills of Tuxedo far more treacherous. . . . At the lodge, in the towers of which it is said are loaded howitzers, the uninvited are confronted with this notice: "Tuxedo Park. Private Grounds. Reserved Exclusively for Members of the Tuxedo Club. No One Admitted Without Permit"

The swells inhabited an extraordinary landscape, a steep-sided bowl of woods rising from the shores of a long, narrow lake, punctuated by stony crags and cliffs. From a distance, the mansions, topped with statues, turrets, and chimneys, looked like huge wedding cakes set down upon the hillsides.

"Prince Pierre," well pleased with his creation, celebrated its opening with a splendid party in May 1886. Seven hundred guests were taken from New York in three trains to the Queen Anne–style railroad station. Horse-drawn buses and wagons painted in the green and gold Tuxedo colors transported them to the Club. Crowds from the surrounding towns assembled to watch them arrive, oohing and aahing at the brilliance of the costumes and the carriages. Gamekeepers dressed in Tyrolean costume were stationed on the roads to wave at the guests; white-uniformed oarsmen toured them about the lake in barges. The evening ended with a magnificent dinner dance. Remarked one rather starchy newspaper account, "All of America's high society was present, by invitation only. Those who weren't invited wished they were."

The Tuxedo Club was the social center of the Park, and its standards for sorting the ins from the outs were ironclad. It was understood that no one unacceptable to the Club would buy land there; newcomers had to rent for a year and only then, if they passed inspection by the members' wives, could they buy. In an oral history for Columbia University, my great-uncle Bertie spoke of the Tuxedo residents' desire to "keep out the unattractive rich." One millionaire, whose income stemmed from a chain of produce stores, failed to heed the hints that he should go elsewhere and kept trying to buy a house in the Park. Finally he went away, after being informed that even if he did succeed in buying, the Tuxedo Association would not supply his place with water and power. I grew up thinking that this snobbery was amusing because it made my parents laugh and because we were on the inside.

One of America's most influential advocates of white supremacy, the lawyer and eugenicist Madison Grant, lived in the Park. His work, *The Passing of the Great Race*, incited hatred against the "darker, lesser peoples" who were "mongrelizing the white race in America." Grant's idea of "native American," contrary to current thinking, was Nordic whites like himself, whose innate superiority demanded that they rule. Hitler admired Grant's work.

When I visited Tuxedo in 1996, I stayed with cousins who had lived there for decades. Much of the old spirit remained. "Private," warned the sign at the stone guardhouse at its entrance; "Private" warned the signs at entrances to the homes inside; "Private" warned the signs posted on trees, lest a potential trespasser decide to follow an inviting wooded path. My cousin's car, which she let me borrow, carried the all-important sticker allowing me to drive in past the guard and into the Park. "Just explore wherever you want, Tops," she said hospitably. "Lots of people know my car, so they'll be waving at you." The first time I drove her car in through the gates I felt once again a flutter of pleasure at being one of the special people: as a child, I had loved visiting my grandmother in Tuxedo, and there was something both gratifying and comforting about being waved in to this fabulous place.

Returning to my cousins' house after a day's work in the little town library, I showed them a clipping from the 1940s about a man named Nathan Berkman who bought a lakeshore mansion from Angier Biddle Duke. As a Jew, Berkman could not join the Tuxedo Club. As a nonmember, he was also not permitted to use the lake. "He has been specifically forbidden to jump into, boat on, or dip a fish-hook into the precious pond," wrote a New York columnist at the time. Moreover, when Berkman held a wedding reception at his house and carefully placed signs on the Park's confusing road system to direct his guests, someone turned the signs around and jumbled them so that the guests got hopelessly lost and the party was spoiled. I was horrified at the sheer nastiness of that behavior and thought my cousins would be appalled, too.

How wrong I was. My cousin's husband smiled. "I was one of the kids who did that," he said, remembering his pleasure in screwing up the Jewish wedding. I was surprised and shocked that he showed no twinge of remorse.

The vicious anti-Semitism with which the Park was founded has faded over the years. More Jews live inside the gates, and the Tuxedo Club these days makes money from putting on bar mitzvahs for nonmembers. But prejudice, like a virus that sometimes goes dormant, lives on.

Not all of my relatives revered their forbears. My mother's younger sister Katharine, nicknamed Goody, became critical of her family's values as she grew older. I knew she had written some reminiscences about how the upper class lived, and so, a few years ago, I went to see her at her New York apartment.

As we sat in her comfortable living room, she spoke scathingly of her grandfather, Richard Mortimer. I had found a picture of him in the course of my own research, in the 1899 edition of a directory called *King's Notable New Yorkers*. The photo showed a balding man with upcurled mustaches, on the same page with John Jacob Astor and Frederick William Vanderbilt. Aunt Goody filled in some details: he inherited a fortune from his father, a Scottish immigrant who manufactured shoddy Civil War uniforms for both North and South, then wisely invested the proceeds in prime Manhattan real estate. Beneath Mr. Mortimer's photo was printed his occupation: "Capitalist."

Although Richard Mortimer inherited the fortune, she went on, he didn't inherit the financial acumen. "My grandfather decided to manage his own money," Aunt Goody told me. "Whenever there was a panic—and there seemed to be quite a few in those days—he was there, losing money."

Mortimer was known for his inability to put on a poker face. Those who saw him arrive from New York at the Tuxedo railway station in the afternoon could tell by his smile or frown whether the stock market had gone up or down that day. And while playing the fierce games of poker that occupied the gamblers at the Tuxedo Club, he had to wear a cravat that covered his throat so that the other players couldn't tell by studying the up-and-down movement of his Adam's apple whether he held good cards or bad. The cravat was held in place with a diamond horseshoe stickpin so big that his friends called him "Flashlight Dick."

Though his abilities were modest, his tastes were not. "Flashlight Dick" built the largest mansion in Tuxedo, the Crystal Palace, named for the grandeur of its conservatory. Imposing stone lions flanked the massive iron entrance gate; busts of Roman emperors lined the long driveway to his front door. Among his interior decorations were a Gobelin tapestry and a fourteenth-century "Christ on the Cross." The window of his south library was a stained glass panel of the Nativity taken from a sixteenth-century Italian castle. With fifty-four rooms on four floors, the house required dozens of servants. If he tired of his home in Tuxedo, he could go to his town house at 382 Fifth Avenue and, while in the city, he could repair to one of his clubs: he belonged to the Metropolitan, Knickerbocker, Union, City, Racquet, Coaching, Riding, and Westminster Kennel clubs. In addition, he and Mrs. Mortimer spent a great deal of their time abroad.

At teatime several years ago at her Pennsylvania farm, my mother, Eve Mortimer Ledyard, began reminiscing to a few guests about the way her parents and grandparents traveled. Sitting in her library with her dogs at her feet, a fire blazing in the hearth and toasted English muffins in a silver dish, she set the scene. Family servants packed up great steamer trunks so large that a child could hide in the bottom drawer, she said, and the family brought along its own linen and silver. The Mortimer entourage included an equerry to make arrangements, a valet, and a lady's maid. "You mean the equerry carried the bags?" inquired an in-law as he balanced his teacup on his lap, listening intently. "No," answered my mother loftily, spreading a little jam on a muffin. "The equerry *hired* the people who carried the bags."

Before leaving on these journeys, Mr. Mortimer took the family jewels for safekeeping into New York to his bank vault. On one occasion, however, he became distracted while on the ferry to the city and walked off forgetting the paper bag containing the jewels. Later, it was noticed in Little Italy that some children were going around wearing diamond tiaras and necklaces of precious stones—a workman had picked up the bag and, thinking it was costume jewelry, given it to his daughters to play with. I don't know whether the jewelry was ever returned.

Mortimer died of heart trouble, quite young. Aunt Goody remembers when, as a little girl, she went with her father to see the wrecking ball smash down the Crystal Palace because the post-Depression property taxes had gotten too high for the family to afford.

Richard Mortimer unfortunately passed along his lack of business acumen to his tall, athletic, and handsome son Stanley, my Grandpa Mortimer. When he was in boarding school at St. George's, Grandpa was expelled, reportedly after being discovered with a chambermaid—so he never went to college. He inherited a share of what was left of Flashlight Dick's fortune, but during *his* brief and hapless period of supervising his own investments, he swiftly lost a few million. Fortunately for Grandpa, he had married an heiress with a fortune sufficient to maintain them both in comfort.

Whatever their faults, both Mortimers, father and son, were highly regarded, popular gentlemen in the family and in their social circles. No one held it against them that they were incompetent, and they seem to have been not at all embarrassed by their failures. But actually earning money—now, there was something to embarrass a gentleman.

My other maternal great-grandfather, Henry Morgan Tilford, was born in Kentucky and went to New York where he became a high executive of John D. Rockefeller's Standard Oil Company. According to my Aunt Goody, after Theodore Roosevelt's antitrust laws broke up the oil giant into regional companies, Tilford was named president of Standard Oil of California—even though he had never ventured out West. She told me that company officials once suggested that he take Mrs. Tilford with him in a private railroad car across the country in order to visit the offices and staff of the newly formed company in the Golden State. But, she continued, rather than endure a journey to what he viewed as a very uncivilized region, he resigned on the spot. Mr. Tilford was far too much of a New York gentleman to sully his shoes with California soil.

I always enjoyed the stories I heard about great-grandpa Tilford, and since the executive offices of the old Standard Oil of California (now called Chevron) were then in San Francisco, I went to the company's History Room to find out more details about his oil company experiences.

What I discovered was truly shocking: Henry Morgan Tilford had been hard-working and resourceful. When still very young, he and two of his brothers left Kentucky for the frontier and went into the oil business. Contrary to what the family thought, they spent years in California knocking heads with competitors, gouging advantageous contracts with railroads and scrambling for market share. They were smart, aggressive, and enterprising, devising new and profitable ways to refine and transport kerosene until Standard Oil bought them out and made them executives with offices in New York.

He continued to succeed. In company histories, Henry M. Tilford stands out as the man who, against all existing wisdom, authorized the huge gamble of wildcatting for oil on the West Coast. It paid off fabulously.

Armed with this information, I went to tea with Aunt Goody on my next trip to New York and told her what I had found. To my surprise, she refused to believe a word of it, insisting that I was mistaken. "He never *went* to California," she said crossly. She stuck to the family version, that he had resigned on the spot in Manhattan rather than visit such an uncouth place. Certainly, he had never *worked* there.

Rather than celebrate Tilford's scrappy and ambitious career in the Wild West, they preferred to pretend it never happened. After tea, as I was leaving and putting on my coat, Goody grumbled, "Wasn't it *fresh* of Standard Oil to make up all that!"

Tilfords, Mortimers, and Pells adopted the attitudes of a class that considered itself many notches above the money-grubbing bourgeoisie. Uncle Bertie was once told that the husband of a young relative had just found a job. "Oh, my dear, I am so sorry!" he said. His papers, collected at the Roosevelt Library in Hyde Park, contain scornful references to businessmen, railing against those who profit by betraying "the confidence of innocent gulls," and against American values "too ready to measure civilization in terms of bath-tubs, radios and automobiles."

I wondered what Mr. Tilford himself thought in his later years about his entrepreneurial youth in the West, whether it was an embarrassment to him after he had arrived in New York. He certainly played the role of East Coast aristocrat: his Tuxedo house was even more impressive than Mr. Mortimer's. Constructed originally for the Wall Street speculator Henry Poor (of Standard and Poor), it still stands, a towering brick structure more like a Jacobean abbey than a residence. Mr. Poor had refused to sell the place when great-grandfather Tilford first asked to buy it. However, knowing that as a speculator he carried certain risks, Poor made a deal. In the event that his investments suddenly plunged and he needed capital, he would sell the house on the condition that Tilford produce half a million dollars within twenty-four hours—back then, a staggering amount of money on such short notice. In 1909, the time came: Poor phoned Tilford saying, "I have agreed to sell you the house." The check arrived an hour later.

A versatile man, Henry Tilford, who could figure out how to refine kerosene, climb the corporate ladder to social advancement, and arrange charming bouquets. A Tuxedo newspaper clipping of the period tells how the former oil pioneer won trophies at the Park's annual flower show, one for having the best chrysanthemums and another for the best group of "Miscellaneous plants arranged for effect." Luckily for my family, he left a great deal of money. After he died in 1919, the *New York Times* reported that his widow was the highest personal taxpayer in all of New York City. Known as the First Lady of Tuxedo, she outlived her husband by many years, dying in 1941. According to my mother, Grandma Tilford lost millions of dollars because she took on her husband's former office boy as her financial advisor and faithfully followed his instructions. "We never thought about money, in those days," my mother used to say, airily shrugging her shoulders over the missing millions.

The generations of my family born before the Depression and World War II lived in a never-never land. "You just can't believe what a cocoon we were brought up in," my mother told me once. "It was such a small world. We were so protected, and we felt we had the right to be." When she was a teenager visiting her friend Pauline-Louise du Pont in Wilmington, my mother got so lost in Winterthur, the du Pont's 150-room mansion, that she had to pick up a telephone and call for a servant to find her and guide her back to her room.

Actually, Pauline's father, Mr. Henry du Pont, showed considerable hospitality in allowing my mother to come. Many years before, he had invited her mother and her to stay. A small girl at the time, my mother had wandered into the front hall and seen a curious, elaborate contraption of glass and water that beautifully reflected light through a series of prisms. By accident, she knocked it over, and the thing shattered on the floor. Searching out Mr. du Pont, the contrite little girl confessed what she had done. He did not tell her that the priceless and irreplaceable object she broke, one of his most dearly prized possessions, had been made especially for Louis XIV. "That's quite all right, my dear," he said kindly, upon hearing the news, then fainted dead away.

The rich and clubbable like my mother lived like protected species though they were anything but endangered. Their meals were cooked and served, their clothing laid out each morning and evening, their offspring reared by nannies, their horses led by grooms to the mounting block. The families entertained on a grand scale: my great-grandmother Tilford had seated dinners of 125 people, one course after another, with a footman in livery standing behind each chair. She never put on her own shoes—her lady's maid did that.

Stanley Mortimer, my Grandpa who later lost all his money, was a good athlete. In one alcove on the far side of the Big Room at his Tuxedo Park house stood mahogany cases for his silver trophies, shelves and shelves of them, large and small. After they were stolen in a celebrated burglary, my grandmother, whom we called Gargy, had them all replaced in sterling silver—whether the originals had been sterling or not.

Grandpa had a few other interests, among them Tuxedo's volunteer fire department, of which he was a ranking member. One night in 1916, he was disturbed at dinner by the shriek of the fire alarm. Rushing to the firehouse, he and the other gentlemen hitched up the hook and ladders and, clinging to the apparatus with one hand, changed from their dinner jackets into red flannel shirts, rubber boots and fire helmets as they sped to a burning inn a few miles away. They arrived only to discover that they had no source of water and no buckets for a bucket brigade.

Their wives followed. "The flames illumined the faces of many society women in the automobiles parked in a circle about the hotel—women wearing heavy furs over the evening gowns in which they had abandoned dinner tables," a New York *Herald* reporter wrote. The luckless inn burned to the ground. Afterward, the Tuxedo Park residents returned to their abandoned dinner tables, the men being permitted to resume their places still wearing their red flannel shirts and high rubber boots while the butlers held their fire helmets.

Because of Gargy's Tilford money, it didn't matter from a financial point of view that Grandpa had no real job. Without an office, however, he needed a place to go during the day. Wherever he was—Tuxedo, New York, or Palm Beach—he belonged to a club. He arrived at ten and picked up the paper. The joke was that by the time his friends arrived for lunch, he had read as far as page two. Gargy referred to his club as his "sandbox," as if he were a child. Once, long after Grandpa had died and a male houseguest wanted her attention, she complained exasperatedly to my Aunt Goody, "What do you *do* with a man who won't go to his club?"

Grandpa's main club was the Racquet and Tennis, at an elegant, brick-and-limestone building at 370 Park Avenue in New York City. Built in 1917 by the renowned firm of McKim, Mead and White, the five-story Racquet Club seems remarkably out of place, an old mansion surrounded by towering glass and steel skyscrapers. The building encloses a world that is just as out of date as its exterior, a world devoted to the creature comforts of its exclusively male members, who can gamble, dine, drink, smoke cigars, shoot billiards, smash balls around courts, or work out. They may not, under any circumstances, conduct business there.

The club maintains a world-class library of sporting books, a gym staffed with trainers, a series of elegantly comfortable sitting rooms and lounges. Museum-quality sculptures and paintings ornament its halls, including a vibrant polo scene in bronze, heroic players and ponies frozen forever at full gallop.

"The Racquet" was a refuge, a home away from home for my grandfathers, my uncles, and my father; Lewie, who rarely used it, was nevertheless a member. Nothing was too much trouble for the staff. When Big Cook bought a pair of new shoes he didn't walk around uncomfortably in the stiff leather, he handed them over to a club employee with the same size feet to break them in. Even today, members are waited on by a carefully selected staff, and on the not infrequent occasions when one becomes incapacitated by drink, he is politely escorted to a taxi and sent home. Other things have changed a little: In my grandfathers' day, wives, daughters, or other ladies who came to the club to meet their men were not permitted in the door—even if it was raining or snowing, they had to stand outside. In my father's day, the club mercifully designated a "strangers' room," a lounge where ladies could sit inside and order tea while they waited. Although they are not ordinarily allowed into the inner sanctums, the club now holds a few dances and other special occasions where ladies can go to the bar, dining room, and the galleries from which to watch games. But its ethos remains overwhelmingly and unashamedly masculine.

A reporter I know, invited once as a guest, revealed how startled he was by the club's changing room, which is most emphatically not a locker room. Instead of rows of metal lockers with benches for seats, he told me, there was a huge, high-ceilinged, dark room furnished comfortably, where men lay around, nude or in bathrobes, on leather sofas and upholstered chairs, chatting and drinking in front of a toasty fireplace. When it was time to dress, the gentlemen repaired to individual mahogany cubicles. In an article about the club, the *New York Times* said of its changing room, "There is no better place for an afternoon nap in New York." A large portrait of Big Cook dominates one wall.

Big Cook (named for some connection with Captain Cook the explorer, not because he was a cute cookie) had been a spectacular athlete and a long-time president of the club who became the top amateur racquets player of his era, winning the national singles championship twelve times.

Racquets, which is most emphatically not racquetball, is one of two obscure English games that played an enormous role in the Pell and Mortimer families; the other is called court tennis. Developed in eighteenth-century England, racquets resembles squash, but the court is larger and, because the walls are made of slate, the ball travels much faster. The few racquets courts in the United States today are all in private clubs, so the number of amateur players has always been limited to men of means. Here is the way Allison Danzig, a sports writer for the *New York Times*, described my two grandfathers winning the national doubles title around 1930: "Time and again [Mortimer] hurled himself up front to volley and half volley under deadly fire, and in general he played with a fire and gusto reminiscent of his palmier days. Pell's soft drop shots, which were so disconcerting to [their opponents] as the ball clung to the backhand wall, were gems of stroke execution, and both the champion and his partner answered the rifle shots of their opponents with a cannonading of equal fury." According to Danzig, "With the possible exception of ice hockey, there is no other game in which the tempo of the play is maintained at so furious a pitch."

In this world, Big Cook was a heroic figure whose reign as champion lasted so long that it showed up in some "Believe it or Not" column. That success served, I think, to reinforce the sense of aristocracy that the men in my family felt. My grandfathers were the best of the best in their league of the well-born.

During my childhood, I assumed this was the way that grandparents lived, occupying at least two houses and never burdened by the need to earn a living. I particularly liked the splendor of Gargy's Tuxedo house, Keewaydin, which was once owned by Pierre Lorillard. Designed by Stanford White on the highest point in the Park, it was far grander than the places my parents owned. A stone and brown shingle villa with two enormous round towers, the house was dominated by a long, splendid living room that you stepped down into from a double stairway leading off the capacious front hall. Whenever I descended those steps, I felt like a princess making an entrance. I loved to lie on the huge polar bear rug before the massive stone fireplace, my face nestled in white fur. The darkly paneled room was so big that the various clusters of comfortable sofas and chairs seemed miles apart, like separate little villages.

Going to stay at Tuxedo wasn't the way most American kids visit Grandma. For one thing, I was never to bother Gargy, whose prayer times in the morning and nap times in the afternoon were especially inviolate. She didn't make pies with me; in fact, she never entered her own kitchen. She didn't brush my hair, or comfort me if things went wrong, or touch me, except for little air kisses. Among the Tuxedo families, form trumped feeling, even when it came to one's own children and grandchildren. Gargy saw hers only when they were clean and polished and at her convenience.

Without being told, I knew I had to show my grandmother a world in which I was happy and popular. If I went shopping with her in New York, the uniformed chauffeur brought the Packard around, assisted us into the rear seat, arranging the soft fur lap robes if it was chilly. He took his seat behind the wheel and awaited instructions. Once Gargy said, "Bergdorf's, please, Badger," he rolled up the glass window separating him from us, and off we went. Once at our destination, he hopped out and opened the door for us. People on the street stared, and I was slightly embarrassed—but Gargy sailed on into the store, where she was greeted by name and ushered into a special room to be waited on by people who had served her for years.

Apart from an occasional lunch or shopping outing, I saw her at teatime, where the conversations varied little. Unfailingly polite, we chatted about the doings of family members, or plans for the evening, or a recent hand of bridge. Gargy, who played the role of Empress, allowed herself a touch of sarcasm, a cutting adjective, a little smile—nuances telling as Chinese diplomacy. Nothing was permitted to displease her.

In fact, Mummy, before whom her own servants and children trembled, turned into a lamb before her mother, who had evidently once possessed a formidable temper. At home, we could tell when Gargy was on the phone: Mummy's voice went up an octave, like a child's, and any pending crisis or disaster was instantly smoothed over into nothing at all. "Hello, Mum . . . the children are all here and doing wonderfully . . . the fox-hunting has been terrific . . . yes, Mum . . . Goodbye Mum."

Gargy's servants addressed me as "Miss Topsy." In Tuxedo, I stayed on the third floor with my young uncles John Jay and Dickie, or "Master John" and "Master Richard," my mother's much younger brothers, who were not far from my age. Gargy first had four children, my uncles Stanley and Henry, then my mother and Aunt Goody. After a long lapse, she had two more boys. John Jay, not even two years older than I, was a baby at my mother's wedding. He was named for our ancestor John Jay, first Chief Justice of the new United States. Miss Grey, the boys' governess, looked after me, too, when I visited. We ate supper early, at the children's table in an alcove of the large dining room, never with my grandparents. We were brought in to see them at teatime in the afternoon.

Down a garden path stood a playhouse equipped with masses of toys, a stove that worked, and small, wheeled wooden horses covered in real hide. Inside the big house, we could ride up and down in the "lift," as Gargy called it—an old-fashioned, tiny, elevator. John Jay introduced me to radio serials, and we would sit on his bed in our pajamas and bathrobes, listening avidly. To this day, the *William Tell Overture* takes me back to the third floor at

Keewaydin, with its splendid view over the Park, as the Lone Ranger and Tonto chase down the bad guys.

When she saw one of her gardeners standing with his hands in his pocket and a cigarette in his mouth, my grandmother fired him on the spot. No matter how late the evening, her maid Margaret waited up for her to brush her hair before she went to bed. And when traveling in Europe, she felt free to phone her butler in Tuxedo to give him an order, irrespective of the six hour time difference. The butler, of course, said, "Yes, madam," without complaining that her call had woken him and his family in the middle of the night.

But my grandmother took good care of servants whom she liked, paying their medical bills and buying houses for them just the way bountiful lords and ladies in feudal times protected their favorites.

The society columnists celebrating Prince Pierre's desire for "the best" neglected to say that he desired it only for his own class. They never described the miserable shanties in which many of his immigrant workers had to live. While building a modern water and sewage system for those in the Park, along with the most lavish of homes, workers in the Slovak and Italian villages had only a few outdoor pumps for water and little by way of sanitation for themselves. They had to heat their houses with kerosene, and they smelled of it all winter long.

The doctor who served both Park and village tended patients in dark, musty lean-tos patched with tin where several families were crammed in together. In those settings, he had to work by candlelight and wash in a tin basin of water heated over a stove while small children crowded under his feet. An hour later, he could be handing his hat to a butler or a "useful man" in a mansion, his footsteps muffled by thick carpet, greeting the patient's day nurse on the way into the sickroom. Dowagers summoned him to look after their pet dogs.

In all the articles and books I read about Tuxedo, the immigrant laborers were never named or thought of as people with feelings—instead, they were condescendingly pictured as extremely fortunate to be where they were. The astonishing thing is that, in the United States of America, they had no rights at all. One history of Tuxedo, *The World with a Fence around It*, sums it up best: "a feudal anomaly in the land of the free." Pierre Lorillard's Tuxedo Association ran the village like a company town. Workers and tradesmen were not allowed to buy the houses they lived in: the Association retained the power of eviction. No one could set up a business without the Association's consent, and a shopkeeper who displeased the Park families with disrespect or exorbitant prices was swiftly replaced.

The swells in the Park imposed their superiority on the villagers in a multitude of ways. Christ may have preached the brotherhood of man, but Park residents on Sunday morning entered the Episcopal church by the grand main entrance while villagers had to go in through a small side door. Tuxedo hired its own police force and, not surprisingly, its residents felt free to do as they pleased. Shortly after the first stoplight was installed outside the park on the village's main street, Mrs. Clarence Busch, a park resident, drove straight through a red. A policeman stopped her and asked why she had driven through it. "Oh, Officer," she asked in some confusion, "Does that light apply to us?"

My mother, an inveterate speeder, recalled a friend of her parents named Mr. Harris, who was for a while a Tuxedo official. "Once, while he was being driven out from New York by his chauffeur," she reminisced. "Mr. Harris was beating the man with his cane to make him drive faster. When a policeman stopped the car and tried to give him a ticket, Mr. Harris arrested the policeman. Those were the good old days!" She smiled.

It was the same in government. The Tuxedo Association, which consisted of Lorillard and some of his friends, hired managers to run everything. One of these was an attractive gentleman named Charles Patterson who lived in the village. Known to workers as Charlie the Pat, he was Tuxedo's political boss. These newly naturalized citizens learned a peculiar version of the democratic process—those who voted anything but Republican lost their jobs and their houses. In order to prevent such misfortune, since their command of the English language was limited, they were instructed to shun the Democratic Donkey for the Republican Eagle. As Italians, however, they were unfamiliar with eagles—the mighty bird looked more like a pigeon to them. So the order went out to vote for "Charlie the Pat under the pidge or loosa the job." And they did.

In those days, servants "knew their places." The mainstay of Gargy's domain was her butler, Alfred England, a tall Englishman with a small paunch and thinning gray hair combed straight back. Gargy, a small, elegant lady with delicate features, met with England in the round sunroom each morning. She gave orders and he, whose overriding goal in life was to please her, saw that they were carried out.

"England, we'll be ten for tea today."

"Yes, Madam."

"England, please have the car ready at two o'clock."

"Yes, Madam."

"England, please tell Mr. Henry when he calls that I will expect him for lunch at one."

"Yes, Madam."

He called my older uncles "Mr. Stanley" and "Mr. Henry," their wives "Mrs. Stanley" and "Mrs. Henry." There were three Mrs. Henrys—I don't know how he referred to numbers one and two after the divorces, but I'm certain he found a properly respectful term.

England carried himself like a sergeant-major in a tail coat. He oversaw the maintenance and cleaning of Gargy's houses, ruling the dozen or so parlor maids and house cleaners beneath him like a king. He fixed the flowers on her breakfast tray, polished the silver, answered the phone, and served at meals. Every afternoon at five, he led a very short, ceremonial procession into the library. He carried an enormous silver tray on which rested the antique silver teapot, tea kettle on its little burner, sugar bowl and cream pitcher, china cups and saucers, and small linen napkins. It must have weighed a lot, but he held it high. A maid in a black uniform and lacy white apron followed respectfully behind, bearing a round mahogany stand laden with tiers of cake, sandwiches, and cookies. And England also filled in as a valet to my young uncles. In the 1950s, visiting friends told tales of watching, amazed, as John Jay stood in his bedroom, arms outstretched, while England put on his coat. As England aged, his eyesight began to fail and he needed glasses. Gargy did not like to have her butler serve dinner wearing his glasses, so she forbade him to wear them at those times. So poor old England had to navigate his way around the dining room table, serving dishes in hand, from one diner to the next.

Eventually, he retired and died. My uncle Henry Mortimer attended his funeral, which featured an open coffin. Uncle Henry later reported to his wife that England was laid out in his coffin, "defiantly wearing his spectacles."

When Gargy died in 1970, the funeral was held at Tuxedo. Uncle Henry took charge of all the arrangements. A tall man with the prominent chin and aristocratic nose that characterize portraits of John Jay, he was currently married to Aunt "Lindah," as we called her, mocking her British accent. Her grandfather had been Lord Curzon, one of the last British Viceroys of India. The Duke and Duchess of Windsor were the godparents for Henry and Linda's baby son.

At dinner the night before the funeral, I sat on Uncle Henry's right. In the course of conversation it came out that I had just separated from my husband. "It's all right," said Henry, patting me on the hand. "The next one is always better." He and his older brother Stanley Jr. (named of course after my grandfather) once had a discussion over which of them had had the better life. "Of course it's me, Stan," Henry is reported to have said. "I've never been without a beautiful wife *or* a first-class butler."

A stickler for formality and detail, Uncle Henry took charge of everything—undertakers, relatives, and staff. The undertakers decided nothing. Henry treated them as servants, and during all the ceremonies they were invisible. They had been somewhat surprised, when called in, to be told precisely how the service would take place. No limousines were rented; only family cars were used. No grief-stricken bereaved looked to them for professional comfort; they were kept strictly in their place.

At the reception after the service there was the best of everything, as Gargy would have wanted: truckloads of flowers, lobsters from Maine, her house impeccably cleaned and shined. One cousin flew with her husband from France, another from Italy. Another, a young man in the Army, had been compelled to remain on duty. This caused much grumbling in the family. Army regulations stated that the death of a grandmother did not merit a leave; the family pulled political strings to make an exception for the boy, but the attempt failed. The boy's father, my Uncle Stanley, contacted the secretary of the Army, Stanley Resor, who also said No. "Well," humphed one relative later, "Stanley Resor is the little shit who married Jane Pillsbury, and what did *she* have but a lot of flour!" I could understand the family's disappointment that a relative could not come, but I was stunned by the intensity of their outrage at being treated like ordinary people.

CHAPTER THREE

Mummy and Clarry

In the long run, people as individuals are no damn good. When things go wrong, they shoot themselves or jump off bridges. That's why the British have lasted so long: there's a form for everything. That's why I've tried to give you children a sense of family.

—Mummy

If someone tries to make me talk about something I don't want to talk about, I don't talk to that person any more.

—Clarry

Clarry was born in 1911, Mummy in 1918. Theirs were the enchanted childhoods of museum-like mansions and airy summer houses, dogs and ponies, beautifully illustrated leatherbound books, and private lessons in the skills required for people of their class: French, tennis, golf, shooting, and dancing. Servants tended to their needs. Their ancestry put them at the inner circle of New York's elite Four Hundred while their genes blessed them with athletic ability and fabulous looks. They grew up in the world painted by John Singer Sargent.

Evie Mortimer was a long-legged, spirited girl with large eyes and thick, brown corkscrew curls. She loved horses and won silver cups jumping her gray mare, Bar Maid, over fences at the Tuxedo Park Horse Show. Her two older brothers saw that their friends were nice to her, assuring that she was popular. But the Mortimer family was cold and formal. Her mother, the grandmother I called Gargy, had little to do with any of her six children; her life centered on her husband, her Pekinese dogs and her friends. Aunt Goody told me that each child in the family was raised

31

under the influence of a particular servant, and each one took on some of that servant's attributes. Their brother Henry, for instance, spent much of his time with an English butler whose job it was to keep the silver shined: Throughout his life, Henry was particularly fond of old silver and spoke in an affected English accent.

My mother was raised by a French governess called Zellie, who stressed the paramount importance of looks and clothes. Mummy—as we were taught to call her, British style—never, ever Mommy—always cared intensely about appearances, for herself and for everyone around her. Whenever I arrived for a visit, whether as a teenager on vacation from boarding school or as an adult from my California home, she scanned me from hair to shoes, and I knew that later on, I would hear what she thought was wrong. "Hair really looks better when it's a little shorter in the front than in the back, don't you think?" she would say, coming into my room while I was unpacking my suitcase. "It makes a better line than the way you've got it."

Goody told me once, "Zellie was a silly woman who lived through your mother and made sure that your mother never thought. I can see it now, Zellie sitting next to your mother and doing her lessons." Gargy didn't consider education important and felt that mathematics induced headaches, especially in girls. Since the family moved from their mansion in Tuxedo Park for a few weeks in fall and spring, to their New York town house in winter, with a vacation in Palm Beach, and summers in Southampton, such schooling as she and Goody had was sporadic at best. One day, Gargy had a chat with my mother, in which it was decided that instead of taking her senior year at Miss Hewitt's Classes, Mummy would come out. Their brothers, of course, went to off boarding school quite young—St. Mark's, in Massachusetts, and then to Harvard, where they joined the best clubs.

In later life, this absence of education stood my mother in good stead: she used it as an excuse to refuse to read directions. She ignored the instructions that came with answering machines or new telephones or a knitting project, instead directing her sons or daughters to come over right away to install a machine or fix her mistakes. "You children did all those workbooks in school. I never did," she said, justifying her helplessness.

While Goody was a baby, she had her own nurse, but when she got a little older, Gargy decided that there were too many servants in the house. Besides the butler and parlor maid, there was a cook, a cook's assistant, and various upstairs and downstairs maids as well as gardeners, under-gardeners, the chauffeur, and a useful man to lay fires and clean up the servants' dining room. The two older boys had a governess, my mother had Zellie, and Goody had her nurse.

After much thought, Gargy decided that the nurse could be done without. Goody, then about five, was to move out of the nursery and up to the third floor of the house, where Zellie would take care of both her and my mother. At the time, Goody said, she was thrilled. But it turned out to be a harsh promotion. When she moved up to the third floor, Zellie declared, "If you realize that I'm going to have to spend most of my time with Evie, you can do as you like. If you don't understand that, I'll see that you get into trouble with your mother."

Zellie cared only about her Evie. She spent hours shopping so that my mother had beautiful clothes, which she tailored to fit. Zellie arranged for her to have fun with her friends and let her sneak out to parties at night. Mummy would have had a bleak life without Zellie, who was as close to a parent as she had, and she credits Zellie with giving her a happy childhood. For years after her governess grew old and retired to France, Mummy corresponded with her.

I believe that the absence of contact with her parents, contrasted with the affection she received from Zellie, imprinted a model on Mummy. She is very proud of having provided her own children with Nursie, the kindly English widow who came in 1941 to care of my younger brothers and sister and stayed until she died at ninety-eight. It also could explain why my mother showed so little interest in what her children felt and thought. She could leave that to Nursie.

My father was the oldest of three children. His mother, Madeline Borland Pell, the grandmother I called "Mam," dominated the family. Clarry's father, "Big Cook" to his grandchildren, seems to have been a rather weak man with an extraordinary talent for athletics. At Harvard, he was captain of the hockey and tennis teams. Like the Mortimers, Mam and Big Cook had a house in Tuxedo. Cook played sports with Grandpa Mortimer in the clubs where they spent most of their time, and the families were the best of friends. Clarry's younger brother, Nelson, was a charming rogue who was killed in a plane crash, and his younger sister, Katherine, known as Tinkie, was a tomboy who could walk down a flight of stairs on her hands. I learned later that Clarry always felt his parents loved the other two more than they loved him.

In the 1920s, Mam decided that life in Tuxedo was too "fast"—too social and too gilded—and besides, a gorgeous, flirtatious woman in the

Park had fixed her attentions on her husband. The family moved to Old Westbury, Long Island, then a distant suburb of New York City marked by green fields and long driveways leading through avenues of trees to imposing mansions. Life was less formal in Westbury than in Tuxedo, with more casual clothes and fewer ceremonious social engagements. Mam and Big Cook could manage with only a small staff of Irish maids and a cook in the house. The parents could spend more time with their children—and they liked to. Instead of a villa in Newport, Mam bought a farm in New Hampshire for their summer place, hoping that her two sons would drink and carouse less in a more bucolic atmosphere. Clarry, who thrived on swell parties and the glittering social life in Tuxedo, absolutely hated the New Hampshire farm.

He grew up playing tennis and hockey and followed his father's footsteps first to boarding school at Pomfret, then to Harvard. Because he turned out so critical and so harsh himself, he must have felt badly treated as a child, and he used to tell how his parents punished him by locking him in a dark cellar. He also said once that if there were disagreements or cross words at the dinner table, his mother simply rose and walked out. Maybe that's why, as an adult, he refused to engage in any conversation that turned controversial.

But, though his mother was domineering and his father was passive, his paternal grandmother, Grandma Pell, adored him. When he went off to Pomfret, she was newly widowed; she sold her Tuxedo house and bought a house in Connecticut near the school so he would have a place to go for Sunday lunch. And when he went to Harvard in 1929, shortly before the crash, she sent him off in style, with a red convertible, a raccoon coat, and a set of tails.

The Depression didn't much affect their lives—since their fathers didn't need to work for a living, no all-important job was lost; no one was evicted from a home, no one had to fire a servant. When I think about these things, it's hard for me to see why both Mummy and Clarry so idolized their fathers, who were cosseted men living on trust funds, concerned mostly with their comforts, their games, and their clubs. Perhaps that's the power of patriarchy—such men didn't need to earn respect; like wealth, it just fell into their laps.

My mother never questioned the rightness of patriarchy nor did she chafe under the restrictions it imposed on women. In fact, it was patriarchy that impelled her to marry Clarry.

When I was grown up, Mummy often told me the story of how, at the age of sixteen, she fell madly in love, but not with my father. Archie Smith, a handsome, well-built oarsman on the St. Mark's School crew, went to boarding school with her brothers. "He had a lot of speed and was very good-looking," she told me with a smile. "He was a little cheap, so my brother Henry didn't approve of him as my best beau." In her vocabulary, "speed," had attractive, sexual connotations, and she was so smitten that she didn't care that his family may not have met Henry's standards. When Archie was a fifth former at St. Mark's—the equivalent of a high school junior and not entitled to have a girl up for the dance weekend—he and my mother schemed together. They got a sixth former to ask Mummy, who accepted his invitation but spent all her time, of course, with Archie.

One summer night several months later, after a party and many drinks, Archie and some friends were driving in a car. A boy reached over and playfully turned off the ignition key, freezing the steering wheel. There was a wreck, and Archie was killed. "I was on the tennis court when I heard," she went on. "I had to leave the game." Nothing about grief or heartbreak, or shattered hopes—just, "I had to leave the game." But she kept a picture of him in his St. Mark's crew uniform, smiling and holding up a huge oar.

After Archie's funeral, his father came to her house with a large, ornate silver mirror. He said, as he sadly gave it to her, "I want you to remember, when you look in this mirror, you are seeing the face that Archie loved." From then on, the she kept that mirror in the center of the organdy-skirted dressing table in her bedroom.

My mother had been so in love with Archie and so devastated by his death that she decided that she would never again know passion. Eager to get out of the rigid Mortimer household, she was ill equipped to live on her own. For someone of her background in 1936, a job or college was unthinkable; the only out that would please her father and mother was to marry well. She made her escape by choosing, from dozens of suitors, Clarry Pell.

She really wanted to marry his family. His mother and father, who were close friends of the Mortimers, were much more fun then hers, playing family baseball games and skating. "I loved the Pells; they didn't have all those butlers and all those footmen, and they were always laughing," she recalled. My father adored her, the most beautiful debutante to come along in New York in years, and they became engaged. At one point, said my mother, she realized that she was not in love with Clarry and tried to call the marriage off. But he took her to an expensive lunch and, giving her a diamond watch, assured her it would work out happily. She relented. She was only seventeen.

Their wedding before five hundred guests was the social event of the 1936 season.

My mother's dress was made of white satin, with a long court train trailing behind her for yards and yards. Her billowing tulle veil was held in place by a wreath of tiny white blossoms. "It was a proud father who gave her in marriage," the local newspaper observed. "The bride is a granddaughter of Mrs. Henry Morgan Tilford, 'First Lady' of Tuxedo Park. Clarry is a grandson of the aristocratic Mrs. J. Nelson Borland and through his father is related to all the more important Pells of the Social Register. Pelham Manor was named for his family."

For their honeymoon, following proper form, the young couple traveled through Europe. Upon their return to Old Westbury, the newlyweds moved into the house that had just been built for them on a back corner of my Pell grandparents' place, at the end of a long driveway. Though it was fairly spacious, it was always called "the Little House," while Mam and Big Cook's was, of course, "the Big House." Clarry commuted to New York to a job in an insurance firm. His eighteen-year-old bride employed a live-in couple to run the household. Nine months later I was born, so a nanny was added. Upper-class children were considered to be so delicate that a white-uniformed professional was engaged to preside over the nursery, a realm where mere parents were ignorant intruders. Big Cook came to visit me every day, and he always picked a pansy from Mummy's garden to wear in the buttonhole of his jacket.

My mother, who still loved to ride, kept her horse in the barn at the other end of the long driveway. She hired a man to look after the horse, never discussing with him in those Depression years where he would live. Actually, she knew he slept in one of the stalls.

She foxhunted with the Meadowbrook Hounds, galloping happily across the great estates and showplaces of her neighbors—Whitneys, Millses, Phippses, Gerrys—leaping over post and rail fences, clattering down little country roads, a great flying crowd of horses and riders at play. She felt lucky to be a woman. "Personally, I liked the status quo when I married and felt I was definitely getting the better deal, which I was," she wrote me in the 1970s, disagreeing with my budding feminism. "No Long Island commuters' crush for me 5 1/2 days a week. Scads of staff (as they say in jolly old Blighty) and someone always to play with, including yourself, whom I adored."

Adoring or not, she certainly didn't like caring for a baby. One of her few trials was my nurse's day off. On those days, my mother would bring me down to my Pell grandparents at the Big House and then flee home with my cries echoing in her ears. Shortly afterward, she solved the problem by hiring a substitute nurse to come in on the regular nurse's day off. However, she came to dislike the way the regular nurse kept the nursery locked so as to prevent her from coming in. Five months later, she fired that one and hired another, one who would at least leave the door unlocked so the new mother could come in and observe before dashing off again.

No one had ever taught Mummy to do anything useful, parenting included, so perhaps it was not surprising that she was less than enthralled with child care. When I was older, she complained bitterly to me about the agony of my birth and the pain of breast-feeding: "You came at me like a shark," she accused. While in labor, she attacked a nurse who was bringing drugs. The nurse instructed her to stop crying and be braver, saying, "It doesn't hurt *that* much." As my mother told the story, she turned on the nurse in fury, demanding, "Have *you* ever had a baby?" And when the nurse answered starchily, "Of course not, *I* would never do such a thing," my mother grabbed at her face and her tiny white hat. Fortunately, the drugs took effect and the angry laboring mother-to-be fell back empty-handed.

Soon she was returned to her life of dinner parties, gardening, polo games, parties, family baseball games, and clothes—while most of America still endured the Depression.

Two years later, in 1939, she had a son who was named, of course, Clarence Cecil Pell III—a huge and beautiful boy to carry on the family name. He was nicknamed Little Cook, after our grandfather. So we were called Cooky and Topsy instead of Clarence and Eve. Just as we were named for our parents, we were supposed to grow up like them.

Cooky had big dark eyes, curly hair, and apple cheeks. The plan for his life was clear: He would follow the path of his father and grandfather, play sports at Pomfret and Harvard as they had, go into a Wall Street business in a desultory fashion as they had, because he would have family money, as they had, and marry a socially prominent, charming girl, as they had.

When he was a baby, Cooky never cried, my mother said. His adoring Nanny kept him on a strict schedule; Mummy bragged about the immense quantities of milk he sucked from her breasts. He napped contentedly on the lawn in a Rolls Royce of a pram, dark blue, solid and shiny, his plump self covered with a satin-lined fur robe. A Labrador curled up nearby, on guard.

Behind the scenes in our house, however, things were going to pieces. At a dinner party given by my Pell grandparents at the Big House not long after Cooky's birth, Mummy met a six-foot-seven, charming and witty lawyer named Lewis Cass Ledyard, who had been at Harvard with Clarry. He was also married and a father. Although she had thought that her passion had died with Archie, Lewie revived it. She and he fell instantly in love. Mummy escaped again.

The two of them had been indulged all their lives, and, after a long affair, they ran off together when Mummy was twenty-three. I know about this running-off in detail—after I was grown and married, my mother used to tell me the story every year or two. Many years later, Clarry's second wife, Cotty, also described it to me. Although her version differed in some details, it basically confirmed my mother's. In addition, I learned about it from letters that Mummy wrote to Lewie while she was still married to my father. I came across these letters in a startling way.

While I was off at boarding school and college, my bedroom was empty. When Mummy was sick or fretful, which happened quite often, Lewie slept there. Once, when I came home from a vacation, I discovered in my top bureau drawer a stack of old letters from her to Lewie. Fascinated and shocked, I read every one from start to finish. They were passionate, filled with frustration that they both were married to others, and longing to be together. In one letter, she said that Clarry had asked her to have a third child in order to hold their marriage together. She told Lewie she could not do such a thing. Poor Clarry, I couldn't help feeling sorry for him in that situation, cuckolded and helpless.

I surmised that my mother had left the letters in my drawer because she wanted me to understand what had happened in her life. Big mistake. When I mentioned to her the next day that I had seen them, she flew into a rage. "How *could* you read someone else's mail!" she scolded. I was so intimidated that I never replied that they were placed in *my* bureau, and I never dared to ask her how the letters got there. I think now that they were left there by Lewie, who for some reason had been reading them in my room one night and then forgot them. But he never said a word, and I never dared to ask him, either. The letters disappeared from my drawer as mysteriously as they had come.

Soon afterward, my younger sister Wendy found Lewie burning a pile of letters in the driveway. "These can hurt people," he said, explaining what he was doing without telling her what the letters were about.

From those letters, and from what my mother told me, I imagine that their romance went like this:

At a former speakeasy in the town of East Norwich, a few miles from Old Westbury, a tall, handsome man with blue eyes, dark hair combed straight back, and a rather full lower lip sits across a table from a lovely woman in a white silk blouse and tailored black trousers. They sit toward the back of the dark, comfortable room and order Scotch on the rocks. They are in love, making smart remarks back and forth like an off-screen Katherine Hepburn and Cary Grant, with every now and then a quick glance around the restaurant to see who else has come in. The waiter is smiling: the man is teasing him about the specials of the day. "Is this turkey hash made from yesterday's leftovers?" he asks. "Is it any good?" The waiter assures him it is delicious, he will oversee its preparation himself, and the two of them order.

After they eat, they turn serious and sad. It is time to separate, and neither one wants to go home. They've had these discussions before: his wife and daughter; her husband and children—and the war that is spreading around the world as Hitler ravages Europe.

They drive around for a bit in his black Jaguar; his arm around her as they imagine a future together. Lewie begs her to come away with him; he has money, he is a lawyer, everything can be arranged. His two sisters have each been divorced so he has seen the process firsthand, and though it is difficult and unpleasant, unhappy marriages can be ended and new ones begun.

The Scotch and the romance and the drama of the looming war overcome her. She agrees: today, she will leave with him. Later on, she will arrange everything and reclaim her children.

They drive to her house in Old Westbury, in through the narrow opening in the pale green wall that bounds the Pell property, past the Big House where Big Cook and Mam live with their unmarried daughter Tinkie, past the stable and down the drive lined with tiny pine trees to the Little House at the back of the property. She goes in the front door while he waits in the car; her husband is at his office in New York, Cooky and I are taking our afternoon naps. She goes upstairs to her room and finds a suitcase. Baffled for a moment, she opens and closes drawers, rummages through her closet. ("I hadn't ever packed a suitcase before," my mother confessed as she told me this part. "But I knew I'd need a lot of jewelry and underwear.") She fills the suitcase, tiptoes into the nursery to kiss Cooky and me goodbye, scribbles a quick note to her husband, and flees out the door.

Lewie opens the car door for her, then steps on the gas, gravel spraying behind as he speeds down the drive. He can barely believe this is happening! She sits apart from him, half aghast at her own temerity, half thrilled. The car rounds one turn by the stable, another by the Big House. He slows down as the car noses into the narrow gate in the pale green wall; he reaches to pat her hand after he shifts down. And then—Crash! The Jaguar rams into the front bumper of a station wagon turning into the drive. Both cars are immobilized, frozen nose to nose in the gateway.

Lewie leaps out. The other driver is Tinkie, coming home to the Big House. "Tinkie! Are you all right? I couldn't be sorrier," he says, coming around to her door.

"I'm fine. It was my fault, I wasn't looking," she answers politely, a little shaken and somewhat perplexed at seeing her sister-in-law in Lewie's Jaguar.

"No, no. It was my fault. I should have paid more attention," he counters. "I think I can just back up and we'll both be fine." He sees her bafflement, but he doesn't respond. Looking backward he inquires, "Evie, are you all right?"

"Just fine," says my mother in a rather small voice.

"There's no damage, really," Lewie concludes, inspecting the two bumpers. He gets into his car and backs up, leaving room for Tinkie to drive her station wagon past him on her way home.

They wave to one another as the cars pass, smiles pasted on their faces. Lewie and my mother drive on for a few miles in silence. She starts to fidget, turning her huge emerald and diamond engagement ring around and around on her finger. "I can't do it. You'll have to turn around," my mother finally announces.

"Evie . . ." he pleads.

"Nope. Take me home. I don't know what I was thinking."

As the Jaguar approaches the Little House, my mother sees my father's car parked outside. "Well, goodbye. I'm sorry." She kisses Lewie, grabs the suitcase, and strides in through the front door. Her heels clatter as she marches down the hall and into the living room. A stricken Clarry is on the phone, calling his parents. "I don't know what to do . . ." he is saying.

"You may as well hang up," she announces briskly. "I'm back."

And so she stayed with Clarry for a little while longer. "I only had one fight with your father," she reminisced to me, years later. "I wanted a divorce and he wouldn't give it to me."

Then, a few months later, she really did leave, and the serene routine of Cooky's and my life turned upside down. Disowned and cut off by her embarrassed parents, my mother quickly got a job modeling. She loved making an impression with her looks: I remember that, when she was dressed up, she seemed remote, more removed from motherhood than usual. It was as if she were absorbed in her own beauty and in the effect she created with it.

I have in a photo album a glamorous picture of her modeling an evening dress. She is seated in profile on an ottoman, looking pensively down, the chiffon skirt swirling in delicate waves around her ankles. My mother was so young, charming and naïve that the experienced models showed her how to put on makeup and what to do.

She earned money and went to Reno, the only place then where one could get a quick divorce. In a small cabin there, she confronted a stove for the first time. When Cooky and I, who were then two and four, were allowed to come and visit her, she cooked peas into black bullets, not knowing you had to put water in the pot. She told me that I loyally ate them anyway. One morning, Cooky climbed up onto a table and tumbled off, striking his head on the stone floor so hard that he needed stitches. It was typical of the scrapes he began getting into. I remember our stay in Reno as an adventure by Lake Tahoe, seeing snakes sunning themselves on the rocks below our cabin, and being closer to our mother than we ever were in Old Westbury. I also have a vivid memory of her speeding off on the back seat of a man's motorcycle.

When we got back to Clarry's after that visit, he was involved with a new woman, a pretty, blonde woman named Lucy Jeffcott, nicknamed Cotty, whom my grandparents regarded as a social climber. I remember her driving up to our house in a convertible with the top down and not liking it. She would be our stepmother for fifteen years.

In 1940, as these things were happening in our lives, World War II was raging in Europe. Lewie, who had a pilot's license, joined the Canadian Air Force and moved to Canada. He gave a million dollars to his wife so she would agree to divorce him, and he sent money to our mother while she was getting her divorce.

Cooky and I lived with our father and our nanny at the Little House while Mummy was in Nevada. Mam was so furious with Mummy that she teamed up with Clarry to help him get permanent custody. I think that Clarry was so humiliated by my mother's very public and scandalous desertion that he, too, wanted to make her pay, so he went along with Mam's plans, and they hired a detective to try to prove that she was an unfit mother.

In a confusing sequence of events that I have never been able to pin down exactly, Cooky and I were kidnapped. As my mother tells it, she missed us dreadfully and wanted us to come to Reno for another visit, which Clarry and Mam would not permit. So she secretly arranged with our nanny to bring us from Westbury back to Reno to see her again. Two days before Cotty and Clarry were to be married, the nanny spirited us onto a train headed west. But this nanny, who had professed loyalty to my mother, betrayed her by secretly letting the Pells know where we were going and what train we would be on.

Many years later, when I asked her to describe that period, Cotty told me that when Clarry found out that we children had gone missing, he scrapped the formal wedding plans, insisting instead that the ceremony take place hurriedly the very next morning ("My mother was so rushed that she wore one brown shoe and one black shoe to the church," said Cotty). Then Clarry, Cotty, and a pair of hired detectives flew in a small plane across the country to Cheyenne, where our train made a long stop ("Not much of a wedding night," grumbled Cotty, remembering). While our train stood in the Cheyenne station, Clarry and the two detectives raced through Pullman cars searching the seats and compartments until they found us. They snatched us off. The train pulled out of the station without us, and when my mother went to meet it in Reno, we were not aboard.

Cotty further complained that she and Clarry and the detectives drove around with us for a few days staying in motels, Clarry sleeping in a bed with Cooky and she in a bed with me. My father registered as "Carleton Palmer," a name with the same initials as Clarence Pell. Then they took us to the New Hampshire farm where Mam and Big Cook spent their summers. We had round-the-clock shifts of armed bodyguards but I remember only one, a man named Lester who showed me his shiny gun. It was Christmas time: I remember sledding into a fence and jamming my lower teeth through the cleft above my chin. I had to have stitches, and I still have the scar. Cooky ate the ornamental berries off a Jerusalem cherry and he had to go to the doctor, too. I got sympathy but he got into trouble.

I don't remember the train or the kidnapping. But I do remember Cooky and me having to go live with Clarry and Cotty. She hired a disagreeable Swiss governess to look after us. Miss Sieber gave us Spam and Del Monte fruit cocktail every night for dinner in our nursery, and ever since then I won't eat either one. Clarry and Cotty, of course, dined later, by themselves, and not on Spam.

After Pearl Harbor, our lives changed again. With the United States entry into the war, Clarry had to enlist in the military. Because he knew how to fly, he chose the U.S. Ferry Command, which transported military supplies and injured soldiers by air. Meanwhile, the legal battle over our custody raged on. My mother asked that, since our father was no longer in the house, she be awarded custody of us. At first, she failed.

Newspapers chronicled the socialites' drama. A clip from the New York *Post* of February 17, 1942, headlined "Pell Guardianship Order Stirs Colony," mentioned the "frisson" that swept Palm Beach society after a court formally awarded us to our father for a term of three years. "Plan will hamper Mother's plans," said the subhead, noting that Mummy was married and living in Canada at that time. "Eve will be permitted to visit the children one day a week, provided that she gives Clarence 24 hours notice." The article added that if she wished to visit us in our nursery, she would have to write him for permission. In case the two could not agree who would have us after the three years were up, the judge named a committee to decide our custody. On this committee were our two grandfathers, Clarry's brother Nelson, and a Wall Street lawyer, a former counsel to the New York Stock Exchange.

Not a single woman. I think now how isolated our mother must have felt, with such men sitting in judgment of her, and her children taken away for three years! But then all I knew was that Cooky and I were shuttled from one place to another. The process felt like a series of abandonments as Mummy went to Reno and Canada, Clarry went to war, and we never knew which family we would be with or for how long.

The legal battle was resolved in a peculiar fashion. According to my mother, a clerk made an error on a court order: instead of giving custody of us to Clarry, the mis-typed document gave us to her. Armed with this paper, she swiftly took us to live with her and Lewie in Canada, where he was teaching novice airmen to fly and she was producing babies. I was deeply relieved to get away from Cotty, the nasty governess, and the Spam.

Once remarried, Mummy and Clarry remained perfect specimens of their class, and they passed its values on to their children. To both of them, "form" was the key—whether it be the way one shakes hands (firmly, looking the other person in the eye) or the way one deals with family and friends (avoiding unpleasantness or messy emotions), or the proper role of gentlemen and ladies (female deferring to male), or the clothing one wears (classic, tweedy, not the latest fashion). "Form" provides the blueprint for handling all sorts of people and situations; it provides a bulwark against the random happenings of life.

In Greek myth, Procrustes was a robber who lived by the side of the road. He invited passersby into his house and forced them to lie on his bed. Then, he tailored them to fit. If they were too tall, he cut. If they were too short, he stretched. No one passed unscathed.

Growing up in an upper-class family was like passing by Procrustes: the child had to be tailored to fit—stretched a little here, shortened a little there. It almost didn't matter how parents treated children or whether they were good parents—what mattered was the child fitting into the class. And if the child could not, or would not, conform, the penalty was severe.

Clarry and Mummy conformed. According to the Declaration of Independence, all men are created equal. But you'd never have sold that to my mother or my father. They knew they were aristocrats; they knew they were special, and they expected to be treated accordingly. People not of their class, which is most everyone, called them Mr. Pell and Mrs. Ledyard. They, however, called others Belle or Ralphie or England or Tim. An old and beloved retainer might address my mother as "Mrs. L," but despite the affection between them, the difference in rank remained crystal clear.

My mother retained a comfortable blindness about the master-servant relationship. "When you get old, your servants become your best friends because they have the same interests you do," she used to say, without a hint of irony. By those "same interests," though, she meant her house, her garden, her furniture, her health, her horses, her dinner parties, and her family. She was not interested in her servants' lives, except to be annoyed when they went on vacation or were kept from work by illness. (There was one major exception to this rule, however: when our old Nursie got sick, in her nineties, after forty-five years of service, Mummy kept her at home, brought up her meals on a tray, and saw that Nursie had everything she needed.)

As years went by, Mummy could not understand why young people didn't want to go into domestic service. "You just can't find people like Helen any more," she told me a few years ago.

I remembered Helen all too well. In 1974, when I was a thirty-seven-year-old mother of three, I flew from my California home to visit my mother at her Pennsylvania farm. As usual, I had breakfast upstairs with her in her large, airy bedroom. A fire burned brightly in the small, brick hearth. Flowered chintz curtains framed the windows, which looked out over acres of green pastures where racehorses, ponies, and cattle grazed. Family photographs, in silver or leather frames, crowded her dressing table, the two polished antique bureaus, and the small side tables. There were brides in white dresses and veils, debutantes in white dresses without veils. There were grandchildren jumping ponies over fences, Gargy and Grandpa looking aloof, several men of the family in tails at a family wedding holding champagne glasses and laughing, Cooky as a newborn in his bassinet. Everything was in its place: the brass drawer pulls on the bureaus shone; inside were rows of neatly arranged stockings, underclothes, handkerchiefs, nightgowns, all washed by a laundress and put away by a maid.

My mother sat up on one side of her large bed eating breakfast from a tray, her back against its white quilted headboard appliquéd with pink and red roses, her curly brown hair brushed, both of her dogs snoozing nearby. She fed them little tidbits of toast and bacon.

I sat comfortably ensconced in a white chaise longue piled with lace-edged pillows with my own tray, complete with little linen napkin, coffee pot, and fine flowered china. Whenever I came to visit, I had breakfast with her upstairs like this, and we chatted.

But this particular morning, there was an interruption. Helen, the downstairs maid in her white uniform, knocked at the open door. She was quite old, with cropped white hair and a wrinkled face. She was so polite that the family referred to her behind her back as "Pardon me," because she said that every time she spoke to us. "Pardon me" was trembling, nearly in tears; bits of china in her hands rattled against each other.

"Pardon me, Mrs. Ledyard . . ." she quavered.

Instantly, my mother saw what happened. While she was dusting in the library, Helen had broken a small antique bowl, and she had come to confess.

"I can't *stand* it!" scolded my mother, furious, from her bed. "I can't keep *anything* in this house. *All* my best things get smashed! People are so damn *careless!*" She vented her rage at the hapless servant for several eternally long minutes. "That china is *irreplaceable*. I've told you I don't know *how* many times to be more careful." Helen stood there, taking it, apologizing from the doorway over and over until the verbal lashing finally subsided.

While this tirade ran its course, I sat, frozen, on the chaise longue, eyes fixed on my breakfast. Spots of egg yolk congealed on the plate; the cream muddied the color of the coffee in its gold-rimmed cup. My mother was relentless in her anger; Helen stood like a butterfly impaled on a pin. The scolding seemed to go on forever, just like the scoldings my mother used to unleash on me when I was little. I didn't say a word. It didn't even occur to me to intervene and tell my mother to stop, although I knew that what was happening was profoundly wrong—I was as frightened of my mother as Helen was. I have been ashamed of my silence ever since, which is probably why I remember the incident so vividly.

Yet my mother, in another situation and without the slightest sense of being a hypocrite, would tell you earnestly that she felt *kindness* was one of the great virtues in the world; she would also tell you how wonderful Helen was.

It was the same for us as children if we damaged something—and we knew never to touch the Steuben glasses on the pantry shelf, labeled in her handwriting, VERBOTEN!

I spent years lying so as to avoid getting in trouble:

No, I didn't spill any ink on that desk.

I didn't make that stain on the rug.

I checked the water in all the horses' buckets, I know I did.

Even today, sometimes a lie will leap from my mouth so that I don't annoy somebody, so that I won't evoke a hostile response.

It's a long way from "Mummy" and "Clarry" to "Mom" and "Dad," a journey that, as their daughter, I would have loved to see them make. But it wasn't a journey that ever occurred to them.

CHAPTER FOUR

These Children Don't Cry

When you are young, class comes as a great surprise.

—Philip Roth, interviewed on "Fresh Air." 9/27/05

I was eight when World War II ended; my mother was twenty-seven. Clarry and Lewie, who had completed their military service, were both thirty-four. By then, Mummy and Clarry's custody war was over, too. Cooky and I would live mostly with her, and she (with help from Lewie) would pay all our expenses. Mummy and Lewie bought a farm on Long Island in Huntington, New York, farther out from the city than Old Westbury.

There were four of us children when we moved there: Cooky and I, who were Pells born before World War II, and Wendy and Cass Ledyard, born during the war. We lived at Whitehackle Farm, Huntington, New York, no street address, no house number, no zip code needed, thank you. My father and his parents (Old Westbury, N.Y.) didn't need those, either, and neither did my grandmother Mortimer (Tuxedo Park, N.Y.) except for her town house in New York City. Outside of New York City, I thought, only common people had house numbers—people like us didn't need them.

Forests and fields extended for miles beyond our one hundred acres, and some of the roads were still dirt. Suburbs hadn't spread out that far, and the

Long Island Expressway didn't yet exist. But Lewie, the fifth generation in his family to become a lawyer, could commute by the Long Island Railroad to New York City, where he began work in the venerable family firm, Carter, Ledyard and Milburn. (His grandfather, Lewis Cass Ledyard Sr., had been J. P. Morgan's lawyer.)

Our picturesque red farmhouse dated from 1795; its white shutters had little moons carved near the corners. Mummy and Lewie loved the signs of its age: axe marks on the low ceiling beams, uneven wide-planked floors, and swirls in the window glass. At six-foot-seven he was so tall that he had to duck his head when he walked through the old doorways. A white picket fence surrounded the spacious front lawn, and twin rows of box bushes lined the brick walk up to the front door. Behind the house, another lawn ran downhill to a circular pond where mallard and Muscovy ducks swam. Drifts of daffodils bloomed there in the spring, dotting the newly green grass around the pond with yellow and white.

They transformed the rundown farm into a country squire's dream. Down with the sagging porch off the kitchen and up with a servants' wing. Away with the plow horses Beauty and Belle; in with the thoroughbred hunters and ponies. Out with the weeds and thistles; in with the pansies and delphiniums. Mummy and Lewie strode across their fields followed by hunting dogs: coon hounds, retrievers, setters, and pointers. They went off on shooting trips, returning with grouse, pheasant, and wild ducks.

We children ran wild: we played hide and seek in the vast haylofts over the horse barn and the cow barn. We climbed the prickly, sweet-smelling stacks of hay bales, tugging them around to make forts and castles, then swung like Tarzan on ropes dangling from the high beams overhead. When our cousins from New York visited, we brought them up to the hayloft and, when they stood, frightened, on the high bales, we grabbed onto the hanging ropes, swung away yelling "City slickers! City slickers!" and hid from them.

We rode from our earliest years, taking our ponies along the country dirt roads and forest paths, building little fences from fallen logs so the ponies would have to jump over them. Sometimes we pretended to be ponies ourselves, galloping along the paths, whinnying, and leaping over the logs. When it snowed, Mummy hitched up a quiet old mare to a sleigh and drove her along the back roads while we tied our sleds and rode along behind listening to the sleigh bells.

If we visited the doctors' offices after falling off horses or getting childhood diseases or for vaccinations, we were stoic. "These children don't cry. They're much more scared of their mother than they are of anything we do," one nurse observed. She was right. If we cried over some injury, or because we were scared of something, Mummy got annoyed. "Stop that! Or I'll give you something to *really* cry over," she would snap.

When we first moved there, Lewie hired German prisoners of war during haying season. Dozens of them arrived on the backs of flatbed trucks, crew-cut, glum, and clad in baggy uniforms. They worked in our fields and were carted away at the end of each day. While they were working for us, our smokehouse where we cured bacon caught fire and our garage, too. Fire engines came, sirens wailing. Afraid that the gasoline pump in the garage would explode, Mummy herded us children far away from the flames, but the firemen put the blaze out in time. We wondered if one of the prisoners had set the fire to get back at America.

At Whitehackle Farm, we produced our own milk, cream, butter, ice cream, bacon, vegetables, poultry, pork, lamb, and beef. We children saw how meat got to the table.

When a cow was to be slaughtered, it was led out from the barn. Billy Crofts, our burly farm foreman, raised a sledge hammer high in the air over his head and bashed it between the horns. It crumpled instantly to the ground and was later butchered. Chickens got their heads lopped off with an axe and flopped around afterward.

Pig killing was the worst. After Billy sliced the live pig's throat, it ran, screaming and bleeding all around the big barnyard until finally it fell over dead. Then its hind legs were trussed and the body hoisted high, pulled by a rope slung over a tree branch. Billy lowered the pig head first into a rusty barrel of steaming hot water. After the scalding, the dripping corpse was hauled up out of the barrel, and Billy slit its belly from top to bottom. Shiny purple guts spilled out as the knife sliced through the skin.

We children took most of this in stride, munching our dinners without thought of the once-living beings we ate. But then came Rammie, an orphan lamb whom we raised on a bottle. We played with him until he grew up and joined the herd. One Sunday lunch months later, instead of the usual roast beef, we had lamb chops. "Children," announced Lewie. "This is Rammie." We screamed, cried, and fled from the table. To this day I wonder what made Lewie do such a cruel thing. Of the two, he was the kind, fun one we loved to be with, and Mummy was the mean one with the sharp tongue.

Our herd of Jersey cows produced Grade A Raw milk. Long rows of cows, their heads held in metal stanchions, lined the two sides of the dairy barn. Above each cow was a sign telling her registered name—something fancy, such as Blue Meadow Royal Duchess. In those pre-cholesterol days, Jersey milk was prized because it had the very highest butterfat content. At the top of each glass bottle was a bulge where the cream collected, labeled with the words, "It Whips." Ours was no ordinary milk.

Lewie was most enthusiastic about some animals you wouldn't find on Old McDonald's farm—fighting cocks. In fact, the farm was named for a particular breed of fighting cock—the Whitehackle. One field was filled with row upon row of large wire cages, each with its own little coop and a trapeze suspended from the top of the cage for the bird to perch on. The cocks had to be kept apart from one another or they would battle to the death as they had been bred to do.

Mummy and Lewie had all these animals in part because they liked them (dogs and horses), in part for food (dairy cows, sheep and pigs), in part for competition (fighting cocks and horses). But a more fundamental purpose was for breeding. They loved thoroughbreds. Even Cooky's puppy "Skipper" had papers and a formal, registered name: "Pine Hills Dusky Prince." Lewie had genealogy charts for the fighting cocks, planning each mating so as to produce the bravest and strongest individuals. He had charts on the Jersey cows, correlating their ancestry with their milk production, butterfat content, and conformation. He researched the bloodlines of the dogs and horses for good noses or speed or the ability to jump fences—in addition to beauty, strength, and courage. Like medieval Europeans, he and Mummy believed that nobility in people was inherited as it is in animals.

There was a complicated hierarchy in our home, where parents were the thoroughbreds who gave the orders while nannies and servants were the commoners who obeyed. As children, we learned that parents were not to be disturbed; if we questioned the order of things, we risked humiliation; and if we wanted something, we should ask one of the staff.

Our daily routine began with Nursie waking us up. We dressed in clothes that had been neatly laid out on a chair the night before, maybe for me a plaid jumper with a round-collared white blouse underneath, white socks, and brown oxfords. In those days, girls were not allowed to wear pants to school. Then I brushed my teeth and combed my hair in my own bathroom, gathered up my homework from the tiny, antique rolltop desk where I studied, and tiptoed silently along the narrow corridor past our mother's bedroom door and down the front stairs, careful not to wake her up.

We sat at the round table in the small children's dining room overlooking the lawn and the duck pond while Mrs. Beveridge, the cook, made our breakfast. A white-uniformed waitress served it to us. (Though the cook and our Nurse stayed on for years, other servants came and went rather often.) We were lucky in Mrs. Beveridge, a plump Scottish widow who had never been a domestic before she came to cook for us. She didn't know that in a proper household, the cook never allows children to enter the kitchen. She not only let us in, she liked us, and she let us take bits of bread dough and braid it or make it into other shapes that she then placed in the huge, black oven for us to eat later. I loved the smell of the baking bread, her kindness and pleasure as she showed me what to do, and the feel of the moist, springy white dough between my fingers. I wished that my mother was plump, had a bun of gray hair, and wore an apron like Mrs. Beveridge.

By the time we finished breakfast, Lewie had ridden around the farm on his horse, supervising the dairy and giving instructions to Billy, the farm manager, who called him "Boss." ("Billy, you better check the fence in the lower field; the cows might get out again." "Okay, Boss.") Sometimes on his prebreakfast tours, Lewie met with Harry Kearney, the old Irishman who trained the fighting cocks, to see how their conditioning was coming along, or how the new chicks were doing in their warm brooders in the horse barn.

His inspection completed, Lewie strode into the kitchen. "Out of the way, Mrs. Beveridge!" he boomed. "It's my turn." He cooked his own breakfast on the big restaurant stove, we children watching as he chopped spinach to make green scrambled eggs or fried up cornmeal mush with sausage. He ate from a special dark blue plate decorated with chickens. When he had changed from riding clothes into his Brooks Brothers suit, we piled into his car. He might use his Mercedes, or maybe the Cadahackle, a black Cadillac hearse that he remodeled to transport his fighting cocks. The Cadahackle looked like something Batman or the Green Hornet might have driven, elongated and vaguely sinister. We then raced at top speed to the town of Syosset, where Lewie caught the Long Island Railroad commuter train to New York and where we waited for our school bus. We'd usually pass the time hanging around Weinstock's store, buying comics and candy with our allowance money. The bus ride to Green Vale School took an hour. We had that long, two-stage commute because Green Vale was considered the best of Long Island's private schools. The local public school in Huntington was out of the question for the likes of us.

At Green Vale, we girls were top students, Cooky was usually in trouble, and Cass daydreamed. Wendy's and my success irritated my mother. "What a shame it's you girls who do well at lessons," she complained. "It's the boys who matter."

The gardener's helper picked us up at Syosset in the afternoon. At home, we did our schoolwork and listened to radio serials, following the adventures of Superman, Jack Armstrong, the All-American Boy, Captain Midni-i-i-ight, and Tom Mix. (We drank Ovaltine and sent away for decoders, badges, special whistles, and other treasures.) We might see our mother arranging flowers in the library or having her tea. Then, at six, we ate supper in the children's dining room.

Mummy and Lewie dined alone in the proper dining room at seven. The waitress, now wearing a black uniform and white apron, lit the candles, announced that dinner was ready, then, after they had left their cocktails in the living room and were seated at opposite ends of the polished mahogany table, passed the food in silver serving dishes. I longed for the day when I would be old enough to join them. I wouldn't be an awkward child any more, and I'd take on some of their elegance.

Annoy our mother and you paid for it. Cooky and I were playing noisily one summer morning, chasing each other around the third floor nursery, then racing down the stairs. "Topsy! Cooky! Come right here!" We froze. "Hurry up!" She summoned us into her darkened bedroom, Venetian blinds keeping out the sunlight, lacy pillows piled high on her white chaise longue. "Can't you remember anything I tell you?" she scolded. "You are the most *thoughtless* children! How can I get *any* sleep at all if you crash around like that! You know the rules." Then, her long bathrobe trailing behind her, she got adhesive tape from her bathroom and taped our mouths shut. "That should help you remember," she said, and, returning to bed, sent us away. I remember closing her door and tiptoeing down the stairs afterward, my lips squeezed tightly together by the tape. By lunch time, she let us take it off.

I found solace in books. Mam, my Pell grandmother, taught me to read when I was four, and from then on I plunged into worlds of myth and enchantment, of stallions and ponies and collies, of witches and fairies, heroes and heroines. I soared on the wings of Pegasus, I thrilled for the Count of Monte Cristo, tears ran down my cheeks when Black Beauty was beaten by a cruel master. When I was six, I discovered Shakespeare. Rudyard Kipling, Robert Louis Stevenson (with the N. C. Wyeth illustrations), Mark Twain, Louisa May Alcott, Harriet Beecher Stowe and the Bobbsey twins—I tore through them all as fast as I could. Though we were forbidden to read before breakfast because that would damage our eyes, I took the risk. At night, I kept a flashlight in my night table and read under the covers.

My love of books, however, cost me my first and only dog. When I was six, my mother gave me a brown and white Springer spaniel named Rusty. Unfortunately, I was supposed to housebreak Rusty, who had a monumental capacity to pee. But when he barked to go out, as he knew to do, I was off in the Middle Ages at the court of King Arthur or flying with Pegasus in ancient Greece. My mother remembers seeing me lost in a book in a big armchair, the dog right in front of me barking piteously, then a yellow stream running across the rug. Engrossed in my story, I never heard him. Many smelly rugs later, she gave Rusty away. I felt terribly guilty, envisioning him beaten like the dogs in the books I read. "I didn't take care of him!" I sobbed into my pillow, working myself up to a damp and monumental sadness. But I never told my mother about my worries, and I did my crying in private. To this day I am the only member of the family who doesn't have at least one dog.

Books and servants, those were the consolations. I could imagine that, however powerless I was as a child, and however desperate to avoid being scolded, when I grew up, I might find another way to live. In books, some adults were kind to children, and children often managed to outwit bad people and live happily ever after. The soft virtues—affection, warmth, consideration—seemed to me rooted in people of the lower classes, like Nursie, Billy Crofts's wife Connie, and Mrs. Beveridge; they were rarely found among the aristocracy, like my parents.

Quite a parade of hired women passed through our house, some more than once because they quit and later came back. One upstairs maid, a plain Irishwoman named Mary, used to come up to my room in the afternoons. She brought with her a glass of clear liquid, which I took to be water, and sipped it as she sat on the toilet seat in my bathroom. I sat on the edge of my bathtub, listening as she talked about her family in the old country. "Ye poor little children," she said to me as she sipped. "I feel so sorry for ye." Mary's soft brogue was soothing. I felt comforted that someone else saw the worries I lived with.

But Mary did not last long. Declining levels in the gin decanter downstairs gave her away, and she was packed back to New York.

At Whitehackle Farm, Mummy and Lewie played out their lord-and-lady-of-the-manor lives. Foxhunting prints and racing pictures hung on the walls;

pale rugs covered the floor. Flowered chintz curtains framed the windows; comfortable chairs and sofas were carefully arranged around the living room and library. She placed flawless bowls of flowers on the antique desks and tables.

I remember once wanting to tell my mother about a new plan for my doll house. I ran into the living room as she sat on the edge of a sofa, fixing some flowers. "I have an idea," I said to her excitedly. "Treat it kindly, it's far from home," she replied, laughing at her own joke as she placed a rose in just the right spot. I was crushed. She wasn't the least interested in me or my idea, so I went away. In fact, she was never interested in what I thought or felt—she didn't talk with me about the divorce, or step-parents, or where babies came from, or even what I liked at school.

My mother had a staff of four to keep the house the way she wanted it: a cook, a downstairs maid, and an upstairs maid who lived in, and a laundress who came in every day to do our clothes and linens. She had Nursie to tend to us.

Many years later, I had words with Mummy over the fact that she hadn't really been there for us as a mother. "Times were different then," she answered, deflecting my criticism. "And what better thing could I have done for you children than to give you Nursie?"

A tiny, hunched English widow, Nursie came in 1943 when Cass was born, and she stayed until she died at ninety-eight. Her real name was Emma Hartin, her hair was white and arranged in neat waves, and she struggled all her life with lumpy bad feet. Nursie, whose status was higher than that of the other help, lived on the third floor with Cass and Wendy, whom we called "the babies." She ate upstairs on a tray and had her own silver teapot, while the other servants ate together in their own tiny dining room off the kitchen. They had a china teapot.

Though she never criticized Mummy or Lewie—Mr. and Mrs. Ledyard to her—she comforted us after we had been scolded or spanked, and occasionally she covered up if we had done something wrong. She soothed us with tea and cookies, the tea hot and milky and sweet. "There, there, never mind," she'd say when we retreated, snuffling, up to the third floor. "Your mother didn't mean it." She wasn't one for hugs, but her kindness and concern for our feelings let us know that she cared. Wendy's fantasy was that Lewie would marry Nursie and take us all to California. Somehow, Out West, things would be easier.

I loved Nursie, and when I was young, I was not fully aware of her complicated status in the house. But when I got to sixth and seventh grade, I became more aware of social class. In my small scheme of things, there were four levels of people: a bottom tier of servants and men who worked on the farm; up a step to teachers, who were sort of like servants and sort of not; up another step to doctors, and, at the top, people such as my parents, who told everyone else what to do. Servants could be—and often were—more lovable than parents, but they were of a lower status and therefore not fit for certain things. Servants, for instance, never went riding or gave orders, and wore their own clothes only on their days off. Some subjects were not to be discussed in front of them; I had seen my parents break off arguments or discussions about family problems when a maid came into the room.

I forget what the issue was, but Wendy, who was then about seven, had some problem that she took to Nursie. I, who was twelve, thought I knew much more about social distinctions than Wendy, and I informed her that she should have taken this issue to Mummy instead of to a servant.

When my mother heard about this, I really caught it. "You must *never* call Nursie a servant!" she exclaimed. "She is more of a lady than most people you'll ever know," she went on, furious. "Go right up and apologize, and never do such a thing again!" I was thoroughly puzzled: Though Nursie wore a uniform like a maid, worked for my mother in the house, and did what my mother said, she was not a maid. I had failed to properly Distinguish, and I apologized. But then, a few months later, I got it wrong the other way. As I was starting dancing class, my mother gave me a small string of Oriental pearls that had been hers. She fastened it around my neck, stood back to see how it looked, and told me it was worth a thousand dollars. To me, in 1949, that seemed like the riches of the Incas. I rushed upstairs to show Nurse my new treasure and boasted to her that it was worth A THOUSAND DOLLARS!

Bad move. When Mummy heard about that, I got scolded for Bragging about Money to Someone of a Different Class. I had failed again to properly Distinguish. Somehow, I never could get the class thing right. During the war, I went to a proper girls' private school where we wore uniforms with neckties and green jumpers. A field was flooded in winter so we could skate, and we were taught to be ladylike and to sew. Cooky, on the other hand, went to a public school near our house. No uniforms, undistinguished buildings, no lessons in manners, no sense of exclusivity. This worried me, so I consulted my mother. "Why does Cooky have to go to school with the raggy people?" I asked. Another big mistake: instead of answering, she howled with laughter—plainly, I was not supposed to mention such Distinctions, and I was teased for years about being a snob.

It was important to Distinguish outside the family as well as inside. My friends from Green Vale School had nannies, too. Mimi Mills's was called Nanny Mills, and Nancy Gerry's was Miss Orkney. They were English and loved having tea with each other. When I went to their houses to spend the night, the nanny unpacked my suitcase. My friends' mothers were as remote as mine. (Actually, more so, since Mummy at least spent hours teaching me to ride, which she wanted me to do.) It was inconceivable to me that a mother would actually do for a child something that the child wanted.

When we lived at Whitehackle Farm, only one other family nearby was of our social class, the Peabodys. But Peter and Patricia Peabody were not allowed to run wild on their place as we were on ours, so Cooky and I found them boring and never played with them. However, a man who worked on their place had twin sons, Lester and Ray, who were ten, as I was, and infinitely more interesting. Ray was skinny and smart, Lester muscular and quiet. We met sometimes in the canvas Indian tent I had been given for Christmas, which stood in our woods, and they taught me to smoke cigarettes. I hated the taste, but choked the hot, nasty smoke down anyway so as not to alienate these most interesting newcomers. With them, I wandered the trails in the woods and played hide-and-seek in our hayloft. After a while, their father moved on to another job.

With the twins gone, the only person around to play with, besides my brothers and Wendy, was Ronnie Crofts, Billy's son. Ronnie was my age, round-faced and plump. He and I climbed trees, explored the nearby woods and waded in ponds in summertime, our feet sinking deep into muck as bubbles of swamp gas floated to the surface and burst. But, though no one ever actually mentioned it, a vast social gap separated us. He never ate at my house or even came any farther inside than the kitchen. I could go to his house, though, where his mother was very nice to me and gave us cookies. His parents, who lived in a little house at one end of our place, called mine Mr. and Mrs. Ledyard, and my parents called his Billy and Connie. My parents owned the house they lived in.

Ronnie said, "Yeah," and "ain't," which I wasn't allowed to do, and he used other words I couldn't say either. If something was funny, he called it "comical." When I used these words in front of my mother, she told me they were "cheap," and I was not to say them again.

Plainly, Ronnie couldn't be a real friend. And he kept breaking my bones.

One afternoon, we were wrestling on the front lawn. He had the advantage in our wrestling matches, being a much bigger, fatter boy against a skinny little girl. That day, after he had gotten me down and I was lying pinned on my back, he rose in victory and as he did so, stepped on my left collarbone. It snapped under his weight. So it was off to Dr. Kurshan, who was used to patching us up after we had fallen off ponies or bicycles; he wrapped up my shoulder in a warm, moist plaster cast.

A year later, Ronnie and I were playing around the cow barn. We sat on a windowsill, wondering if we could jump across a narrow space and land in the dairy window a few feet away. If we missed, we risked a longish fall to the ground below—it was an interesting proposition. While we sat there speculating, Ronnie gave me a little shove. I tumbled off the sill, hit the hard ground and broke the same collarbone again.

Back then, I figured those were just accidents—he was very sorry, very nice—and I didn't stop playing with him. Now, I wonder whether he was envious of all that I had, and whether my injuries were what we used to call "accidentally on purpose."

Unlike us, Ronnie did not have to learn manners.

"Curtsy to grown-ups when you say, 'How do you do.' Look them in the eye, and don't shake hands like a dead fish." If my parents had people over for dinner, we went around the room saying Goodnight to each one when we had to go up to bed, squeezing their big hands, looking over their cocktails into their eyes. Wendy and I bobbed up and down in curtsies, with left knee bent, right foot out behind.

"Stand up when a grown-up comes into the room. Open doors for people, and don't go rushing through them." Sunday lunches, when we all ate together, could be ordeals. No elbows on the table, never push your food with your thumb, and don't let the food pass the danger line—the painted border near the outside of the plate—because you might spill. Tip the soup bowl away from you, and if there are several knives and forks, use the ones on the outside first and work your way inward. When the dessert plate and finger bowl are put in front of you, pick up the finger bowl with its little doily and floating pansy blossom, then set it behind and to the left of the plate.

The penalty for forgetting these things was a sudden, sharp pain. Mummy or Lewie reached out an arm toward the offending child and, with the middle finger, flicked an ear. Sometimes there was a warning, sometimes not. Mummy was a little more likely to flick but Lewie's flicks were harder. It was a toss-up which one to sit farthest away from.

Every now and then, on a weekend afternoon when the maids were resting, there would be a knock on the front door. One of us children answered it, and there, on the porch, were Mummy and Lewie. "Ve are the Russian Ambassador and his vife. Ve haff come to pay a call," they said. In this exercise, we had to welcome them, invite them to sit on the sofa, give them tea, and entertain them, which meant making conversation after the business of the cups, saucers, lemon, cream, and sugar lumps was completed. "Lovely weather," we said. "Are you enjoying your stay in our country?" and such other politenesses as we could come up with while Mummy and Lewie, with an occasional giggle, played their parts.

I don't know why they picked Russia to be from. Maybe it was because the Cold War was beginning, and the real Russian ambassador had taken over the Ogden Mills estate not far away for a country retreat. When we went to ride our horses through there as we always had, armed guards shooed us away. But at our mock tea parties, we children were too well brought up to mention anything so controversial as politics.

As I look back now, Mummy and Lewie were training us in more than manners; they were teaching us to be charming. Charm, as put by Nelson Aldrich in his book *Old Money*, is the ability to make others feel good about themselves. You always ask the other person about his life, his interests, his family—and, listening attentively to his answers, you draw him out even more. One drawback of learning to be charming is that you must become slightly dishonest, slightly misleading, as you show your extraordinary interest in whatever the other person is saying—and, of course, you must conceal any negative feelings in the effort to please. I became quite good at entertaining and dissembling—and correspondingly bad at learning to know or to say what I really felt. The one was valued, the other was not.

Our training came in handy for my mother. One day, she invited a lonely bachelor from a neighboring farm over for dinner. This was such an extraordinary event for him that he arrived a full hour early, while she was still taking her bath. Rather than put herself out by rushing, she simply sent me downstairs to greet him and give him a drink, knowing that I could make conversation until she was good and ready to make her entrance.

In making that conversation, there were words I could use and words I could not. My mother told me never to say "cute"; instead, I was to say, "What a *cunning* puppy, or baby, or whatever." Saying "cute" was something like having pierced ears or ankle bracelets: people of our sort didn't. My stepmother Cotty even made up a paragraph of forbidden words that she used when instructing her sons Peter and Haven, my Pell half-brothers who were roughly the same ages as Wendy and Cass. "*Doris* (pronounced by her *Daw-ris*) lay on the *divan* in her *wealthy home,* surrounded by *gorgeous drapes,* nibbling on a *tomay-to* picked from the grounds of her *estate,* and putting on her *hose.*" Correct, of course, would be lying on the *sofa* in her *big house* with the lovely *curtains,* nibbling on a *tomah-to* picked from her *place,* and putting on her *stockings.* We probably would never meet someone named Doris, but if we did, we wouldn't say "Daw-ris" but "Dah-ris."

As future aristocrats, we had also to master a variety of pastimes. Most important to my mother was my ability to ride horses. Consequently, I rode from the time I was a baby, sitting in front of my mother on her saddle. Horse-crazy myself, I spent hours with her on and around our horses. We rode out together from the stable through the woods and fields, sometimes to the schooling field down the road where she gave me lessons. She trained me for horse shows, standing in the center as I rode in a circle around her. "Heels down. Hands down. Kick with the outside leg so the judges won't see. *Get that pony on the right lead. Pull his head around harder. Harder!* Use your spurs!"

Around and around we went, Lucky and I, until we got it right. Sometimes Lucky did not want to jump the fences we practiced over. Then I kicked, whipped, and urged him forward with all my might, and sometimes he would stop anyway. I bumped my nose on his neck, or fell off, or just was mortified that this had happened. Then I would reorganize, whirl Lucky around, squeeze hard with both knees and, kicking and whipping, go at the fence again.

My mother's favorite—and my terror—was Shotlo, a nervous brown thoroughbred. I hated Shotlo because he was too strong for me and he knew it. One day she told me to jump him over the fences in our schooling field. Feeling my fear, he started off at a canter. Galumph, galumph, galumph went his strides, hoofs rhythmically striking the ground, a short interval of lift between each stride. But the beat got faster and faster until he was racing, nose extended, belly low to the ground, the fences approaching much too fast. As we neared the first one, he shortened his stride jerkily, hurled himself up and over, and sped to the next. Another wild leap. I tried to shorten the reins, hoping not to tangle them up or lose the tight hold one of my fingers had on his mane. I didn't want to fall off, and I didn't want him to hit a fence, which could send us both crashing to the ground. But most of all I didn't want to get in trouble with my mother. Two more leaps. Shotlo, mercifully, slowed to a canter and a trot, and we were done.

I never told my mother that I was afraid because I couldn't stand to be found wanting, or ridiculed. Riding horses, liking what she liked, was the best way to earn her approval. From the time I was ten until I was twelve, my mother took me out of school for two weeks each fall to go with her and Lewie for a foxhunting vacation in Maryland. My teachers objected, but they had no voice in the matter. Besides, I had an A average. Mummy herself looked after me on those Maryland trips, which meant that I could mostly do as I pleased, and they were wonderful.

Cooky wasn't fond of riding. From time to time, though, he had no choice. I remember one day when Mummy had him jumping the fences in the schooling field on Grandpa, a big chestnut horse. He managed all right until the last one, the widest, where Grandpa jumped big and Cooky fell off. He lay still. "Get up! Get up!" my mother ordered, but he didn't move. He'd been knocked unconscious in the fall. This became a family joke, one of many at Cooky's expense—the time Mummy yelled at him when he was out cold.

Besides riding, we had to learn golf, tennis, poker, canasta, bridge, and backgammon. We had to gamble for real stakes and to shoot guns. The idea was that you had to know how to Do Things, otherwise no one would like you or invite you for the Weekend. (Either of these would be terrible fates, she implied, although at age nine and ten, being asked for a Weekend seemed rather distant.) And, said my mother, still looking to our futures, "Most people after dinner have nothing at all to say; a game makes a much better evening."

The evenings of bridge instruction were torture. My mother sent us to get the folding card table, its special blue felt cover, and the cards from the tiny bureau drawer next to a sofa. We carried in chairs from the dining room and sat. She dealt the cards. "Lead from a doubleton or a singleton or fourth best of your longest and strongest suit," she explained. The words and cards all ran together in my head. Then she told us exceptions to the rules and exceptions to the exceptions until I was completely confused: "Well, yes, by the book you should play the spade, but since the dummy is out of clubs and you're doubled, use your diamond," she might say. Petrified, I stared at the cards in my hand. Often I played the wrong one and got called stupid, and sometimes I fled from the table, humiliated and in tears.

If I was good at a game, of course, that was different. Then I was praised and pleased. But I never could relax. The games were too fierce, the rebukes too angry, the sarcasm too biting. There was more at stake than plastic chips or pennies; my standing as a child rode on which card was played. It became my self who was being eaten up piece by piece, checker by checker, as my mother jumped my men and removed them from the board.

Even family baseball games on summer evenings, rare as they were, brought more anxiety than fun. I remember being at bat, my mother pitching. Something made her want to end the game, so instead of pitching gently, she slammed the ball past me three times, striking me out. The determined look in her eye as she pitched told me that, at that moment, I was just an obstacle to her. Trudging back to the house, I was scared as well as angry.

When they were bored, Mummy and Lewie used us children as amusements. Lewie would put boxing gloves on Cooky and me and make us box each other while he watched. And once, after a particularly drenching rain, either Lewie, or Billy under Lewie's direction, put Cooky on a half-grown steer in a field and, with a halter and rope, led him around for a few minutes. The steer trotted along, right up to the edge of an enormous puddle with Cooky bouncing along on top and smiling. But not for long: with a quick jerk of the rope, the steer was stopped and turned. Cooky, naturally, tumbled off forward into the puddle as Lewie and the assembled farmhands roared with laughter. Someone was there with a camera—to this day, I have a small black-and-white snapshot of Cooky right afterward, covered in mud and face all scrunched up, standing ankle-deep in muck. But he wasn't crying.

Mummy had no patience with tears. One night in the bathtub when I had had a bad day in fifth grade, I was down in the dumps. No one listened to me or cared what I felt. I sat in the hot water and wallowed in my misery, pushing myself back and forth, making waves in the tub. I bawled away, awash in self pity and bathwater, feeling bitterly unloved. Suddenly the bathroom door flew open and my mother thrust her face in. "*Stop making yourself cry!*" she ordered, and, slamming the door, vanished.

Rarely, it was possible to defy authority and succeed. Each summer, Nursie took a vacation to visit her relations in Canada. For those two weeks, Mummy hired a temporary nurse from an agency in New York to look after us. But in 1949, when Cooky and I were away visiting our Pell grandparents, the replacement was an especially grim woman. By then, Mummy and Lewie had had a third child together, our little brother Michael, who was nearly a year old. The temporary nurse would not let Wendy or Cass play with the baby, and she didn't let the children have any fun at all.

"When the nurse put Michael outside to nap in his pram and then went inside," Wendy told me many years later, "I grabbed the pram and pushed him all the way down to Mrs. Crofts' house." Mrs. Crofts was Billy's mother, a sweet old lady who lived nearly half a mile away on a far corner of the farm and was very fond of us children. "Mrs. Crofts gave us tea and something delicious, as usual," Wendy went on. Mrs. Crofts also got in touch with our mother, who came home from wherever she had been. "I told Mummy that the person was mean. Mum didn't scold me, and she fired the temporary. Then, for two whole days, she looked after us herself!" Wendy said, still amazed at the novelty. Nursie, scandalized at what had happened in her absence, never took another vacation until we were grown up.

Sometimes, my mother made her children into accomplices. To keep from getting speeding tickets, she instructed us, back in those super-patriotic postwar days, to pretend that we were American tail gunners and she was the pilot. We had to search the skies out the back window for Japs or Nazis—the police—and tell her if we spotted one. We knew how cops lurked under bridges and hid behind billboards, and she usually didn't get tickets when we were on the job.

Local police, whose palms perhaps had been greased, gave Lewie no trouble about his fighting cocks. The *Game Fowl News* came regularly to our mailbox; Lewie's silver cockfighting trophies were displayed on mantelpieces and other tables in our house. Every now and then a big tournament would be held at Whitehackle Farm.

All year long, Harry Kearney would get our birds ready. He made his rounds every day feeding and watering and training, followed devotedly by Girly, a graying, arthritic coon hound. As part of his regime, Harry ran the cocks on a carpeted treadmill like fierce, feathered hamsters; he threw them up in the air repeatedly to strengthen their wings as they fluttered down. For fighting practice, he sparred them, strapping miniature boxing gloves over their heel spurs so they couldn't hurt each other. Harry was legendary in the chicken-fighting ring for his ability to revive a wounded cock in the ring. He would take its bloody head right into his mouth for a moment, do something to it, and get it battling again.

When a tournament took place, station wagons filled with caged birds and their keepers drove in from as far away as Boston and Virginia. Our house was full of guests. One regular was Mrs. Marian du Pont Scott, at that time a short, middle-aged woman with gray hair and a big nose who had once been married to Western actor Randolph Scott. But that had ended long ago, and Mrs. Scott devoted herself to raising race horses and fighting cocks on her sumptuous Virginia estate.

Tournaments lasted for a couple of days, one fight after the other all day and into the night. One area in a barn was cleared out and a ring set up inside with chairs and benches all around. At the start of the fight, two handlers stepped over the little wall into the ring, each carrying his contender. The birds looked proud and haughty, their round yellow eyes flashing anger. The handlers, holding the cocks, approached one another so that the birds' beaks touched. Each tried ferociously to peck the other. Then each handler put his cock down on the floor. Immediately, the birds flew at one another in a blur of feathers, wings, beaks, and claws. You could hear the clash of feathered bodies and the riffle of wings beating. The cocks were armed with short metal spurs strapped to their legs; these would slice more smoothly into the opponent's body than the cock's natural, rough spur. Each had had his comb and wattles trimmed so as not to expose more flesh than necessary. Spectators crowded the ring, offering and taking bets—the odds changing from moment to moment as the fight progressed.

The combatants battled to the death. Some fights ended in seconds: with a lucky strike, one chicken at the first clash dealing his rival a mortal wound. Others dragged on interminably as the cocks gave and received blows. Weakened from injury and loss of blood, they kept at it until they were fighting on instinct alone. If it happened that both chickens could barely move, the referee drew a line in the sand for each. The handlers placed their birds behind the line, and whichever one would still attack the other earned points.

These fights were cruel, bloody and illegal. Sometimes I couldn't bear to watch any longer and had to leave. But other times I brought my money and bet, especially during the year when Harry Kearny had a heart attack and I had helped Lewie train the cocks. I knew each one, its strengths and weaknesses, and I loved my role as helper.

We children loved the excitement and energy and strangers in our barn. But for weeks afterward, we had lots and lots of tough chicken for dinner.

Although Mummy believed that form and good manners mattered, she had no qualms about being rude to those she regarded as her inferiors. She especially hated the Sunday drivers who came out from New York

City to look at the rich people's "homes" and "estates"—which we called "houses" and "places." They sat in their cars and gawked at the ducks on the ponds, the horses grazing in our fields, the rolling countryside. "Why don't they stay where they *belong*!" she complained when her headlong rush from one place to another was frustrated by the dawdling sightseers. She tailgated frighteningly close to the backs of their cars, waiting for a straight section of the winding, two-lane roads so she could hurtle past them. And she considered it an intrusion when developers built tract housing near Whitehackle Farm. She hated it when these developments and construction of the Long Island Expressway blocked off the riding trails we used, and she scoffed at the small, new houses with flat, ugly roofs. All these lower-class people on their quarter-acres were infringing on our territory, spoiling our rides, and cluttering up our roads with their cars.

When an Italian family named Rizzo set up a public riding academy a mile away from Whitehackle Farm, confrontation became inevitable. Soon dozens of citified horse renters began trooping through our place. They bounced unsteadily down the dirt road that separated one part of our property from the other, clutching the horns of their Western saddles, shrieking with fear and pleasure. Apart from noisily invading our privacy, the riders allowed their horses to trample a strip of my mother's holy lawn bordering the dirt road. The grass that she so prized became ragged and sliced by hoof prints. My mother was also furious at runaways galloping through the place, and she worried that an out-of-control horse could collide with one of us children on our bikes.

One horse renter, who had the ill luck to be riding along our road while my mother was gardening, refused (or was unable) to obey her order to steer his horse off the lawn. After he failed to respond to several commands, she picked up a sack of lime and flung it at him. He returned to the Rizzo's barn like a powdered ghost, sputtering with rage. After that, Lewie had his farmhands cut a trail around the upper border of Whitehackle Farm so that the riding academy horses would no longer pass in front of our house on the dirt road.

When she wasn't gardening or riding horses, my mother's clothes were tailored and chic. She shopped at Bendel's and Bergdorf's and Hattie Carnegie, and she dressed me as carefully as she dressed herself. She did not wear ethnic clothes and neither would her daughter, as I discovered when I asked her to get me a bright, full peasant skirt to wear when our class performed at Parents' Day. The sixth grade girls had been learning polkas, I explained, and Miss Blake said we should have white ruffled blouses and colorful skirts. "Everyone else will have one," I assured my mother, believing that argument to be irresistible. "You're *not* everybody else," she answered. I was standing beside her as she knelt, transplanting pansies from containers into a flower bed. "*You're* not everybody else," she repeated, and that was that. I would not have a peasant skirt to wear that day even if every other sixth grade girl at the very private Green Vale School in Glen Cove, Long Island, New York, did.

Caught between two people I had to obey, my mother and Miss Blake, I fretted for days. My teacher said I had to; my mother said I couldn't. My mother wasn't the kind of parent you could talk to if you were in a jam. But I had friends, and luckily, a girl in my class named Kate Babcock had a more understanding mother, along with two bright skirts and two ruffled blouses. She let me wear her extra ones on Parents' Day. I don't think that my mother came to see our dances, but that didn't matter. I got to dress like every other girl in my class, and that was all the relief I needed.

Yet, truly, I was not like everybody else, nor were my brothers and sister. We were instructed and reminded of our differences at every turn. We didn't go to public school, we didn't have a Mom who cooked or cared for us, we didn't use certain words because they were "cheap," and our clothes were chosen for us without regard to fashion. Like my mother, I looked down on little boys whose mothers dressed them up like miniature men in long pants, fedoras, and snap-on bow ties. Such outfits were American, ugly, and *wrong*. My brothers wore gray flannel knee pants with knee socks, striped ties, dark blue blazers, and gray or blue caps. Their clothes were modeled on those worn by children of the English upper crust—attractive and *correct*. While American girls wore dresses hemmed midway between knee and ankle, mine and Wendy's ended just at our knees, the way little French girls wore theirs.

I knew I was supposed to grow up to be like my parents, but sometimes that seemed to me like a good future and sometimes it didn't. So many orders to give, so many people to scold, so many things that could go wrong, like a cook whose soufflés were too moist in the center, or cows escaping from pastures and trampling the pansies, or a maid smashing an antique bowl. Wearing beautiful evening dresses and sparkling jewelry, foxhunting to my heart's content, those things seemed fine. But I didn't like the upset, the annoyance, the unspoken taboos. It was hard to figure out how to navigate a tricky landscape of social caste without being allowed to mention a word of it.

CHAPTER FIVE

Cooky and His Fathers

Nice game, Mortimer.

—Clarence Cecil Pell Sr.

I go from the club car to the car club.

—Clarence Cecil Pell Jr.

I want to speak French with a Japanese accent.

—Clarence Cecil Pell III

I need now to jump forward in time to tell you what happened to Cooky and about the WASP, self-righteous patriarchy to which he was heir. The male heads of families in our circles were not as a rule distinguished by wisdom or generosity of spirit. In fact, instead of welcoming him into its ranks as it should have, that patriarchy behaved like Procrustes, chopping and stretching the little boy in a futile attempt to make him fit into a bed for which he was not at all suited.

(There were side effects on me: what they did to Cooky demonstrated how dearly one would pay for defying our upper-class system, and accounts, to some degree at least, for my ingrained fear of saying what I think or asking pointed questions.)

One of the things to watch for is the effect that diminishing fortunes had on the men in the family. As you have seen, my grandfathers Pell and Mortimer lived lives fully insulated from the worries of middle-class America; the gates of Tuxedo Park kept such concerns firmly at bay. But outside events such as World War II weakened that barrier, and as the world changed, their class privilege, and the fortunes of their sons, declined. Clarry's inheritance was much smaller than Big Cook's—since his private income was not enough for him to live on, he had to hold a job—and Cooky got barely anything from Clarry. Fathers had it easy, sons less so—and since the fathers never had to cope with as much as the sons, they usually didn't provide either useful role models or sound advice.

Moreover, they were entrapped in a kind of ancestor worship. Clarry, for example, tried desperately to please Big Cook, to think like him, and to match his athletic achievements. But despite his best efforts, he couldn't be his father. He didn't have the money, he didn't have the temperament, and he wasn't as good an athlete. But he doggedly played on in racquets tournaments until he finally eked out one national title at the age of forty-three.

Not only did he play the games his father played, he tried to think the way his father did: he divided things into good and bad, using as the standard whether his father would approve or disapprove. Just as Big Cook did not allow his children to call him "Daddy" or "Father" but made them call him "Cook," Clarry did the same. Clarry thought that shampoo was for women and sissies; he washed his straight black hair with plain bar soap, the way his father did.

Like his father's, Clarry's code was rooted in the sanctity of a few hallowed things: his aristocratic ancestry, the private clubs where he played games, Harvard of course, and the social status that assured his place in a neat, hierarchical universe. In Big Cook and Clarry's view, people with white skin were superior to others; men were superior to women; and the Episcopalian Church had the right idea about God.

Clarry didn't like basketball, which was a "wrong" sport played by "niggers;" a word he used without hesitation, just as he complained about Guineas and Wops and Kikes and Hebes and fairies. Growing up in the 1940s and '50s, I thought that "Jew" was a bad word. (Lewie's attitudes were no better: when asked why, at 6'7", he didn't play basketball at Harvard, he answered, "Why would you want your nose in a nigger's armpit?")

Clarry played racquets into his fifties, hockey into his seventies and lawn tennis into his eighties. But the game that meant the most to him was the arcane sport known as court tennis, which he and other devotees called "real tennis." (Its other name is "royal tennis.") What to most people is tennis—the popular game played today by Roger Federer and the Williams sisters—Clarry ostentatiously called "lawners," for lawn tennis, which was once its name.

There is little need to distinguish court tennis from lawners these days, since court tennis has so few practitioners, but Clarry maintained the distinction.

As an Anglophile obsessed with class, he exulted in the exclusivity, history, and social distinction of court tennis, which had its origins in a twelfth-century French monastery and spread across the Channel to England. At one time, it became so popular that workers began neglecting their jobs. A royal edict was then issued banning common people from playing. Henry VIII enjoyed his games at Hampton Court, which is one of the places where Clarry played on his annual trips to England.

The game, which requires athleticism and strategy, is so intricate that there are jokes about the inability of the gentlemen athletes to manage by themselves. Sometimes the club provides a hired professional (called a "marker") to keep score for them. From time to time the marker may call out, "Chase the door," or, "Chase better than half a yard," and the players must know what he means. Another joke is that, because so few people play, anyone who steps on a court instantly achieves national ranking.

In the 1970s my father raised money to build a court at Newport, and, twenty years later, my younger half-brother Haven Pell raised money to build one near Washington, D.C. Clarry, of course, was inordinately happy that Haven had followed his lead. After attending the opening, he called one day to tell me how wonderful the Washington court was. "I guess you and Haven are the only father son pair to build tennis courts," I said, thinking to please him.

"No, we're not," he happily corrected me. "There was Edward the Second and Edward the Third."

Imagine Cooky, who was happiest playing and working on the farm, faced with Clarry and his values. If Clarry had been flexible and imaginative, their connection might have been easier. But my father disliked change. He brought all three of his wives home to the Little House that was built for him and Mummy. His routine didn't vary: On weekday mornings, Clarry descended the stairs to take his place at the head of the dining room table. Belle, the black cook, brought him eggs and bacon and coffee while he read the *New York Times*, second section first. As the antique clock chimed 8:00, he left the house and drove to the East Williston station where he caught the train to New York.

When he was a young man, he rode into town with the ordinary commuters. But after he was middle-aged, he boarded a special club car on the train outfitted with comfortable wicker chairs and staffed by a porter. As he walked down the aisle to a seat, he nodded good morning to friends. ("Morning, Grant." "Morning, Pell.") After finishing the paper, he pulled out his pen and whipped through the crossword puzzle. At the Jamaica station, my father transferred from the club car to a limousine that whisked him and a few others to their Wall Street offices. He described this commute with a satisfied smile: "I go from the club car to the car club."

The company Clarry worked for insured airplanes. But the clubs he belonged to and the sports he played meant far more to him than his job. After work, Clarry went uptown from his office near Wall Street to the Racquet Club for games and drinks before heading back out to Long Island for more drinks and dinner.

But for all his devotion to the world of clubs and class distinctions, my father was cheap. He detested taking taxis and prided himself on his encyclopedic knowledge of the fastest, least expensive way of getting around New York—the subway. He went to a dentist in Jamaica so as not to pay Park Avenue prices, he bought his shoes at a discount store, and he once scolded his third wife because she paid full price for some toothbrushes. He even violated the Racquet Club rule against members spending the night there, stretching out on a couch after a late dinner so as to save himself the price of a hotel room.

Clarry gave up his custody claims to Cooky and me on the condition that he not be responsible for our expenses. But on occasions such as my graduations or coming-out party or wedding day, Clarry showed up—having not paid a cent or helped to arrange anything—to dance the first dance or walk me down the aisle, publicly assuming the father's role. Lewie and Mummy, who had paid for everything, were unfailingly gracious.

I wondered why Clarry did not pay our tuition at Green Vale, as the divorced fathers of my friends did. Did he not care about us? That was only one of many things that confused Cooky and me. And we never knew exactly where we belonged.

When our parents split in 1940, Cooky was only a baby. He was suddenly detached from his doting Nanny and his secure routine in the nursery at the Little House. An upsetting series of events followed: we were shuttled back and forth between parents and grandparents and fought over in a nasty custody battle; our mother married Lewie and had their baby Wendy while our father married Cotty and had their baby Peter. Cooky and I suddenly became older half-siblings with step-parents. All this happened against the tense backdrop of the war. Lewie was stationed in Canada, Clarry in Delaware, and no one knew just what would happen next.

By the time that Cooky and I were awarded to our mother in Canada, he was about three and, no surprise after so much upheaval, began wetting his bed. On the nights that this happened, Lewie took him down to the basement and spanked him with a dog collar. But, though my mother sat on her bed, hands over her ears so as not to hear his cries, she and Lewie believed that naughty, bed-wetting children had to be spanked. If you spoiled them, or let them get away with anything, they would turn out badly. (As an adult, I found the baby-raising manual that my mother used, the one that preceded Dr. Spock. I was shocked at its relentless and dire warnings about the need for rigid scheduling no matter how much a baby cried. Feeding every four hours, period. Toilet training completed by the first birthday. Failure to maintain rigid discipline in infancy inclined the child toward juvenile delinquency in school and failure in adult life—consequences that would have been unacceptable.) It became a family joke that you could read "Ledyard" in mirror writing on Cooky's backside, from the imprint left by the metal nameplate on the dog collar.

One of the things that confused Cooky and me was the matter of fathers. In spite of the spankings, we liked Lewie much better than we liked Clarry because he was so much more fun. We wished we were Ledyards and that Lewie was our real father. It was hard to like Clarry, who was critical and brusque, yet we were supposed to love him. The nice one wasn't ours, the mean one was. Moreover, the two of us never fully belonged in whichever family we were with. One day when we were at Clarry's, Cotty's mother was visiting. Our little half-brothers Peter and Haven called her "Grandma." But when Cooky called her "Grandma," she snapped at him. "I am not your grandmother," she said. "And don't you forget it. To you, I am Mrs. Jeffcott."

At a time when divorce was relatively uncommon, we lived in a family of marriages that didn't last. Lewie's two sisters had four husbands each: one year, we acquired some nice new stepcousins when Aunt Totty married Mr. Jackson. But it wasn't long before, after we had gotten to know and like them, they, along with Mr. Jackson, were gone, and Aunt Totty was soon Mrs. Turner. Who knew when our parents might run off again?

Many years later, I was startled to learn that Peter Pell was also confused. When he was little, he had no idea who Cooky and I were or why we came to visit. Peter told me, long after we were grown up, that his father used to say, "I'm going to get the kids." Clarry would drive away and come back with two children, Cooky and me. Peter didn't know why these children came to visit; he didn't know that his father was our father, too, and that his father had once been married to our mother. No one explained us to him, and of course he didn't dare to ask. A governess finally clued him in.

Even after the grown-ups made their final bargain and were settled again on Long Island, Cooky's troubles continued.

He was always dropping things and bumping into things and forgetting things, so he was constantly scolded and punished. He knocked china ornaments off side tables and dropped the baseballs he was supposed to catch. He repeatedly injured himself in bizarre ways. On one occasion at Whitehackle Farm, he threw a rock up at a scythe that was hanging on the barn wall. The scythe fell, slicing through most of his arm. After that healed, he tumbled off a small motor scooter that we had, ripping great patches of skin off his face. He was accident prone, his parents said. Our otherwise kindly grandfather, Big Cook, called him "Boob," and "Little Useless." One whole summer, he was called "Rockhead."

Upon arrival at Green Vale School, he announced on the first day of first grade, "I am Cooky Pell and I am full of hell!" Though Mummy and Lewie roared with laughter, the school was not amused. He was immediately suspended. That moment marked Cooky as a bad boy, and he remained more or less a bad boy the rest of his life.

When he was having trouble in second grade, Mummy and Lewie used to chuckle over his report cards. Mrs. Valentine, his teacher, used words and concepts they didn't understand. She expressed her concern over his poor motor coordination. "Motor coordination! Motor coordination!" they scoffed, ridiculing the unfamiliar phrase. And, of course, they didn't bother inquiring further into Cooky's school problems and continued to scold him for being so clumsy.

Perhaps they laughed at the report cards from Mrs. Valentine because neither of them could imagine having a child who was flawed in any way. I think now that Cooky had a learning disorder as well as emotional problems, but in those days he was considered disobedient and lazy. If he would just concentrate and try harder. . . .

Cooky's behavior put our parents into bad, angry moods, thereby making things worse for me. Instead of trying to protect him, I rolled my eyes at his doings and wished he would act right. Now, I look back on those times with shame—instead of identifying with and protecting Cooky, I identified with our parents and wanted him to shape up. Cooky was just as hopeless when Mummy sent him to find the pale blue sweater in the second drawer of the large bureau on the left as he was at hitting a forehand on the (lawn) tennis court, and since he often spilled his milk all over the dining room table wherever he was, he got into trouble at both Mummy's and Clarry's. In fact, he got so accustomed to punishment that one day, when Mummy was returning a toy that she had taken away, he said, "Don't give it back. I'll just get to like it and you'll take it away again."

It was harder to be a kid at Clarry's than it was at Whitehackle Farm. The households differed in spirit because Lewie and Clarry lived such different styles of upper-class life. Lewie had more money than Clarry, and he didn't feel compelled to mimic his father. If the farm with its cockfights represented the freedom of the upper crust to break the law and do as it pleased, my father's house in Old Westbury was the other side: the upper crust baked hard and rigid.

Lewie, Cooky's other role model, had been a playboy given to fast cars and good times, as happy flouting convention as Clarry was following it. In his teens, one story went, Lewie had disguised himself with a false beard and run away from Groton, a very strict, old-line boarding school, on a motorcycle. But because of his family's status, he was not expelled. President Franklin Roosevelt, who had been a friend of old Mr. Ledyard, was Lewie's godfather. One evening after a party in Washington, Lewie lurched drunkenly up the White House steps and demanded to spend the night. (They took him in.) While at Yale Law School, he staged cockfights in the basement of the exclusive Fence Club, and he had adventures with rumrunners. In the early 1930s, together with five other Harvard students who also resented Prohibition, he went one night to a tattoo parlor. Each was marked with one letter so that together, their arms spelled out "REPEAL." Lewie had one of the "Es." He also got a skull with a snake crawling through it and several other designs.

My stepfather thought nothing of going foxhunting in his tuxedo after dancing and drinking all night long. It wasn't hard to see why my beautiful, passionate young mother had fallen in love with him—a dashing, handsome, and exciting fellow with a delicious sense of humor. Lewie knew how to be a bad boy and make it work.

Clarry, who liked the rich and well-born, wasn't wild or even playful. He diligently practiced at the obscure sports in which his father had so excelled, and he stayed for decades as vice-president of the insurance company.

Lewie, however, who had gone to work after the war for Carter, Ledyard and Milburn, quickly tired of his white-shoe family law firm and quit for something surprising: a dollar-a-year job for New York's Legal Aid Society defending indigent people accused of crimes. All day long, he represented thieves, burglars, con men, and drug sellers—so successfully that his clients dubbed him "Lewie the Springer" and asked for him the next time they got hauled into court. But after seeing the same clients return year after year, he grew disillusioned about the value of his work.

Lewie told us stories about the odd people he met, like a woman who insisted that space aliens were broadcasting messages into her head. "Madam," he told her, "the trouble is that you are not properly grounded. You have seen how big trucks drag a chain along the road so as to ground the electricity?" He fashioned a small chain of paper clips, attached it to the hem of her skirt so that it dragged along the ground, and assured her that the messages would now cease. She left quite satisfied.

But it was the ostensibly virtuous Clarry who got nailed for cheating on his income taxes and Clarry who was arrested for drunk driving and punching out the cop who arrested him. The press found out about his arrest, and a huge photo of him disheveled and battered filled the back cover of a New York scandal sheet.

The range of tolerable behavior for children at Clarry's was more constricted, the expectations more menacing than at the farm. At the farm, Cooky could play with his dog and tag along after the workmen on the place. When his black cat, Crazy, had kittens in the barn, he named them Eggy, Yolky, and Mousie, and tried unsuccessfully to teach them to swim. (Crazy taught her babies to avoid him after that.) When Mummy asked him what he would like to do when he grew up, he said, "I want to speak French with a Japanese accent."

He thought up other odd things. One summer, we went to visit Lewie's younger sister Dorothy in Southampton. The grownups went to a huge ball on Saturday night, and on Sunday morning our Aunt Dot, as we called her, had a very strange experience. She was something of a hard-drinking, good-time woman, so she put a glass of water by her bed Saturday evening to ease the next day's hangover. But each time she reached for the glass that particular morning, it moved away from her. This happened several times, and Dorothy, completely puzzled, began to wonder how much she had drunk the night before and what it might have been.

After a while, though, she saw that when the glass moved away, it was being pushed by a small finger. She then discovered Cooky, who had sneaked into her room early that morning and hidden under her bed. He remained still as a mouse till she woke and reached for the water. "It was a sensation rather like *Gaslight*," she reminisced years later. Aunt Dot, whom Cooky christened "Auntie Mame," adored Cooky and delighted in his escapades. Unfortunately, hers was a minority opinion.

Cooky liked to compose and sing little wandering songs. But that didn't go over at Clarry's, where originality was frowned upon. Every act was a performance to be judged. There was no escape: we had to play tennis or baseball or pick-up sticks or something that forced us into success or failure, and even the way we ate was scored up or down.

I didn't like going to see Clarry, and Cooky hated it. Wendy tells me how he used to cry and sometimes try to run away before we went. Clarry criticized everything, and he possessed a great talent for making his irritation evident.

Because I was a girl and could never belong to the really important clubs anyway, it didn't matter quite as much if I served up a double fault or dropped a grounder. I didn't bear the burden of being Clarence Cecil Pell III, heir to an athletic and social legacy. But I didn't completely escape. When Cooky and I went to our father's for the weekend, I knew I would have to play tennis. The games were risky: in serious matches when I was at the net, I was fair game—opponents sometimes slammed a ball at me as if I were a target. If I played well, I reaped heaps of praise. If I played badly, I suffered sarcasm, withering looks, and anger. With my father as with my mother, I prayed not to mess up and get scolded. Please God let this ball over the net. Please God let the serve go in.

How he hated defeat! We lost the finals of one father-daughter country club tournament when I was about ten—as I recall, because I double-faulted at a crucial point. For the whole forty-minute drive back to his house, he glared at the road ahead, silent, fingers clenched around the steering wheel. I didn't dare say a word. Today, when I go on a tennis court, I cannot control my right arm properly, and though I am not a bad athlete in other sports, I often can't return even an easy shot. Years later, it was a great comfort to me to learn that one of Clarry's Racquet Club friends had been so traumatized by his first game of court tennis with my father that he avoided the game for twenty years.

Cooky suffered the worst of our father's ill temper. I winced when Clarry snapped "Nice work," as Cooky missed another easy forehand on the tennis court or struck out another time at bat. With frozen face and irritated sigh, Clarry let him know what an utter failure he was. If Cooky tried to please our father by telling how he could start the tractor at Whitehackle Farm all by himself, Clarry crossly changed the subject.

When I reflect now, I imagine that, to Clarry, the thought of his namesake on a tractor was yet one more painful reminder of how Lewie Ledyard had damaged his life. Clarry disliked farms; he wanted a gentleman sportsman for a son, not a kid atop a John Deere.

Cooky didn't have friends. He developed a fondness for sick animals. It was embarrassing to be the sister of such a monumental fuckup. I gloried in my role as the "good" child. But something about that superiority felt a little corrupt then, and it feels awful when I think of it now. By colluding with the grown-ups, I accepted the system that rewarded me and punished him.

Once I left for ninth grade in boarding school, I stayed away from home as much as I could, and I was so focused on my own life that his troubles became a sort of background noise to which I paid little attention. Although my mother tried to arrange friends and social engagements for Cooky, those failed in welters of miscommunication and awkwardness. In their own minds, our parents meant well. It was just that their ideas of what was acceptable had so little to do with the real needs of children. Even I knew from a young age that they didn't want to know what I really thought and felt. They wanted a happy little girl who would curtsy, play tennis, ride horses, say the appropriate thing, and grow up to be just like them. They wanted the same from Cooky. And he would not, or could not, adapt.

To admit that anything was wrong with their goals for Cooky, or the way they were bringing him up, would mean that there was something wrong with the way their parents had raised them—or even, perhaps, with the values by which they lived.

We continued on as Cooky the bad little boy and Topsy the good little girl. Divorce couldn't be bad for children, claimed my mother: "Just look at Topsy." I had skipped a grade in school, looked happy, and had friends. She blamed "bad luck" for Cooky's accidents and for the problems that plagued him in school.

In deference to the value Clarry placed on family tradition, and because he agreed to pay half the tuition, Mummy allowed Cooky to be sent off to Pomfret, the Connecticut boarding school that Clarry and Big Cook had attended, even though she thought it was rather second-rate. Cooky had a stormy career there. Instead of finding the refuge and acceptance that I found at my boarding school, Garrison Forest, he was often in trouble and not well liked. He endured hours upon hours of "slate," the prep school punishment of sitting at a desk and copying out an assigned text. He was thrown out for a year; then, after a successful session at another school, Pomfret took him back.

Even his big triumph at the school was spoiled. A fine oarsman, Cooky rowed on a championship crew and in his senior year was elected Commodore. But before this honor was formally announced to the school, he told his father, who told Big Cook. Thrilled, they immediately wired him a message of congratulations which was seen by school staff as it was being delivered to him. Because of this, Cooky got scolded for premature boasting, even though he had informed only his father. The new Commodore was humiliated before the school and nearly lost the honor.

A school report card from that year dated May 1958, illustrates how his life went:

> As commodore, Clarence takes the inspiriting nature of his role rather too seriously. With the record of last year's crew driving him on, I'm afraid he's communicating an anxiety about results that has not been as helpful as he had hoped. . . . Clarence feels compelled at times to provide verbal exhortation. The net result is antagonism.

One of Cooky's schoolmates remembered how desperately my brother sought solace in women.

"There was one girl within twenty miles of our school and Cook found her," he told me.

Cooky misbehaved in the ways bad boys of our class traditionally did, getting tossed out of school, drinking, womanizing, and driving fast. He looked like a young gent: tall and clean-cut looking, with wavy brown hair and a huge smile. His manners were wonderful, Mummy always said, and he made great cocktails as he chatted up her friends.

By the time Cooky graduated from boarding school, sons of alumni were not automatically accepted to Harvard. Even if he had wanted to, there was no way Clarence Cecil Pell III could follow in the footsteps of Clarence Cecil Pells Sr. and Jr. to Cambridge. But Cornell accepted him, and Mum spoke brightly of a career for him in agriculture. He had made some close friends and he had a lively social life.

Once again, things went horribly wrong. In his sophomore year, Cooky got a girl pregnant. At that time, I was married, living in San Francisco, and six months pregnant with my first child.

I jumped on a plane and flew east. All the parents were terribly upset. After all, this was 1960, when premarital sex and babies outside of wedlock were shameful, and abortion was illegal. There were heated arguments about what should be done. Lewie took the old school position that a gentleman had to do the right thing. I argued that Cooky ought not to have to live the rest of his life with a woman he didn't want to marry, but that idea went nowhere. Mummy said, "If they don't get married, it's too hard on her. If they do get married, it's too hard on him."

The young woman was Cathe Jackson, a Wellesley student whom Cooky had been dating; her parents lived in Pennsylvania not far from Mummy and Lewie. Cooky first said he would marry her; then he said he wouldn't, then he said he would. During these drama-filled days of tears and anguished back-and-forth, Mummy even suggested that Cathe have the baby and give it to her to raise. Finally, Cook decided to marry her. He called his closest friend Andy Guest to come quickly and be best man.

But on the morning of the wedding, while Cook was on an errand, Andy talked to Cathe. "This is a strange conversation to have on this day," he began. "But you should know that Cook is involved with another woman [whom I will call Marie]; she's at Cornell." Cathe told Andy that she was crazy about Cook and hoped to make the marriage work anyway.

They were married in a tense, sparsely attended, church ceremony. A friend of the family gave Cook a job with a lumber company in the Northwest, and off they went. Some weeks later, my mother wondered how they were getting along. So, rather than make the effort to investigate the situation herself, she sent Wendy, then only eighteen, to visit them and report back.

Things were going badly. Cooky was staying out late and pretending to some of his co-workers that Cathe was not his wife. She was lonesome and miserable. To make matters worse, Cook left love letters from Marie to him on top of his bureau where Cathe would be sure to find them.

At the end of the summer, they went east to have the baby in Pennsylvania. My mother rented a small house for them just down the road from her farm. Cathe flew back while Cook drove, letting Cathe know that he would stop and visit Marie for a while on the way. The baby was a little late, and the wandering father drifted back in time for his birth.

My brother didn't name the boy after himself, Clarry, and Big Cook; instead, he called the baby Thomas Nichols Pell after Tom Nichols, a friend who was a class ahead of him at Pomfret. Tom was one of the few people who had been kind to him there.

According to Cathe, Cooky was something of a split personality: "He could be very cruel, or he could be a loving father and husband. He could be charming, but he was arrogant with people whom he thought were beneath him, like waiters or clerks or my friends." She was amused that Cook, who had several younger siblings, including John Ledyard who was then about two years old, panicked the first time he saw his baby on the changing table. "He's deformed! See how his legs are all bent!" Cathe, who had spent years earning money babysitting, explained that all newborns are folded up like that at birth; they straighten out as they grow. "He had never seen one naked before," she told me. "He was used to Nursie caring for the babies up in the nursery, out of sight."

Cooky and Cathe separated after a brief, miserable time together. As he had promised, he went back to Marie. But unfortunately, as I learned later, by then he had gotten involved with a third woman. It's hard to believe, but in 1964, to redeem the pledge he had made four years earlier, he again married a woman he didn't love, Marie. This ceremony, a formal wedding with all the trimmings, was another nightmare. Cooky was so drunk that he could barely walk down the aisle. In an exercise of group denial, none of us said a word about his condition, and probably no one offered to help him. At the country club reception afterward, my family ignored the brides' parents and relatives, and any semblance of manners, clustering instead around a television set, absorbed in the running of the Preakness Stakes.

The next day, I learned that, after he and Marie drove away from the reception, Cooky stopped the car at a red light. Without a word, he opened the car door and fled into the darkness.

That marriage didn't last long, either.

I saw Cooky briefly in the summers when I brought my children east to see their grandparents, but otherwise we didn't keep in touch. Soon,

Cooky was living alone in a Philadelphia apartment, twice divorced, and still frantically pursuing women. At my mother's insistence, he saw a psychiatrist. When he had visitations with his son Tom, who now lived with Cathe in Philadelphia where she attended art school, he brought the little boy out to Mummy and Lewie's farm. Cathe was often angry with Cooky because he was hours late to pick Tom up when he was scheduled to, and equally late bringing him back. As a rule, the parents did not have much to say to each other as the child changed hands, but one evening, in early 1966, Cook said to Cathe, "My Army Reserve unit may be called up soon, and I may have to go away for a while. I want you to know that you are a really good mother to Tom." She remembered that because it was so out of the ordinary. A few days later, he called to say that he could not pick up Tom as planned. He added, "I'm having trouble with my mother; I cannot get along with her. She is making me see a shrink I hate, so I just lie to him."

A week or so later, I was cooking dinner at home in San Francisco when the phone rang. It was my mother. I remember standing by the washing machine, holding the receiver of the wall phone in my hand as her words came through: "Your brother has shot himself."

The police had called her. The death had occurred days before, they said; a friend had asked them to check Cook's apartment after he did not answer messages left on his answering machine and he had not been seen for a few days in the usual places.

I flew home.

My mother, who was then forty-eight, wanted Cooky to be buried in his Army uniform since he had liked being in the military. No one had the nerve to tell her that his body, having lain undiscovered for so long, had become too bloated to fit into it.

The same Episcopal minister who had married Cooky and Cathe performed the liturgy for the dead. But he made no eulogy: neither he nor anyone else mentioned Cooky's name or said one word about him or his life. We sat silently, about fifty of us, through the prayers, psalms, and Bible readings.

When it was over, the family filed out behind the coffin to the strains of "Onward Christian Soldiers" and climbed into long black limousines. We were aghast when the hearse carrying Cooky's body took a wrong turn on the way to the cemetery, needlessly prolonging the sad drive and keeping us trapped in the same kind of frustration and anger we had felt so often when Cooky was alive. Even after we finally arrived in the peaceful Quaker cemetery, there was trouble—the excavation for his grave was dug much closer to the graves of another family than my mother had expected, and she was upset. Even in death, she wanted a greater distance to separate her family from ordinary people.

My father came down from New York grim and silent, asking no questions.

In the long days that followed, my mother endlessly played a reel of audiotape that was taken from Cooky's apartment, hoping to hear his voice and perhaps a clue about why he ended his life. She didn't find one. For years afterward when she was alone with me, Mummy reminisced obsessively about him and his last days. She dwelt on his attentiveness to her friends and his love of his son. As always, she blamed his troubles on a lot of very bad luck, with no mention of the way she had been as a mother.

Clarry kept a photo of Cooky in his bedroom. It had been taken when he was three or four, a beautiful boy with huge brown eyes and apple cheeks wearing a white shirt with an Eton collar, an apple in his chubby little hands. My father stuck a piece of black Dymo label tape on the bottom of the picture frame: "CCP III, 1939–1966."

After Cooky's death, I felt more shocked and stunned than sad. I didn't actually miss Cooky in the way that I have missed close friends who died—where you feel that you want to call that person and then suddenly realize you can't because the friend is dead, and then you feel the pain and loss. But what do you do about the self-inflicted death of a brother you didn't really like that much, but who was the one person on earth who shared your genes, who was kidnapped with you and scared with you, who went back and forth from mother to father with you, who lived the closest thing to your own life? And—here is the truly awful part—the worry that maybe, if I had been a kinder child or a braver child or even a less cowardly child, I could have spared him some pain. I could, perhaps, have stood up for him against our ignorant, angry, critical parents. But back then, such defiance didn't occur to me.

Sometimes Mum blamed Clarry because he had been mean to Cooky. Once she blamed me for dominating him when we were small. Many, many years later, she speculated that if our family had lived "Out West," he might have been able to be happy.

Now that I am no longer young, I miss Cooky. I wonder what kind of a life he would have made, if he had been able to make a life. But he couldn't, and so he is a shadow over me, the brother I couldn't love when he needed me.

CHAPTER SIX

Escape From Home

All things good of the head and heart has she, she will go far, this little girl.

—My high school yearbook quote

A senior has betrayed her trust.

—Miss Offutt, headmistress

When I went away to school at thirteen, I left Cooky and his tribulations behind. He continued on his troubled trajectory. But so far as I was concerned, things began to look up.

The 1950s that most teenagers experienced—bobby socks, poodle skirts, saddle shoes, and *American Bandstand*—were forbidden territory to me. Not one friend of mine attended a public high school—they went to boarding schools, almost all of which in those days were single-sex. After seventh or eighth grade, the boys left home for places such as St. Paul's or Exeter in New Hampshire; the girls, after eighth or ninth grade, for schools like Farmington, in Connecticut or, if they liked horses, Foxcroft in the South.

I couldn't wait to go. Getting away offered a hope of relief—no angry mother to please, no troubled younger brother to take the attention I wanted, no going back and forth between Mummy and Clarry. I left home as soon as I was allowed—after eighth grade.

My mother favored Foxcroft, a girls' school with an ultra-snobbish reputation set in Virginia foxhunting country. Its headmistress, Miss Charlotte, was legendary for her highhandedness and her love of the military. She was great friends with the commandant of the Marine Corps and, in that spirit, insisted that her girls learn discipline. So Foxcroft girls slept outdoors on sleeping porches and drilled with mock rifles in military formation. Equally important, perhaps, they took a course in servant management.

Although she ran the most exclusive girls' school in the country, Miss Charlotte had a thoroughly practical attitude toward diversity: she was reported once, back in the 1940s, to have addressed her student body about an incoming student in words something like these: "Girls, we will have a Jewish student here next year. I expect you all will be very nice to her, especially since her father is paying double tuition." When one Foxcroft alumna, a good friend of mine, became involved with a Marine whom her parents didn't like, Miss Charlotte rang up the Marine Corps Commandant and had the young man transferred from his cushy assignment to some remote outpost.

Unlike my mother, Lewie was put off by Foxcroft's heavy emphasis on social position. As they were deciding where I would go, Mummy talked him into going to visit the school with her. But he made a bargain: if Miss Charlotte said anything snooty, I couldn't go. Until the end of the tour, Mummy told me later, it looked as though I'd be headed there. All went well as Miss Charlotte showed them around the lovely grounds, describing the fine education Foxcroft provided. But, just as Mum and Lew were about to leave, Miss Charlotte said something like, "And you know whose daughters are here," then ticked off a list of Vanderbilts, Mellons, Whitneys, du Ponts, and other prominent families. That did it. Even though my best friends from Green Vale were going to Foxcroft, I was not.

Lewie had another card up his sleeve. He had a daughter from his first marriage, a redhead named Evelyn who was a year older than I. Known fondly as Jeep, she was a strong, athletic girl who lived with her mother and stepfather in Providence, Rhode Island. I hated it when Jeep came to visit because she wasn't subject to the same rules as we were, and because she was so much better at sports than I. Mummy and Lewie always pitted us against each other—in races, in throwing and catching, on horses—and I always lost, unless my mother rigged a particular riding contest so I could win it.

Jeep went to a boarding school called Garrison Forest, in the Green Spring Valley outside of Baltimore. Lewie took me to visit Garrison in the summer before my ninth grade year—for some reason, my mother didn't go. A bit casual about my education, she had not entered me on time as she should have, and I think the school was already full. But Miss Offutt, a small, plump, and charmingly vague woman who was one of the two headmistresses, chatted with Lewie after taking us around. "What a shame that we don't have a space in ninth grade," she said. "Maybe Topsy will come in tenth." Lewie nodded his head. Then, as an afterthought, he asked her, "Has it ever happened that a girl you didn't expect simply arrived at the start of the school year?"

Miss Offutt thought. Yes, that had happened once. Lewie asked what she'd done, and she said, "Well, we just took her in."

He smiled. "Now I know what we'll do with Topsy," he said. Whatever influence was or was not exerted, a place was made for me. Soon afterward, the school let him know that I was accepted.

So, in September 1950, a grimy Pennsylvania Railroad coach sped me and my huge green, monogrammed leather suitcase south from New York toward Baltimore. On the train, I spotted some clusters of girls a few years older than I making elaborate gestures with their cigarettes, gossiping and giggling, with fashion magazines in their laps. They turned out to be "old girls" returning to Garrison. I also spotted some who looked like new girls: we nervously eyed each other, and a few of us began awkward conversations. Others sat alone, encased in new tan polo coats, too terrified to speak. It might seem odd that I was sent off from home for the first time all alone, but I was not the only one whose parents were too occupied to accompany their fledgling daughter to boarding school. Also, I was hardened by years of experience going back and forth from one parent to another; Mummy and Clarry were accustomed to my departures. I felt brave and expansive because I had an older stepsister at the school, even though we weren't really friends.

As we pulled into the dingy Baltimore station, though, worry seeped into my head about leaving home. Who would I ask when I needed to know something? Would people like me at this new place? I had not been popular in seventh and eighth grade in Green Vale, perhaps in part because I was so young for my age and small, having skipped a grade, and so behind the other girls in development—no breasts, no waist, no period. More important, perhaps, I was quite self-absorbed and not very nice. I remember feeling like a social failure in those years, not being invited to the parties where my classmates played Spin the Bottle with boys. At least Garrison Forest had no boys.

I got off the train buoyed by the fantasy that drew me South to begin with—Garrison Forest would become my Tara, and somewhere in the Maryland countryside the boy who would become my Rhett Butler was waiting. Faithful black servants would love me, and spirited steeds pawed in their stalls for me to ride them. No matter that the brisk, poodle-cut gym teacher who met us in the station and checked off our names on her list looked as though she belonged in a locker room, not on a veranda. A new stage of my life was beginning. Perhaps at boarding school some magic would transform me from a skinny ugly duckling into a full-fledged swan, a Scarlett O'Hara who was nice.

The brown wooden buildings of Garrison Forest perched on a gentle hillside that sloped down from woods behind the school to the tennis courts and hockey fields below. Stone pathways across enormous lawns linked the buildings together; flowers and trees dotted the inviting landscape. The school was comfortable and relaxed. Both Miss Offutt and Miss Marshall, the two headmistresses, had her own dog with her at all times.

Miss Offutt, the gentler of the two, was accompanied by a smelly old spaniel. She smiled often, frequently oblivious to the time of day or the demands of schedules. She was also a Catholic. The only other Catholics I had encountered were the Irish and Italian maids and laundresses who worked in the houses of my parents and grandparents, so her religion struck me as odd. I knew she was a woman of some stature, being a headmistress, but she did not fit into the social hierarchy as I understood it, and I remained confused about her and the handful of Catholic girls who attended our otherwise Episcopal school. Why did they have that lower-class religion, I wondered.

We dressed in blue cotton uniforms by day, with brown oxford shoes and dark blue blazers. Every so often there were surprise inspections: we had to line up in two rows outside of study hall after morning prayers while monitors checked to see that we hadn't put on sneakers, that our oxfords were properly shined, and that we wore regulation color belts. If your uniform wasn't perfect, you got a demerit, which meant you would be punished for fifteen minutes on Saturday morning—cleaning bridles at the stable, raking leaves, or walking loops around the hockey field.

For dinner, we changed into shiny silk dresses, although whatever outfitter the school used sent them out with droopy ankle-length skirts. But my mother saw that mine were smartly shortened to just below the knee. We could wear our own clothes as well as lipstick on Friday evenings and

Saturdays; Sundays we had to get dressed up for church in the mornings, and Sunday evenings we were back in our uniforms again for evening vespers.

My new classmates came from moneyed suburbs all across the country: Lake Forest, the Main Line, Grosse Point, and Burlingame. One of them didn't last long. Elizabeth Busch, a fourteen-year-old beer heiress from St. Louis, decided after a week or so that she didn't like the place, so she pawned her diamond rings and ran away. We never saw her again.

I loved the school. Classes ended at lunch, leaving afternoons free for riding, sports, and friends; I could foxhunt once a week and gorge myself on tea and cinnamon toast at the hunt club afterward. A quick student, I could finish my homework in the afternoon study hall and spend the evening study hall sprawled in the library reading novels. Some of my happiest times were spent at Garrison Forest.

My roommates and I didn't really get on, but sometimes we stayed up after lights-out, talking. Three of us were tomboyish northerners; Sallie Simpson and I even got into a fight after climbing trees one day, pelting each other with small hard green apples. But Mary Barringer, who was tall and slinky, hailed from South Carolina where she lived in a hotel managed by her father. She was used to being waited on, adamantly opposed to exercise, and knew how to dance the shag. She also knew much more about boys than we did. One night we were talking about sex—rather, Mary was talking and we were listening, sitting cross-legged on top of our beds. She was telling us in her Southern drawl what we would have to do on our wedding nights (it's rather a sign of our antiquated times that we never even *considered* that we might do anything before then). "His *thing*, ya'll know, it'll be *big*," she warned, "And he's gonna want you to *play* with it!" Aghast at such a prospect, I dove under the sheets.

Garrison Forest had both boarding and day students—in fact, some of the day students in my class had been there since kindergarten. They had come up through Garrison's lower school. I became close friends with some of them, and they invited me to go to out with them on Friday afternoons and to visit their houses on weekends.

With them, I saw an intriguing social class. Many of my new friends just walked into their kitchens and made hamburgers or sandwiches! There was no live-in cook to annoy or to shoo them out; their mothers made dinner. The girls had *dates* with boys; "Who are you dating?" they asked one another. Like "cute" and "boyfriend," the word *date* had never been permitted in my vocabulary. On the very few occasions when that had happened, I didn't "date a boyfriend," I "went out with a beau." These girls had felt college pennants and posters on their walls and very ordinary furniture. I had beautifully framed old hunting prints on the immaculate pastel walls of my room at home and antique bureaus to hold my clothes. These girls giggled and sometimes talked back to their mothers, and the mothers even seemed to enjoy the banter.

Things that could never have happened in my house took place regularly in theirs. Boys came over. The girls spent hours in pin curls. They colored their hair with rinses; they wore Bermuda shorts and toreador pants. Their kindly mothers chatted with them about things they were interested in, friends and boys and school. On Friday afternoons, the girls went to an ice cream parlor near Gilman, the boys' school where their brothers and friends went, and watched football games and flirted. No one scolded them, at least not hard. Parents seemed to be delighting in the development of their daughters. I had never seen anything quite like it, and I accepted every invitation I got so I could see more.

But visits with day students were rare events: most of the time I was at school, where we were being prepared for our future. Our teachers told us that we were destined to be leaders in our society, that we were very fortunate and that we had an obligation to be of service to the less fortunate. As budding Ladies Bountiful we took up Christmas collections for the black maids who cleaned our rooms once a week, we were very polite to the black grooms who looked after the school horses, and we supported a Greek foster child named Maria, who like Orphan Annie never aged but stayed eight years old for the four years I attended the school. We had to go to church on Sundays and got scolded when some girls put only pennies into the silver, velvet-lined collection plate. We hated the garter belts and nylon stockings we were supposed to wear to church, since panty hose had yet to be invented. We drew brown lines down the backs of our bare legs with eyebrow pencils so it would look as though we were obediently wearing stockings with seams.

Garrison in those days was a quirky place. Miss Marshall, her German Shepherd at her side, taught Ancient History. A tall, mannish woman who had once been muscular, she had very curly brown hair, a sagging face, and an athlete's slightly pigeon-toed way of striding in her sensible shoes. Intensely religious, she sang in the school choir at Vespers, and occasionally she got so carried away with emotion that tears rolled down her cheeks. The girls who sang next to her thought at times they smelled whiskey on her breath.

Miss Marshall, who took her Episcopalian faith seriously, wanted us all to believe as she did in Christ, resurrection, and life after death. One day in class, she presented us with what she called irrefutable proof that souls physically exist. Scientists, she said, had put a monkey on one side of a scale, balanced it with exactly equal weights, and killed it. At the instant of death, said Miss Marshall, the monkey's side of the scales fell—thus proving it had a soul that actually departed from its body when it died. This was very interesting stuff indeed. She didn't say where the monkey's soul went, or how much it weighed, and I never thought to ask until this moment at my computer, more than fifty years later.

Actual experiences of Christian brotherhood and sisterhood, however, languished. No black, brown, yellow, or red girls attended our school. One girl, Liza Dietz, was rumored to be half-Jewish. It was whispered that her father, Howard Dietz, had written "Dancing in the Dark" and other classic songs, so that probably offset any anti-Semitic prejudice that might have affected her.

Not until college did I go to classes with other than white girls, and very few even then. My attitudes toward race mirrored the way I had been raised. I thought that people of other races were, along with everyone who wasn't like me and my family, of a lower class. They might be perfectly nice, perhaps, but not suitable for the life that I had because they weren't us. I didn't think they would appreciate rare American antiques or well-bred horses or the sarcastic wit my family enjoyed. At Garrison, where maids and the men who worked in the stable were all black, I would have felt uncomfortable with a black classmate, and I was afraid of black men. I didn't think about segregation; when *Brown v. Board of Education* came down from the Supreme Court the year I graduated, I wasn't aware of it. My classmates and I smiled condescendingly at blacks and Jews who drove big Cadillacs, while our own fathers in their big Cadillacs seemed entirely natural and fitting.

In four years there, I thought very little about the caste system in which I lived. Yes, yes, we had been given a great deal and we should remember the poor, but that was as far as it went. The civil rights and feminist movements of the 1960s would not happen for a decade, and it did not occur to me to think about segregated schools or Americans who could not vote, much less the limited options open to women. Only one teacher, the frightening, brilliant, and eccentric Mrs. Taylor of the sharp tongue and unwashed, sculpted hair, came close to examining the issue of our privilege. A tall, pale woman who wore the same purplish velvet jacket for weeks at a time, she arranged her classroom so that we sat around tables instead of in rows; she made us read and prodded us to think. She was our English teacher our last two years, and no one in my class ever forgot her. I will always remember what a tiny percentage of the world's population is white and well off, and I will never use "like" as a conjunction.

Before I got to Mrs. Taylor, however, I was busy becoming somebody. The first weeks of ninth grade brought two surprises: I was elected to the sought-after dramatic club and, though I couldn't carry a tune, chosen to be a cheerleader. Moreover, I was one of the most experienced riders in a school where membership in the Riding Club was prized above all else.

The four years at Garrison were among the most peaceful of my life. There, unlike either of my homes, the environment was benign and predictable. The rules on Tuesday were the same on Wednesday. For me, as for some of my classmates, this was the closest to a normal existence we had ever known. Moreover, through friendships with the day scholars in my class, I got to meet boys and go out with them. On vacations, I visited classmates in Baltimore as often as I possibly could. Halfway through Garrison, that goal became much easier to reach: Lewie retired from Legal Aid, which Mummy had never liked, and sold Whitehackle Farm. He bought a larger place in the hunt country of Unionville, Pennsylvania, where they could ride all day without encountering a parkway or a housing development. By then, I had a driver's license and could speed south to Maryland at a moment's notice for parties and visits with my Garrison friends.

Our senior class yearbook pictures show me cheerleading, riding, belonging to clubs, and co-editing the literary magazine. The person who emerges from inscriptions written in my book by friends is a peppy, cheerful girl who got good marks, spent hours on the phone with boys, broke rules, kept smelly riding clothes in her closet, and was known to dance around in a hat, underwear, and high heels. After what felt like success and acceptance, I became rather outspoken and wrote reams of terrible essays, stories, and poems. I was riding high. I was one of two who were voted Most Likely to Succeed.

But that year I was also a love-struck seventeen-year-old, and I got caught in a major crime. I had gotten to know Peter Alexander at parties in Baltimore. He and I went out together for several months starting in junior year, and he came to visit me that summer when I was with my father and Cotty on Martha's Vineyard. A tall, athletic young man whose father was a conservative newspaper columnist, he was Miss Marshall's nephew.

On weekends and some afternoons when we were seniors, we would meet in the woods behind the school. He was my true love—one of a long series of true loves—and extra special because, I fancied, he was a bad boy being made good by the love of me. Peter had a long record of mischief. He had been found drunk under a Stutz Bearcat at the age of fifteen; he gambled and went to cockfights and race tracks. He said he had even gone "all the way" with a girl. He assured me that he didn't respect her, while he did respect me. This, in the 1950s, was very important. I didn't do any more than light necking then, and I got panicky when at a dance I could feel a boy's *thing* press against my body.

A tall, strong, sandy-haired boy, Peter was a champion wrestler. Whenever I could, I went over to Gilman to watch his meets. No one lasted long in the ring with Peter. Like a huge spider he circled his hapless opponent, reached out a long arm, and tangled him to the mat within moments. He flashed me a grin when he won. I felt like a gun moll whenever he did that. My mother liked Peter the best of any person I've ever been involved with. She thoroughly approved of the way he was bad. He had a sense of humor and good manners, and he rode horses well.

He boarded at Gilman, but only five days a week, and he had that Ford. My last year at the school, instead of going straight back to my room after our late study hall, I sometimes sneaked over to the end of a lane just behind Senior House. Peter waited there for me in his car; I climbed in, and we necked and talked until the very last moment before I had to run off to get in my dorm before the curfew.

All went swimmingly until one evening when I was walking down the stairs at Senior House on the way to dinner. Our housemother, Miss Hall, called me into her room. A frowsy-haired, stout, and dedicated woman who had taught at Garrison for forty years or more, she had charge of the seniors. A massive German Shepherd accompanied her everywhere.

"I've heard you've been seeing Peter *Elexander*," she said. She always pronounced it like that. "Oh no, Miss Hall, I haven't." She repeated the accusation. I denied it again and went off to dinner, shaking. It was a Wednesday and my favorite meal, but the pork chops tasted like cardboard and the sweet potatoes like glue.

A week went by uneventfully, so I thought I had gotten away with it. But then I was summoned into Miss Offutt's office. "Topsy," she said to me sadly, "You didn't tell Miss Hall the truth. You were seen with Peter Alexander. I can't say who saw you. You must be suspended for a week." I flashed back on one afternoon when I had been in the woods with Peter and Mrs. Whitman, the senior riding teacher, had gone by on a horse. She must have told.

I frantically called Peter at his school. "They've found us out!" I told him. "I'm being suspended. What shall I do?" He had no answer.

That night, a severe blizzard blanketed the East Coast. Because of the snow, I could not get to my mother's farm in Pennsylvania so I was put on a train to New York, to Clarry. Shaken by the enormity of what had happened, I worried northward through Wilmington, 30th Street Philadelphia, North Philadelphia, Trenton, Newark, and New York to Pennsylvania Station. "All out please," called the conductor. Dreading what was to come, I lugged my suitcase from the train and up the escalator. At the top stood my grim, stone-faced father. Silently I followed him to the subway, coated in shame. Never one to engage in personal conversations even at the best of times, he sat rigid and wordless as we hurtled along underground.

But Clarry was taking me just where I most wanted to go. For two weeks a year, socialites displaced basketball and boxing fans at Madison Square Garden as horses and riders from all over the world converged for the National Horse Show. Clarry hated horses, he hated horse shows, and he hated to be embarrassed when his children got into trouble. Radiating annoyance and disapproval, he had to go and meet Cotty at a place he despised. I followed meekly behind, too afraid to break the wordless dynamic that bound us as we sped toward our destination and his wife.

Cotty adored the horse show. As a member of a ladies' committee, she attended every night dressed to the nines, watching the horses, flirting with the riders, and drinking with her friends. She herself had not ridden for decades; I thought she liked the social angle better than the horses, and I self-righteously scorned her and the other ladies who fawned all over the Mexican colonels and Irish lieutenants on the jumping teams.

When the show was over that evening, the three of us drove in silence out to Westbury. Clarry treated me like an outcast, but in a few days the snow melted enough that I could be sent to my mother's.

She took the whole episode lightly, noting with amusement that I had at least had the wit to get involved with the headmistress's nephew, which undoubtedly lightened my sentence.

But I dreaded my return to school and my fall from grace. I knew that Miss Offutt had spoken to the school, her speech beginning, "A Senior has betrayed her trust."

As the taxi left me off at Garrison, I hung my head, grabbed my suitcase, and trudged across the lawn toward Senior House. "Hey, look who's back!" came a welcoming cry. It was Bee Shriver, a friend from my class. She broke the ice, and my crime was not mentioned again. The romance with Peter crumbled under the strain of what had happened, and I got interested in a handsome Princeton sophomore instead. And despite worrying that my suspension might keep me from being accepted at college, I got into all of the colleges I had applied to.

When I graduated in 1954 with my class of forty-two girls, Dwight Eisenhower was in the White House, the Army-McCarthy hearings dominated the news, and family togetherness was the prevailing ideal. At our commencement ceremonies on a soft June day, stiff corsets called Merry Widows pinched our waists and pushed up our breasts. I won the Riding Cup and, after it was over, we packed up clothes, riding boots and stuffed animals into our parents' station wagons, and drove away.

CHAPTER SEVEN

Debutante

...Like as a virgin riseth up, and goes,
And enters on the mazes of the dance;

—Dante, *Divine Comedy*, Canto XXV

Girls like me began our training at the age of eleven or twelve, when, with velvet dresses on our skinny bodies and party shoes on our clumsy feet, we were taken to dancing class. There, we learned the box step, waltz, Charleston, Mexican hat dance, and the all-important art of making conversation with boys. The man who taught my dancing class was a former amateur boxer from an old New York family named William de Rham. Mr. de Rham must have fallen on hard times; he was particularly interesting to me because he had once been married to Lewie's sister Totty, the first of her four husbands, so he was my ex-stepuncle. The only time I ever had to dance with him, he held me quite close to his prickly gray suit and I noticed through my haze of anxiety that he reeked of body odor.

Mr. de Rham, who carried himself erect as a top sergeant, was not afraid of hurting the feelings of his elite little charges. I remember an agonizing waltz with my fellow student Harry Bingham, the two of us selected to perform in front of the class. I struggled vainly to keep in step with the agile Harry as he spun round and round in perfect time to the recorded music. "That's it, Harry," called out Mr. de Rham, "If she won't turn fast enough, just *push* her."

Dancing class ended with grammar school. In ninth grade, we future debutantes from New York families took the next step: attending formal dances in the city at Christmas and Easter. No sock hops, these. There were four of them: the Metropolitan and the Get-togethers, the Holidays and the Colony—the Mets, the Gets, the Hols and the Cols—with balls at Christmas and Easter vacations, every year until we came out.

A committee of ladies accepted or rejected the girls who applied. I don't know that there were rigid social standards for boys, though certainly in those days no blacks would have been admitted. There had to be enough of them to be dancing partners for the girls, and so their origins were less scrutinized.

Being a Pell, I was automatically invited to these dances. Families such as ours, I sensed, belonged as a matter of birthright. Some other girls, however, had to go to teas with their mothers so they could be inspected by the committee ladies, and only those who were approved received the engraved invitations.

I was vaguely aware that something odd was going on in this process, something quite different from what happened at school or at the horse shows where I competed. It seemed that my classmates were included or excluded based on criteria that had little to do with academic success, athletic ability, or good behavior, the standards we had been judged by in the past. The accents of their parents, whether they had had nannies, the houses they lived in, the style in which they dressed—and of course whether their mothers were known to people like my mother—seemed to be the factors determining who was chosen and who was not. Since I was among the elect, it didn't occur to me to question this sorting-out. Perhaps I might have wondered if a friend of mine had been rejected, but all my good friends—Sue Martin, Natalie Fell, Nancy Gerry, Kate Babcock—were also accepted, no questions asked, no tea party inspections endured.

But once I was in, my worries began. It was up to us girls to invite boys to be our escorts. Isolated in far-off boarding schools as thirteen- and fourteen-year-olds, we had to arrange for at least one and preferably two boys for each dance. (The two boys per girl ratio was to prevent wallflowers, the extra boys providing a reservoir of dancing partners.)

To line up escorts, we wrote the boys from our schools; the long-distance phone in those days far too expensive and frightening. I worried when deciding whom to invite: A boy I liked? One who liked me? A safe old friend? Dozens of sheets of writing paper were crumpled up in false starts. "Dear Crawfie," I would begin. (Crawford Blagden was the son of friends of my parents and a close friend of my young uncle, John Jay Mortimer. I had known Crawfie for years, so he was the one I asked first.) "It was fun seeing you in Tuxedo this summer. I wonder if you would like to go to the Junior Holiday with me on December 18th? Please let me know." Hmm. Was this too forward, saying I'd had fun with him? Or should I be even more enthusiastic, and say that I had had "lots" of fun? And should I sign myself "Sincerely," as in a business letter, or, more affectionately, "Love"?

Then I would look at the finished letter. Did the lines run too much uphill? Were they too wobbly? Was the handwriting too blotchy and unfeminine? I never mastered that cute, rounded semi-printing that my popular girl friends used, the i's dotted with little circles, no matter how slowly and carefully I moved my pen.

Acceptances by boys brought high exuberance and shrieks of relief; rejections led to brooding, further fretting over who else to try, and more stacks of crumpled notepaper. Social success and failure hinged on the small envelopes trickling in from New England boys' boarding schools. (The boys didn't seem so uptight about the impressions created by their letters—they mailed back any old penciled scrawl, for which we girls were desperately grateful.)

Another challenge to our social skills: The girl had to get herself and her escorts invited to a dinner party before each dance. We girls could organize a bit together: ". . . if you have your grandmother give a dinner before the Hols and you invite me, I'll get my mother to give one before the Gets and I'll invite you."

My mother's behavior showed me that these dances mattered; she spent hours marching me up and down Fifth Avenue in search of evening dresses. (We never called them "gowns.") She sped from Lord and Taylor through Bonwit Teller, Saks, Altmans, and Bendels, with me trotting dutifully behind. On arrival in the right department of the store, she began selecting dresses for me to try on, brushing rejected frocks aside with contempt. She treated the sales people like servants. One day, particularly annoyed, she exclaimed, "These dresses are made for fat little *kikes!*" Mortified by her behavior, I smiled weakly at the saleswomen, hoping they would realize that I was not prejudiced like my mother.

Skilled in the art of presenting herself as a beautiful woman, Mummy did well by me. After a dress was chosen, seamstresses were ordered in to shorten skirts and insert what were called "rosettes" into the front of the dress to make up for my flat chest. No one was so common as to call the rosettes "falsies." My mother was not modest in her approach to sex appeal; where my friends' mothers usually chose gentle pastel hues for their teenaged daughters, she went for brilliance. My best dress was lipstick red, with a sort of satin shelf under the bosom and a halter top—quite risqué for the pallid fifties—and guaranteed to draw the attention of teenaged boys. If bright colors would attract more dance partners, I was game, even if my friends with more conservative mothers were slightly shocked. (I remember arriving at a summer resort to stay with a Garrison classmate and unpacking my short white evening dress with hot pink sash and matching hot pink shoes. "You're not going to wear those, are you?" asked my friend's younger sister, horrified by the neon colors. Of course I was.)

After the dress had been bought and fitted, and the boys and the dinners lined up, the day finally came. I took the Long Island Railroad from Whitehackle Farm into New York, changing trains at Jamaica, then the subway or a cab to Gargy's vast penthouse overlooking Central Park. (Unlike parents of today, my mother saw no need to supervise my party preparations, and there was certainly no eager relative in the front hall with a camera to record the scene.) At Gargy's, I had tea and a little chat with her and whichever aunts, uncles, or cousins had dropped in.

Then I had my bath and, with the help of Alice, Gargy's French maid, I dressed. First, on went the Merry Widow. Still enthralled with Scarlett O'Hara, I did my best to cinch in my waist, which required Alice to do a lot of tugging while I sucked in my stomach. Next I put on stockings, silk underpants, one or two crinolines, and silver or gold evening slippers with narrow straps that felt fine at first, but by midnight would be biting into my feet. Then came the small Oriental pearls my mother had given me, three gold charm bracelets, little earrings, lipstick, and powder. My hair had been done at the hairdresser's and combed into a smooth page boy. Last, over my head with the dress, a careful inspection in the mirror, the white gloves, white bunny-fur jacket, little silver evening purse, and down the hall to wait for the boy(s) to arrive.

Then came the introduction of the boys to my grandmother; "Goodnight, Gargy," I said, and down we went in the elevator to the chilly, Christmas-y air of the streets, hunting for a taxi to transport us to another fashionable East Side house or apartment. The boy paid the taxi driver and up we went to greet the girl who was giving the dinner and her mother or grandmother.

After that, we took taxis to the hotels where the dances were held, usually the Plaza or the Pierre. (I remember how much, when we were in the taxi, Anson Beard, a cheerful boy with a particularly engaging smile, liked to pat my bunny-fur jacket, but only in the most innocent places.) The splendidly uniformed hotel doorman opened the taxi door, and out we stepped, accepting his deference like the elegant young ladies and gentlemen we were supposed to be.

Once there, girls clustered in the ladies' room, primping and chatting nervously in the warm, female atmosphere. Someone always needed a last-minute Kotex, or an aspirin for cramps, or a comb to borrow because she'd forgotten hers. I stood in front of the mirror and smiled at the silent, black-uniformed maid stationed there as I molded my hair into the smooth shape it was supposed to have, enjoying the security of being with the other girls. But after a few minutes, we had to pull out the cardboard admission tickets from our little purses, place a quarter in the china saucer for the maid, and leave our sanctuary to join the waiting boys. We passed through the receiving line of committee ladies—dreary-looking mothers in evening dresses—smiling politely, shaking limp hands, and murmuring, "Good evening."

Then we were truly in the arena, a vast, high-ceilinged ballroom in the center of which stood a cluster of black-clad boys like a flock of penguins. Couples danced around the cluster in the old-fashioned way, holding one another and fox-trotting to the beat of Lester Lanin or Meyer Davis. Above the dance floor, in boxes, sat the committee ladies and a few hen-pecked husbands. My mother, who didn't bother herself with my search for boys and dinner parties, would not have been caught dead in that situation.

The challenge for the girls was to get danced with by as many boys as possible. Nice, attractive ones would be best, but quantity beat quality on this brilliantly polished playing field. The key to success lay in becoming a girl whom boys didn't get stuck with; the goal was to be so entertaining that many boys would cut in on you several times a night. You could be discussing the poetry of T. S. Eliot with a studious one, then smile gracefully over his shoulder at the approach of another as he raised his hand to cut in. As the poetry student released you, you moved into the arms of the newcomer—with whom you had previously been chatting about the Rangers' star hockey player—and then you smiled regretfully over the hockey fan's shoulder to indicate how much you longed to continue the poetry conversation. On a good night, I carried on a dozen interrupted conversations that way, several of them with boys whom I had never met before. My attention could switch from one boy and his subject to another boy and another subject in a flash as I smiled, adjusting my brain and body to each new partner's style without missing a beat.

On some electric evenings, I would dance only a few steps with one boy before another cut in. But occasionally, I would get stuck with the same boy for song after song, both of us miserable and flat out of things to say, longing for the moment when the orchestra leader stopped the music and instructed, "Everybody double-cut." Jane Anderson, who had been in my class at Green Vale, was a tall, ungainly girl, with limp, straight, muddy blonde hair, a good brain, no visible sense of humor, and a poker face. She was doomed from the start in this competition, and I hate to think of the fortitude she had to summon up to get through these evenings. Anyone could read the unhappy body language from tall, serious girls like her, stiff and miserable, who were dumped from one boy to the next all night long. Boys (but not girls) who were stuck could double-cut when they felt like it, pawning off an unpopular girl on someone else and trading up to someone prettier. When that happened to me, I summoned up a sickly smile and tried to make bright conversation with my new partner, but I felt like damaged goods and he knew it. The ultimate nightmare, if you were a girl, was to have a boy wave a five-dollar bill behind your back—a bribe for anyone who would cut in.

But for the most part I was lucky—reasonably pretty, small enough to attract the short boys who liked dancing with someone even smaller, and possessed of an unusual nickname. Also, since I had been schooled in the art of making conversation from the days when Lewie and Mummy knocked on the front door pretending to be the Russian ambassador and his wife, I could chat up my dance partners. I was perky, and I had learned—on the foxhunting field, on the tennis court, and with my parents—not to quit. Dead air was not an option, and I was determined to make my dance partners like me. The game back then was pretty straight, and it would have been cheating to gain popularity by giving out sexual favors. You had to succeed using your looks and personality. You didn't want to be known as "fast."

There was one Latino boy, perhaps the son of a United Nations diplomat, who always danced with me at these parties. Maybe my tanned skin was familiar to him, about the same shade as his. One evening, we had left the dance floor to get some punch, and on the way back we went down a stairway into a short corridor. There, with no one else in sight, he took my hand in his, and as I stood still, he turned and kissed me. "*Tú eres linda*," he murmured. Astonished and with no idea what to do next, not understanding a word of what he had said, I pulled back and headed for the dance floor as if nothing had happened. He never kissed me again.

Back at Garrison Forest after the vacation dances, I waited hopefully for letters to arrive. That was the road to romance: if some boy met you at a dance, liked you, and wasn't too shy, he would write. After waiting a calculated interval, I would write back, carefully calibrating again how to close, taking a hint from the closing he had used—which might range from the bland "Sincerely," to the exciting "Love." We got our mail at recess at Garrison Forest, gathering in a crowd under the stairs in Moncrieffe Hall while a girl read off the names from the envelopes as she handed them out—so that it was public knowledge whether you got letters or not. As with dances, so with letters; it didn't matter who was writing you as long as you got mail. My personal record was a day when I got letters from seven boys.

But it wasn't just about social status. How I wanted to be loved! To be cherished, to matter to someone! Like my friends, I soaked up *True Romance* comics, though their silly plots rarely varied: the girl always fell for a rich, selfish fellow, ditching the humdrum steady guy who'd always loved her; then she got into trouble while the flashy one split and the good guy rallied to save the day and win her hand in marriage. Unlike the love comics with their democratic teachings, however, I'd never have a future with a good-hearted mechanic—my husband would have to come from a background like mine.

Sometimes I was a little unclear about the implications of social class. I had met and played with "unsuitable" boys when I was little—Mummy and Lewie teased me because one year when I was about ten, I befriended a townie in Southampton, where we went for several summers. A handsome, friendly, freckle-faced boy, who would have been utterly acceptable had he come from a rich family, he had the misfortune to summer in the same place where he wintered. I think his father worked in a local store, and his mother was a housewife. I rode my bike around with him, and we played tennis on the macadam public courts; in fact, I had more fun on the public courts with him than on the grass courts of the Meadow Club with the socially prominent boys. "How many *thousands* of dollars do we pay to belong to these clubs, and she ends up on the public courts?" asked my mother in mock horror. I continued hanging out with him that summer but, after going off to Garrison Forest, I stopped befriending townies.

Just as the Hols and Cols and Garrison itself were pit stops on the road to a proper marriage, so were the places I went in the summer: Southampton,

Long Island, with my mother and Lewie; Martha's Vineyard with Clarry and Cotty; Dublin, New Hampshire, with my Pell grandparents; and Tuxedo with Gargy.

I liked the New York dances and the summer colonies, too. I learned there that I could be attractive to the opposite sex, or at least to some of them; that my class of people went where they pleased, that catering to boys brought sweet rewards. And along the way, I found that other people's parents were much nicer than my mother and my father, and far easier to please.

To be sure, there were excruciating moments. Once, as a thirteen-year-old in ninth grade, I had to give a dinner at Gargy's before a Junior Holiday. Gathered in her elegant apartment, with its high ceilings and Louis XVI furniture, my teenaged guests and I struggled to live up to our formal, adult clothes and surroundings. An ornate Napoleonic clock ticked away on a mantelpiece, the marble floor of the foyer gleamed brightly, the polished silver shone. England, the butler, took the guests' coats and asked what they would have to drink. A black-clad maid with frilly white apron passed hors d'oeuvres, circulating around the immense drawing room. We teenagers were overwhelmed. Once seated around the large, candlelit dining room table with England and the waitress passing silver platters of food, we could think of absolutely nothing to say.

Silence hung over our table; embarrassment filled the room. All of us, boys and girls, were quite unfamiliar with the opposite sex, except as objects of fantasy. For weeks and months in our single-sex schools we had anticipated these dances and hoped to find romance, but once faced with the actual situation, we were struck dumb. "Where do you go to school?" we asked each other, though we pretty much knew already. "What's it like?" You certainly couldn't ask some boy if he had been homesick, or say how weird it felt to be in a setting far more suitable for Cary Grant and Katharine Hepburn than for bashful teenagers. We longed for sophistication and smart repartee, but we were stuck in acne and awkwardness.

Luckily, some of the girls at my dinner were going to Foxcroft, the boarding school in Virginia whose headmistress so admired Marine discipline. Students there had to march and drill with wooden rifles. A couple of the pluckier boys began asking the girls about that: "Do you really carry guns? Do you want to be soldiers?" But by the time the soup course was finished, the topic was worn thin. Tepid discussion of Foxcroft's other odd accoutrements, such as its outdoor sleeping porches, carried us through most of the main course. So when a second embarrassing silence fell, and a boy dredged up yet another tired question about the military drill, we all nervously laughed at our absurd situation—and the school's peculiar militarism got us through dessert.

There were other, worse, moments. Before one winter Get-Together, I had not been invited to a dinner party and I hadn't been able to line up even one boy for the evening. I didn't dare tell my mother or Gargy about the situation; that would have been a terrible admission of failure, and, embarrassed and feeling inadequate, I was worried that they would scold me. (It never crossed my mind that they might provide help or support.) I had no idea where to turn. Finally, I dredged up a very nice but plump and unfashionable fellow, Joe Plumb, who went to a boarding school no one had ever heard of and who had never been to one of these dances before. I had heard that my blonde, sophisticated Garrison Forest classmate Jenepher Burton was giving a dinner that evening, and I hoped against hope that, though we were not particularly close friends, she would invite me. But she didn't.

When Gargy asked me a week before the dance where I was going to dine, I panicked and, instead of taking advantage of a chance to tell the truth, I lied, and said, "At Jenepher's." The next evening, when I saw Jenepher in the ladies' room during another dance, in a desperate attempt to get her to ask me, I squeezed up next to her at the mirror and asked pointedly, "Where are you going to dinner before the Get?" She avoided my question, eyes front as she carefully put on her lipstick. I was mortified to have been so pushy, even more upset at being unsuccessful, and still desperate about what to do.

As it turned out, Gargy often played bridge with Jenepher's grandmother and must have said something to her about the dinner. The grandmother said something to Jenepher and so Jenepher was forced to include me. It was clear as soon as Joe and I arrived at the dinner why she had not wanted to include me in her evening: she had planned an intimate foursome with her best friend and their two boyfriends, all four as polished and urbane as Joe and I were nervous and dorky. They looked at us as if we were unwanted intruders, which we were, and, instead of the intimate and easy chat that the four close friends had looked forward to, they were obliged to make stiff, general conversation that included us. I felt guilty for thrusting us two outsiders on them, but somehow justified because I hadn't known what else to do—sort of a defense of necessity. The ruined dinner didn't last long, and soon I was dancing away in the ballroom of the Hotel Pierre. But in all the years since this incident, on the few occasions when I have seen her, I have been too embarrassed to mention it to Jenepher.

Another time, I behaved much worse. For a Christmas vacation dance a year later, I had lined up two boys for the evening. I had a crush on one of them, a rather mischievous dark-haired boy named George Carter whom I had met while visiting my Pell grandparents on their New Hampshire farm. The other, Harry Justice, was a sweet, gentle boy who had liked me and been a good friend for some time. However, I didn't find him so sexy and exciting as George. So when, toward the end of the dance, George suggested that we sneak out early and ditch Harry, I eagerly followed him out the door. Days later, Harry wrote a letter telling me of his distress, standing alone near the exit as people filed out, searching the crowd for my face. He described how people had teased him and laughed as they went by: "Left you behind, has she?" But I was off necking at my grandmother's with George, who, as any reader of love comics could have predicted, turned out to be not such a nice person after all.

Embarrassed though I was about behaving badly to Jenepher and Harry, the most painful experience of these dances involved my father. The dance committees sent out tickets to the girls beforehand; I was always careful when packing my suitcase at Whitehackle Farm to check the little drawer in my mother's desk where she kept the tickets and to bring the right ones with me to my grandmother's in New York. But one day when I looked, there was no ticket for the Colony. I didn't ask my mother for fear of touching off her anger. (In our family, the less you had to do with Mummy, the better.) I left for the city a trifle worried but certain I could get in by giving my name to a hostess at the special table by the entrance.

When my escort, Bobby Gilmor, and I arrived at the dance, I went over to the table and gave my name to the motherly person there. A buxom lady with a few wisps of hair escaping from her bun, she wore a long pearl necklace around her wrinkly neck, a diamond brooch on the silk collar of her long beige dress. To my surprise, she did not immediately smile and direct me inside but told me to wait. This was embarrassing, but Bobby and I did as we were told, standing awkwardly at the entrance as crowds of couples passed us on their way in. Several uncomfortable minutes later, we were permitted to enter.

The next day, I happened to visit Clarry's house. When he arrived home from work, he summoned me into the living room, where he became coldly furious. Evidently my mother had forgotten to answer the invitation and send in the fee for that dance. But, because some of the committee ladies knew who I was, they allowed me in anyway. One of them had phoned my father in the morning to tell him what had happened. In an ominous tone, he informed me that the incident was *very* serious. Mrs. Brewster had called him at his *office*. A lady never phones a man at his office, he went on, except in a dire situation. Plainly, he was holding me responsible for this horrendous breach of etiquette. My face flushed. I felt confused and miserable—at fault, evidently, but what could I have done differently? The subsequent dinner was strained and unhappy.

Later, when I mentioned this humiliation to my mother, she just laughed. "I don't see why he got so upset," she said, dismissing it lightly. "It was just a matter of bookkeeping."

I didn't realize then what was going on. I did not foresee that, as the years went by and docile Topsy grew into rebellious Eve, my father would always choose obedience to the code of his class over loyalty to me.

But Topsy had a long way to go before developing any hints of Eve. For my friends and me, the debutante year meant a dizzying round of dances in cities up and down the East Coast. There were summer balls, autumn balls, and Christmas balls. My friends and I took for granted the extraordinary amounts of money our parents spent on these affairs—one orchestra and sometimes two, rivers of Champagne, baskets of flowers hanging in an enormous, airy tent for the summer parties or a palatial hotel ballroom in the winter, an elaborate supper at midnight, a made-to-order dress. Those were just the basics, and they added up to thousands and thousands of dollars—all for one evening.

My turn came in June.

Although by 1954 Lewie and my mother had moved from Long Island to the farm in Pennsylvania, my debut would be in New York because I came from a New York family. So she and Lewie teamed up with three sets of parents to give a June dance on Long Island where their daughters would come out together, a not uncommon arrangement among families who had known one another for generations and wanted to share expenses. The four of us had gone to Green Vale together and at various times I'd been best friends with each one of them. We had stayed over at each other's houses, passed notes in class, and compared nannies and parents. Sue Martin's mother and father had been married and divorced even more often than mine; in fifth grade, we were inseparable. Natalie Fell was the most popular, beautiful and athletic girl in our class. In third grade, she had tried to teach me to run fast by grabbing my hand and pulling me across the school playground. Nancy Gerry lived right near my father's house; we had ridden our ponies together for years, and, when I was ten, she had told me where babies came from.

We were known as Fell, Pell, Gerry, and Martin. Natalie's name came first probably because she was the most popular but also because the party was to be given at her parent's mansion. Bendel's made my dress, which was of course white, with cap sleeves, a princess waist and wreaths of embroidered pink flowers on the long, belled skirt. I went with my mother to a cramped New York office where a lady, who I suspect had fallen on hard times, maintained card files listing the names of suitable guests. As she read off the names, we said Yes or No.

I felt curiously absent from my own debut. For some of my friends, it seemed to be a time when their mothers felt particularly close to them, and they planned the big event together. But I had no interest in closeness with Mummy. Seventeen now, I stayed away from home as much as possible, visiting friends and going to parties. Flirting, dancing, driving around with boys, giggling with my girl friends, borrowing a big car and racing it to see my Garrison friends in Baltimore—that was fun. But at home on the Pennsylvania farm, it seemed that all my mother wanted was for me to run errands and exercise horses. She didn't want to talk with me about my friends, my beaus, or any of the other topics with which I was absorbed. She was only thirty-six at that time and looked about twenty-five. She had four younger children: Cooky, who was away at boarding school, and the three Ledyards, Wendy and Cass, who were twelve and eleven, and our baby brother Michael, then only six. She had a large estate and a household to manage, plus her horses to ride, races and dinner parties to attend, and bowls of flowers to fix. Besides her involvement with her own life, she did not want to interfere with my freedom, she has since told me, in part because she felt she had had so little freedom herself when she was young.

But from my point of view, besides being totally self-interested, she was always ready to criticize—for walking instead of running to get her a sweater, for wearing blue shoes with my brown tweed suit, for doing a sloppy job cleaning my horse's bridle after riding, for not having a clean pair of white gloves for church. In order to dodge her temper and the errands she wanted done, I went home only to leave off my dirty laundry, say where I was going next, and pack for another visit to a friend.

By staying on the move, I avoided discussing the coming-out party with her. I remember going to Debbie Dilworth's ball in Philadelphia, where her father was the mayor, the week before mine. I spent that night as a guest of Debbie's married older sister. I suspected that Mummy would summon me home the next day to help with my party, but I had other ideas. I hopped an early morning train to New York to visit another friend, even though I had packed only a summery cotton dress besides my evening dress, and had brought no white gloves along. I never had gone to New York without a proper outfit before, but escape outweighed decorum.

I had been right. Mummy telephoned Mayor Dilworth himself early that morning to track me down, routing him out of bed, but I had already flown the coop.

On the night of my debut, Mummy and Lewie stayed with friends, and I stayed with my father in Westbury. Cotty did my makeup too heavily, powdering my dark skin until it was several shades lighter. Peter Alexander was my escort, as we had arranged before I got suspended from Garrison, my last date with him. Many of my friends from Baltimore came up for the event, and once the dancing got going, I remember having a whirl.

Photographs of the evening show me dancing and laughing with many boys, waltzing solemnly with my father (who contributed not a dime to this effort but showed up to dance the first dance with me), posing with my brothers. But the most striking photographs feature my mother. Unlike the other mothers, who dressed quite modestly in long, pale dresses, Mummy wore a short, sexy black dress with a plunging neckline. She looked like a totally different species from Mrs. Fell, Mrs. Gerry, and Mrs. Davison, Sue's mother. I don't remember any contact with her at all. The party ended at six in the morning with Patty Weymouth and some boys diving into the Fells' swimming pool still wearing their evening clothes.

While our party was splendid enough, the ultimate coming-out party that year was Cathy Mellon's, held at her family's horse farm in Middleburg, Virginia. Certainly we were all privileged, but she was more so. I did not know her well, but she had gone to Foxcroft with Natalie, Nancy, and Sue, and once I had visited her gorgeous house. Her bedroom had beautiful, small paintings of sailboats on the wall—I had no idea until later that they were by Raul Dufy.

Cathy's party was lavish, even by our standards. In addition to the flower-bedecked tent for dancing, the Mellons had transformed one of their barns.

The horses had been removed and each stall cleaned and painted, then made into a mini-restaurant in a theme to match the food being served there. In one stall you could get oysters; another served hamburgers, others served ice cream, pastries, hot dishes, strawberries, and so on.

About midnight, the dancing stopped. We turned our attention to a spectacular display of fireworks that soared, exploded, and cascaded in brilliant colors over the hunt-country pastures. For the hundreds of us who went, jaded though we may have been by other grand evenings, this was the one to remember.

I was thoroughly happy that night, being just where I wanted to be and doing just what I wanted to do. All I knew was that the Mellons were very rich and very nice. I had no idea then that they owned Gulf Oil, and I had never heard the phrase "robber baron."

In fact, I felt superior to families such as the Mellons or Rockefellers and slightly sorry for them because of their notoriety. Their grandfathers had been "in trade," which was vulgar, and I remembered hearing somewhere that an ancestress of mine had considered them too nouveau riche to enter New York society. But the Rockefellers I knew seemed shy, very nice, and slightly awkward, except for Michael, a bright, bespectacled young man who danced with the energy of a dervish and later perished on an expedition to Papua, New Guinea.

And as it turned out, my snobbish belief that my own family had never been "in trade" proved quite wrong. As I discovered in researching this book, the Pell who returned from Canada after the Revolution made a lot of money importing wood and marble to New York City from Vermont, the Mortimer immigrant from Scotland sold Civil War uniforms, and my great-grandfather Tilford was a hard-driving oil pioneer on the rough-and-tumble California frontier. Unlike my Aunt Goody, I'm glad now that Henry Morgan Tilford had the wit and gumption to make his own way. But I probably wouldn't have liked it back then.

Gathering of Pell family beneath portrait of John Pell, second lord of the manor, 1956. I am in the front row next to Claiborne; my father is standing, wearing a white jacket and dark tie. The fishmonger Pell, Cousin Rodman, the rightful heir to the lordship at that time, is third from the right. *From author's family album*

Portrait by Aunt Olive Pell of her husband, my Great-Uncle
Bertie, and his son, Claiborne. *Courtesy of Senator and Mrs.
Claiborne Pell*

Richard Mortimer house, Crystal Palace, Tuxedo Park. *From author's family album*

Henry Morgan Tilford. *Image copyrighted by Chevron Corporation and used with permission*

Gargy and her mother, Grandma Tilford, in Palm Beach. *From author's family album*

Gargy and Grandpa Mortimer at Tuxedo Horse Show. *News Photo Service*

Grandpa Mortimer and Big Cook, with racquets bats, probably
before a tournament. *Courtesy of Richard and Lynn Mortimer*

Gargy and Grandpa with their children, about 1935. My mother is seated on the right, Aunt Goody on the left, John Jay on Gargy's lap, Henry and Stanley at the back and Dickie between his parents. *Phyfe photo from family album*

My mother on her pony. *From author's family album*

My father and his younger sister, Katherine, known as Tinkie.

From author's family album

Wedding of my mother and father, June, 1936, in Tuxedo Park.

H. R. E. Phyfe photo

Mum and Lewie in 1954 before the Tuxedo Autumn Ball. *From author's family album*

Me on Greybud, Jeep's pony, at Piping Rock Horse Show, about
1946. I remember being petrified. *Freudy Photos Archives, LLC*

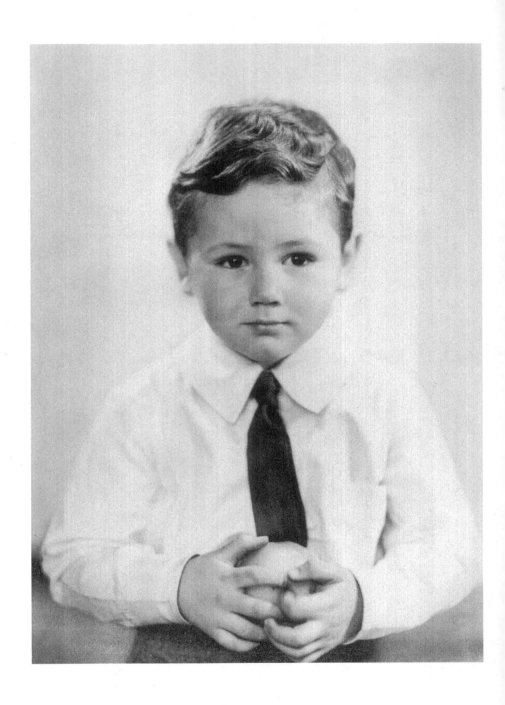

Cooky as a young child. *From author's family album*

EVE PELL

"Topsy"—"Topper"

WEST GROVE, PENNSYLVANIA

Entered 1950

"All good things has she of the heart and of the head; she will go far, this little girl."

Perpetual pep . . . "Why, Topsy, I didn't know you were a senior!" . . . Professional innocence . . . Absolutely no marks under H.C. . . . Unsurpassed in complicated love life and non-fumigated riding clothes . . . "Yes, as a matter of fact, my grandfather was an Indian!" . . . Four o'clock tea and English muffins . . . "Won't somebody contribute to the Riding Club library?" . . . Ingenious talent to say the right thing—but occasionally at the wrong time . . . "Evil Pell" . . . Annual attraction for Baltimore—its horses, hounds and men . . . "Someday He'll Come Along" . . . Attempts to sing on key . . . Always enthusiastic . . . Determined and unique.

Always saying: *"Fill up your hat with mud and pull it down over your ears."*
Where found: *On a cloud*
Remembered for: *Her Sunday visitors*
Appropriate song: *"I'm an Indian Too"*
Pet peeve: *"Where did you get that sunburn?"*
Waterloo: *Getting ready for hunting on time*
Suppressed desire: *To suppress the Confederacy*
Animal resemblance: *Mink*

41]

Garrison Forest yearbook page, 1954. *Courtesy Garrison Forest School*

My mother, aged 36, with me, aged 17, at my coming-out party.

June, 1954. *Freudy Photos Archives, LLC*

Clarry dancing with me at that party. *Freudy Photos Archives,*
LLC

Bridge game at Pembroke West, Bryn Mawr College, about 1956.

Alfred Eisenstaedt/Time-Life Pictures/Getty Images

Herbie and I leave our wedding, May 16, 1959. *Stephen Colhoun photo*

Me with baby John, 1967. *From author's family album*

Herbie and I, about 1958. *From author's family album*

The only photo I know of that has the Ledyards, Cooky, and me together with Mum and Lewie, on my wedding day at the farm in Pennsylvania: Cass (kneeling), Michael (standing), Jeep, Lewie, Mummy with baby John on her lap, Wendy, me, and Cooky. The building behind us is our brood mare barn. *Stephen Colhoun photo*

I'm with my mother and Lewie at the Essex, N.J., hunter trials, about 1957. *Freudy Photos Archives, LLC*

I'm interviewing George W. Bush in the 2000 campaign for a PBS documentary. *Photo courtesy of Center for Investigative Reporting*

Paul Jacobs. *Photo courtesy of Saul Landau*

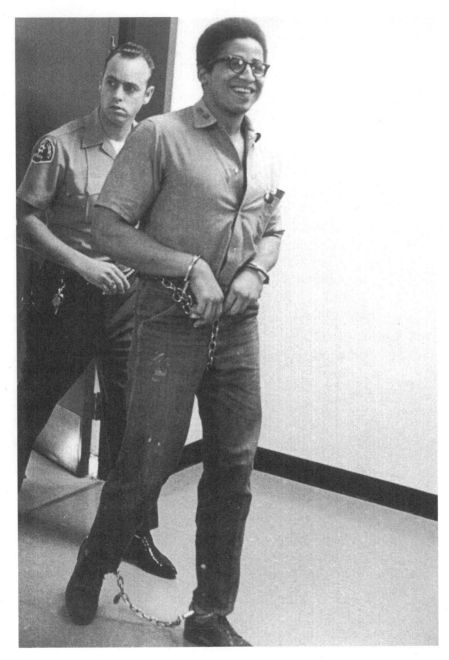

George Jackson at the courthouse in Salinas, 1970. *Dan O'Neal*
photo and It's About Time

Revolutionary
Memorial Services
for

George Jackson
Field Marshal, Black Panther Party

Date of Birth:
September 23, 1941

Date of Death:
August 21, 1971

Program for George Jackson's funeral, 1971. *It's About Time*

John, Daniel, me, Peter, and Mark Dowie, about 1973. *Anne Dowie photo*

Marching for a cause with other journalists and activists. *From author's album*

Winning the Dipsea Race, 1989. *Gene Cohn photo*

I'm with Daniel McLaughlin, my oldest son, his wife Francine Miller, and my grandchildren, Cade and Bryn, in 2001. We are in Golden Gate Park, San Francisco, modeling clothes for a local magazine. *Marc Joseph photo*

Awakenings

Only our failures marry.

—Unofficial motto of Bryn Mawr College

I went to college to be interesting to my future husband and to pass the time until he showed up. It never occurred to me that I might someday work for pay. Around the time when my stepsister, Jeep, was going to Sarah Lawrence College, she was offered a job in New York City. When Lewie heard of this, he insisted that she refuse. She argued that she would earn money. "*Prostitutes* earn money," he snapped, and that was the end of that.

Not one of my mother's or father's female friends worked, so far as I knew, and they certainly would have been insulted to be called "women." They were "ladies." Ladies existed to marry gentlemen, manage families, arrange flowers, and run houses. They were not the same species as female employees. After all, if a lady could not even telephone a man at his office, as my father angrily told me, how could she possibly work in one?

But I felt I had to do something. Staying at home as a post-deb, foxhunting and running errands for my mother, didn't appeal. My father and stepfather held contrasting views about my immediate future. Lewie, Harvard '34, informed me that only ugly girls went to Radcliffe; he made it clear that I oughtn't to consider it, if I were going to college at all, which was certainly not necessary or even desirable. My father, Harvard '33, took his views, of course, from our family's past. His mother had spent a year at Barnard, which meant to him that some higher education for young ladies was appropriate. Pells were Harvard men, and the nearest thing to Harvard at that time was Radcliffe, so I should go there. But, oddly enough, he never troubled to take me to Cambridge and show me what splendors Harvard/Radcliffe might have in store. Maybe, in his heart of hearts, he thought the 'Cliffies were ugly, too.

In fact, it was my teachers at Garrison Forest who arranged my future. I was accepted at Radcliffe, Bryn Mawr, and Vassar, and so far as those teachers were concerned, it was no choice at all. Most of them had graduated from Bryn Mawr College, on the Philadelphia Main Line. They wanted me to go there too, in part because they believed the place would suit me, in part because it was good for Garrison's reputation to have its students accepted to such an elite institution, and perhaps because it was a college known for upper-class girls who shed the baggage they grew up with and went on to accomplish things.

My mother, whose priorities were different, didn't care about my education—her convenience was what mattered. Because Bryn Mawr was only about forty-five minutes away from the Pennsylvania farm by car, I could gallop horses for her at home before going to class.

Bryn Mawr suited me, too. I was very competitive, and it was then considered the hardest girls' college to get into because it was both intellectually demanding and very small—together with its graduate school, the college in 1954 enrolled about 750 students. Bryn Mawr did not have a Phi Beta Kappa chapter since, it claimed, anyone who went there would be Phi Bete at any other college. I liked the attitude.

Little did I suspect that the college's fierce belief in the equality of women might begin to undermine my deference to men, along with my inherited ideas about ladies and the kind of life they should lead. M. Carey Thomas, a woman, founded Bryn Mawr after she had been forced to sit behind a screen while attending classes at Johns Hopkins Medical School; it was the first women's college to award the PhD degree. Its informal motto: "Only our failures marry."

By 1950s standards, it had no rules. It seems absurd now, when men and women live together at college. But it was a big deal then that you could cut classes and, if your grades were all right, you could stay out every night until 2 a.m. Unlike the other women's colleges—Vassar, Smith, and Wellesley—Bryn Mawr treated its freshmen like adults. Those other colleges seemed too girly, I thought, though I never bothered to visit any of them.

Besides, my close friend since ninth grade, Sheila Janney, was graduating from Foxcroft and heading for Bryn Mawr. I had visited Sheila at her family's spacious place in Northeast Harbor, Maine, every summer since I'd known her; we'd played tennis, gone to dances, and bicycled around Northeast Harbor in packs of prep school teenagers. She'd had much the same foxhunting, country-squire upbringing as I, but she was straighter—not the sort to be suspended for necking with Peter Alexander and then lying about it. Red-haired (the society magazines called it "Titian-tressed") smart and athletic, Sheila was highly competitive as well, and strictly brought up. She flashed a wide smile and was enthusiastic about all the things we were supposed to like: sailing, sports, the summer dances at the Kimball House, and Sunday evening church services outdoors under the fragrant Maine pines. We planned to room together.

On the sunny September day when college began, I envied her. Her high-powered lawyer father had taken time off from his firm to drive her up from their home in Maryland's Green Spring Valley. Mr. Janney was carrying bedspreads and books and suitcases into our rooms, seeing that Sheila was comfortably settled. In a repeat of my Garrison Forest experience, none of my many parents and stepparents bothered to take me to Bryn Mawr. I loaded up the family station wagon, the extra car kept for us children or the men on the place to use for errands, and drove off alone. I told myself it wasn't a big deal: I was used to getting myself off to boarding school, and I would never have thought to ask one of my parents to take me. Still, I wished they would care whether I had enough pillows and blankets, even if they were not interested in my books or higher education.

Self-pity was short-lived. Bryn Mawr was a dream campus. Its ivy-covered stone buildings were linked together by pointed arches, huge shade trees spread out over spacious green lawns, and the library cloister was an oasis of wisdom and tranquility. Sheila and I lived at Pembroke West in a comfortable three-room suite, our tiny bedrooms separated by a large, cheerful living room. Our meals were served to us by uniformed black maids in a high-ceilinged dining hall. Venus, a soft, plump, pillow of a woman, managed the hall switchboard and took our telephone messages. We were all called "Miss"—amenities I took for granted; I had always had my room cleaned and my meals served to me.

But Bryn Mawr was not Garrison Forest. Most of the students had attended public high schools; many were Jewish, with a sprinkling of blacks and Asians, and all of them were very, very smart. Many of these young women were uncomfortable at being called "Miss," or having their meals served and their floors swept by others. For some of them, going to Bryn Mawr represented both a triumph over their social and economic circumstances and the door to a bright future; it was not merely a method of filling in the years between coming out and getting married.

Hugely excited about being away at college, these non-preppie freshmen sat around in the smoker just to the left of the front door to our hall, which they called a dorm, dragging on their cigarettes and playing bridge. They talked enthusiastically about upcoming mixers with boys from neighboring Haverford College. A college "mixer" in a dreary gym, with records spun by a DJ, potato chips and Cokes, seemed a far cry from debutante balls. I headed off to football weekends at Harvard and Yale.

From the start, most of us from boarding schools held ourselves apart. We shunned college activities such as group singing on the steps of Taylor Hall, ceremonies with lighted lanterns, Maypole dancing, and hoop rolling. Having lived away from home before, we found these rituals stupid. While it may seem contradictory since I cared about doing well in school, it never occurred to me that college mattered all that much, or even that I would want to graduate. My Garrison teachers may have had ambitions for me to become an educated woman, but my parents didn't share them, and at first, I didn't either. Surely a husband would appear before my four years were over.

In private, we preppies mimicked the accents and demeanor of our non-preppy classmates, and we both scorned and feared the trio of lesbians—we were sure they were lesbians—in our class. One of them was fat, one was skinny, and one was Polish; they stayed to themselves as much as we did, but probably not for the same reasons. There was no women's movement then, no gay liberation, and we were not their friends.

The six or seven girls from boarding school who roomed in Pembroke West that freshman year merged into a clique. We had an unwritten dress code: tartan skirts, knee socks, tasteful blouses, smooth hairdos, no makeup. (In those days, you couldn't wear trousers to class.) If one of us became "pinned" to a boy, she wore his fraternity pin on her collar instead of dangling it off a breast as the high school girls did. We didn't call colleges "schools." "Where did you go to school?" meant, to us, "What boarding school did you go to?"

Appearing superior was nothing new. As a small child, I had been sent around Whitehackle Farm giving orders to adults—"Mummy says we'll have the cheese soufflé tonight, and please don't overcook it." "My mother says to saddle up the gray horse this morning, and be sure to put on the double bridle." Having learned that bearing and attitude of authority at home, I believed that I was not subject to the same constraints as ordinary people. I was certainly not about to endure indignities such as freshman hazing.

In late September, Bryn Mawr tradition called for a very pale version of Hell Week. Freshmen were to wear beanies and do whatever seniors told us: sing silly songs, kneel down before them, make up poems. These activities, we were told, were to last all week and come to a climax on Saturday morning. The seniors warned us to prepare for something truly dreadful.

Sheila and I thought this was ridiculous. We put up with the hazing until Friday morning, sometimes refusing the silly commands and sometimes obeying with poor grace, but we were determined not to go through with the whole thing. So we invented pressing reasons why we had to be away for the weekend—my mother suddenly became ill as I recall, and I forget what disaster befell the Janneys. The older students were upset with us. Again and again, earnest seniors urged us to stay, trying to impress us with the importance of Bryn Mawr traditions and the need to get through the Saturday morning ordeal. But we held our ground and took off Friday after classes, pleased to be escaping.

But when we arrived back at college on Sunday night, we were mortified. Vases of wilted flowers clustered in the dimly lit hallway outside our rooms. The climax of hazing that we had dodged had actually been a surprise welcome. We learned that seniors had gone around to the freshmen's rooms early Saturday morning, placed massive bouquets outside the doors, and woken each one with a song. I felt abashed and sorry, as though I had committed a social blunder by opting out. I even felt a fleeting moment of envy for the freshmen who had woken to the surprise serenade by the seniors; they had been welcomed with warmth and affection, but by acting superior we had shut ourselves out.

While I was happy to hold myself apart from my classmates when it suited me, I also learned that, in some situations, being ordinary might have felt better.

I didn't dwell on these thoughts for long because, right after Hell Week, something happened to take my mind off Bryn Mawr almost entirely. In the years when my mother and Lewie took me out of Green Vale to go foxhunting in Maryland, I developed an enormous crush on a steeplechase rider there named Laddie Murray. Horsy girls like me, and adult women, too, went bananas over race riders as if they were rock stars. The most charming and successful one, Mikey Smithwick, had his choice of lovers. Rich women fell madly in love with him, and one heiress was believed to have committed suicide after he broke up with her.

But I preferred Laddie. I had first seen him at a stable when I was eleven; he was a glamorous nineteen, and he was educated, too, unlike the other trainers and jockeys whose lives were devoted solely to horses. He grew up in an old Maryland family that had fallen on hard times. Laddie went to Princeton and, when the Korean War began, joined the Marines. The crush lasted, and when I got to Garrison, I wrote his initials all over my blue loose-leaf binders. BHM, Benjamin Huger Murray, again and again and again. EP + BHM; EPM (for when we were married, because of course I would be Mrs. Murray). I designed an assortment of monograms, circular and diamond-shaped, to embellish our future towels and sheets.

Later on, I heard that Laddie had fought in Korea and been grievously wounded; he had been awarded a Navy Cross for extreme bravery under fire. Now recovered, he was beginning law school at Penn, in nearby Philadelphia. Unlike the callow college boys I went out with, here was a man who had been to war and suffered deeply.

In October, my mother phoned me at college with an appalling suggestion: "Why don't you call up Laddie, Tops, and invite him for the weekend?" Having people for the weekend was a normal thing for my parents to do—a house party to amuse themselves and their guests, and just what I had been trained for, learning all those sports and games. Sometimes three or four people would be invited, sometimes just one. People would arrive on Friday in time for drinks and dinner. On Saturday, depending on the season, everyone would go foxhunting or shooting, or perhaps with an elaborate picnic to the races or a polo match in the afternoon. Then would come tea and a time to bathe and change clothes, followed by cocktails and perhaps a dinner dance at a club in celebration of an important horse race. On Sunday there would be an enormous breakfast, church for those so inclined, then lunch with roast beef and Yorkshire pudding, after which people would take their leave.

This weekend with Laddie would be a very scaled-down version of a house party, since only he and I were coming, and I don't recall that there was a big race scheduled. We would most likely just go foxhunting on Saturday.

My old crush rose up like a fountain. I could think of nothing else. I had no idea how far in over my seventeen-year-old head I was about to plunge.

Despite those years of training with the Hols and Cols, it took days for me to work up the nerve to call him. Closeted in the narrow, unpleasant kitchenette in Pem West, which reeked of the strange foods cooked there by an African student, I plunked a dime in the pay phone and dialed. Laddie answered. "This-is-Topsy-Pell-my-mother-said-to-ask-you-to-come for the weekend," I blurted. He said, "Yes, I'd like to." He would pick me up at college on Friday. I hung up the phone and panicked; what would I ever say to him when we were together? It was like having a date with a movie star. The week dragged by in a haze of anticipation and dread.

Late Friday afternoon it began to rain, and by the time we were driving to the farm, thunder kicked in. Feeling as if I were cast in an old black and white film, I sat frozen beside Laddie as we careened down narrow country roads slick with running water. The road started to flood. Trees fell. At one point, I had to take the wheel while he removed his shoes, stepped into the driving rain and waded ahead of the car, his tall, thin body illuminated by the headlights, in order to be certain that the pavement hadn't been washed away. Neither of us suggested going back. Mostly, I stared straight ahead through the drenched windshield, not daring to look at him—though I sneaked a few glances at his jagged profile. I was too overcome at being with him to have any presence of mind; the storm was not nearly as awesome as sitting beside my heartthrob in his ancient coupe.

By the time we arrived, I was head over heels. He was brave; we had gone through a terrible storm together; we had defeated the elements. I could not believe that I was actually with the man whose initials I'd scratched all over the blue cloth cover of my ninth grade three-ring binder.

But the weekend was a disaster. My mother, still young and glamorous at thirty-six, loved horse people, especially younger men with whom she could flirt. On Saturday night, of course without consulting me, she had invited people for dinner. I was sitting in the library, the fire cheerfully burning in the fireplace, waiting with Laddie and Lewie for the guests to arrive. My mother, as usual, didn't come down until most of the guests were already in place. She always made an entrance, and this one was particularly effective. Dressed in a tight red blouse and black velvet trousers, flashing her brilliant smile and pushing out her breasts, she received homage from everyone in the room but me. It was no contest.

"Isn't it wonderful to have Laddie in this part of the world!" she exclaimed. She charmed him, laughed at his jokes, and plied him with sherry. She even sat him at her right hand at the dinner table and acted enthralled with everything he said.

I felt ugly and tense and inadequate, making tepid conversation about horses with some boring trainer while my mother was moving in on my heartthrob. Lewie didn't help: he regaled Laddie with tales of the Royal Canadian Air Force in World War II while Laddie entertained him with stories about races he'd ridden, horses he'd known, and the quirks of their owners and trainers. I was invisible.

But after that weekend, Laddie began calling me and asking me out. He had little money, so we ate pizza and Chinese food in cheap restaurants (the first pizza and Chinese food I had ever tasted) and occasionally went to movies. On the weekends, we went off to steeplechase races in Maryland, Virginia, or Pennsylvania. While there, we stayed at houseparties—he in one room and I in another. He rode races on Saturday while I watched and cheered, and we went to hunt club parties at night. I didn't care about college at all, though I managed to do enough work to make the dean's list just for the sake of vanity.

I was so crazy for Laddie that I stopped seeing the young men who were my own age. I was always with older people, either around the races or going to dinner with some of Laddie's long-time friends from his Princeton days, now married businessmen raising families in the Philadelphia suburbs. But whenever we went to my house, which was often, my mother took over, flirting with him and chatting him up. That made me feel shut out and miserable, but I took hope in the thought that I was inching closer toward that fantasy monogram, EPM, and my future life as Mrs. Murray.

As a freshman advisor, he lived for free in a dorm at Penn. One Saturday evening we were in his room, making out on his bed. Some freshmen must have seen us go in together, and the lights go out, because after a while they gathered right outside his door and began calling to him. We could hear them chuckling. "We really need you!" called one. "We know you're in there," taunted another. I was panicked and mortified. We were trapped, wordless, with the door shut and the lights out, until finally they got bored and went away.

The next year, Laddie moved from the dorm into a dingy apartment in Philadelphia near the law school, and each time I went there we necked. He began asking me to sleep with him, which I resisted out of sheer terror.

Our dates turned into wrestling matches, and I always left feeling upset and guilty. In the fifties there were bad girls and good girls, and I didn't want to switch categories. Moreover, birth control wasn't easily available, and the pill hadn't been invented yet. I still remember with admiration one friend of mine who simply made an appointment with her doctor and ordered up a diaphragm—in those days, that took courage.

Each time I turned him down, Laddie became angry and withdrawn. I hated the silent drives back to college afterwards. When, I fretted, would he ask me to marry him? After that, we could have all the sex he wanted.

One night, as we were necking in his car outside Pembroke West, Laddie explained why he always picked me up so late on Friday afternoons—about 5:30. He had a weekly appointment with a psychiatrist that day. He confessed that he was confused, angry with his parents and himself, and troubled. He felt that he had talents he could not use, that he needed to deal with deep problems. I knew that he could be quite moody, but I had thought that was my fault for not being sufficient entertainment, sexual or otherwise.

I was so naive that I didn't understand the import of what he was telling me about himself and his situation, but I did realize that it was bad news: he wasn't about to propose. What was the matter, I wondered, like the self-centered college freshman that I was—why wasn't I enough? My teenage fantasies were being fulfilled because I was with him. But being with him hadn't turned out to be as much fun as I had expected because he was so often glum and because of my mother's behavior. Now, on top of all that, it turned out that my idol was miserable.

I had been raised to think that anyone who felt bad was not trying hard enough. Resolving "inferiority complexes," the lingo of the day, was simply a matter of self-discipline; my mother said that only very peculiar people went to psychiatrists. This was 1955, a time when mental illness of any kind still carried a dreadful stigma. Belonging to a family that steadfastly ignored the depression, alcoholism, or narcissism that afflicted many of our relatives, I was shocked at what he was doing but also curious.

Early in my sophomore year, we had a scary scuffle. He was grabbing my breasts, reaching for my underpants, and pressing himself against me hard. I fled from his apartment and back to college on the train. But when he called the next day to ask me to take the train back in to Philadelphia and come to his apartment, I knew I wouldn't fight him off again.

I walked over from Thirtieth Street Station and rang the bell. He stood at the top of the long, dim stairway, dressed in an undershirt and khaki trousers, looking unkempt and unhappy. I slowly climbed the steps. Without a word, he took me in his arms and led me to his small, messy bedroom. He took off his clothes and mine as I lay on his bed. I was too frightened to respond when he kissed me or when he lay on top of me. But we did it anyway, quickly and, for me, painfully. Then he stood up and dressed; he had an appointment with his psychiatrist, he said, and rushed out the door. "You wait here," he ordered, as I lay on the rumpled bed.

I put on my clothes and walked the afternoon streets of Philadelphia, a virgin-no-longer who smarted between the legs and could not contain her tears. As I crossed a bridge over the Schuylkill River, I considered jumping off. I considered taking the train directly back to college without meeting Laddie at his place as he had told me to. But, obedient as ever, I returned to his apartment; we spoke briefly and afterward, I took the train to Bryn Mawr alone. I was miserable and certain that everyone who saw me would somehow know what had happened.

Then followed a time of terrible anxiety: Would I get pregnant? As we kept on having sex, I awaited my period each month with dread. When it arrived, I was doubled over with cramps for at least a day, which I took as a paltry, pathetic atonement for my sin.

Contrary to my fantasies, our sex was neither fun nor romantic, even when I borrowed Cynthia Butterworth's gold ring to look married and he took me to a rundown hotel for the night. So I spent hours in the Reserve Book room in the college library, reading through the various volumes that told about intercourse and how to do it. If I had studied for my classes the way I studied Havelock Ellis and other authorities on sex, I would have gotten a great education. But hard though I tried, their advice on reaching simultaneous orgasm was of no help to me. So I went to a lecture on Family Life at the college. The sturdy middle-aged teacher began by looking over the assembled students and saying, "Not all of you will get married." That got my attention. I listened especially carefully to the few words she said about the mechanics of sex—after marriage, of course—and noted the books she recommended reading—all of which, of course, I had already read. Afterward, there was a question and answer session. So, a bit flushed with nerves, I raised my hand. "Suppose someone reads all the books and follows the advice, and it still doesn't work?" I inquired. The teacher brushed me off and quickly called on someone else. I was mortified, and for all the embarrassment I suffered for asking such a self-incriminating question, I learned nothing. Her brush-off reinforced old baggage: though I was asking about something that mattered intensely to me, she dismissed my question—just like my parents. I felt ignored and humiliated.

Though Laddie was invariably polite to my mother and Lewie, he told me privately that he thought they were snobbish and had bad values. He held more liberal political beliefs than I was used to. He believed that poor people should have a better chance in life, and he criticized racial segregation. Since I was upset with Mummy and Lewie anyway, his arguments gave me more ammunition and ennobled the resentment I felt toward them.

Growing up, I had buried myself in novels, histories, and lives of the saints as well as comic books. My heroes were Robin Hood, the Scarlet Pimpernel, Wonder Woman, Queen Elizabeth, Joan of Arc, St. Theresa of Avila, Helen Keller, Mahatma Gandhi. I knew in an abstract way that there were other ways to live besides the narrow, class-conscious, New York aristocrat life I had been brought up in. I liked listening to Laddie talk about politics. Except for Jenny Ballard, the sole vocal supporter of Adlai Stevenson for president in 1952 at Garrison Forest School, he was the only liberal Democrat I really knew.

Laddie broadened my social horizons, too. When the Marine reserve unit he captained held beer-drinking nights at a working-class bar in Camden, New Jersey, across the river from Philadelphia, he sometimes invited me and I was thrilled to go. With pop music blaring from a noisy jukebox, my manners from the Hols and Cols nevertheless came in handy as I made conversation with the Polish carpenters, Italian truck drivers, and waiters in his unit, and their wives, too. The lesson I had learned in society, to show interest in other people and get them to talk about themselves, traveled well. Laddie's men adored him, the war hero whom they referred to as "Loot" (for Lieutenant), and they were prepared to like his girl friend, too. It was a long way from Cathy Mellon's coming-out party, but I was glad to be accepted in that Camden bar. Acceptance by his men brought me closer to the "Loot," and I was showing myself and him that I was not just a little snob.

With Laddie, I established a pattern of falling in love with smart, rebellious, and difficult men who did not treat women very well. I also established another pattern: desperately upset that Laddie wouldn't marry me, and on increasingly poor terms with my mother, I went to see the college psychiatrist, a bespectacled young man named Smith, who had a receding hairline. I saw him at the college once or twice; then he signed me up as a private patient, and I had to commute into Philadelphia to his office for sessions there.

Looking back, I think my decision to see Dr. Smith marked another crack in my insulation from the real world, an admission that my upbringing was inadequate to cope with the problems I faced. I was miserable, confused, and out of my depth. I was starting to see that an interesting, worthwhile life might exist outside the upper crust, and though I had been raised to look down on anything different, perhaps there were reasons to explore further.

At the same time, I wanted desperately to be understood, to be loved for myself. But none of my parents and stepparents showed any interest in what I was going through. I saw no sign of help coming from them, or from Laddie either. My dream of marriage, the solution I counted on, evaporated.

I had done the things I was supposed to do: learn manners, follow the teachings of my parents, hit backhands, conjugate irregular French verbs, and jump horses over fences. I could waltz and instruct servants. But none of these skills equipped me for the situation I was in or the pain I was feeling.

I was a stranger to my own feelings. A girl like me was not supposed to feel negative emotions such as fear or anger, certainly not to express them if they happened to turn up. So I stayed, for the most part, polite and positive. But things happened at college, particularly my relationship with Laddie, that I couldn't manage. As I searched through the self-help books about sex, I stumbled onto the work of Erich Fromm, a psychoanalyst who wrote *Escape from Freedom* and *Man for Himself*, books that criticized authoritarianism and espoused liberation from restrictive social systems. According to the case histories Fromm cited, patients' angers and fears could be attributed to real causes, and their lives could improve dramatically once those things were understood and dealt with. What a vista stretched out! Maybe there was another way; maybe my parents were wrong; maybe my anger and confusion, instead of being marks of inadequacy, were somehow justified.

On a less elevated level, I was following Laddie's advice. He believed that psychotherapy was a useful thing, and, perhaps seeing that I needed help, he had suggested that I try it.

So I lay on a brown couch on Wednesday afternoons, week in and week out. As I recounted the events of my childhood, I got even more upset with my mother and father. Why had Clarry agreed to give up custody of Cooky and me in exchange for Mummy and Lewie paying our expenses? It felt as though he had sold us. Why was my mother so critical, so lacking in warmth or understanding? Dr. Smith listened and took notes; he seemed distant and unsympathetic. He did suggest that I not marry Laddie, at least, not right away. I didn't like that. The more I saw Dr. Smith, the more sullen and anxious I became. Nothing was going right.

I tried something different—a direct approach. It was the end of sophomore year and the start of summer vacation. While we were seated in her parked station wagon outside our stone house, I tried to talk to my mother. "I need to say some things to you. It hurts my feelings when you scold me, and you just care so much about what I look like . . ." I began, intending to accuse her of ignoring my inner self and my real needs.

"Of course I care how you look," she interrupted. "You've always been well turned out. I always thought you were such a happy child, and that we had such a good relationship."

"You scold so hard, and you never say you love us," I persisted, but I was weakening in the face of her refusal to react the way I had hoped she would. Her face set, her eyes narrowed a bit, her classic chin jutted out as she looked out through the windshield.

"*My* mother never told me that she loved me, I just knew she did, and it was never a problem," Mummy answered crisply, as though there were something wrong in me to have raised such an issue. "And you should have heard the way she spoke to me when I stepped on the gravel in the driveway outside her window and woke *her* up from her nap! Now *that* was a scolding!"

The tables were being turned: instead of her feeling sorry for me, I was supposed to feel sorry for her. This was not working.

But though my mother brushed off my feeble accusations and complaints, our conversation in the car evidently affected her. The next morning she lay in bed in her darkened bedroom, curtains drawn, crying softly, too upset to get up. Taken aback by the drama of her reaction, I clutched up my courage and stepped over the threshold into her huge bedroom. Though it was summer, the small logs in her fireplace were neatly piled, the balls of crumpled newspaper beneath, ready for a match. In the dim light, her dark hair stood out against the monogrammed white pillowcase, and she seemed quite small under the lace-trimmed coverlet, clutching a handkerchief to her face. "I'm sorry you feel so bad," I said, about halfway meaning it. "I'm going to New York. I do love you." She continued to snuffle and did not answer. I turned around and walked out, still feeling misunderstood, righteous, and thoroughly pissed off at her emotional collapse. I left the house and, caught up in the theatre of it all, took a train to New York. I wondered, as the train stopped in North Philadelphia, if I would ever go back to the farm again.

Perhaps because people in my college class got summer jobs, and because most of them intended to have careers, I had decided some weeks earlier that a job would be the answer to my problems. Weekly sessions on Dr. Smith's couch in Philadelphia had brought me to the realization that, as long as I lived the life my parents wanted, I would stay dependent on them and stuck in their value system. In order to continue living a life of horses, beaus, and parties, as I had done the summer after freshman year, I would have to accede to their way of life and stop being hurt and angry. Even if I had wanted to live that way, I had no trust fund with which to support such luxury. A stab toward independence seemed like a better idea.

Without my becoming aware of the change, two years at Bryn Mawr had shredded my post-debutante aversion to the world of work. While I did not like the informal motto of the college, "Only our failures marry," I must have absorbed some of the underlying rationale that assumed that each Bryn Mawrter could, would, and should accomplish something.

Coincidentally, my father had promised to get me a summer job in New York after my sophomore year. He had somehow met Robert Young, the actor who later starred in the television show, *Marcus Welby, M.D.*, and boasted to me of his influence with Mr. Young and the interesting things I would be doing that summer, thanks to him. But although everything was supposed to have been arranged, I heard nothing from Young's office. Finally I called there myself as the college year was about to end, only to be rebuffed by Mr. Young's secretary, who denied that there was any such job and seemed never to have heard of me. I was devastated, having bragged about this great opportunity for weeks to my friends. My father was no help at all.

Nevertheless, after such an unrewarding confrontation with my mother, I had no intention of spending the summer at home. I fled from the Pennsylvania farm that morning to a prearranged destination. Two girls who had been a few years ahead of me at Garrison had a vacancy in their New York apartment, because a third, who had paid her rent well ahead, had moved out unexpectedly. I took a taxi from Penn Station to their First Avenue address, moved in with them and pounded the streets searching for a job. I had never worked before, and I couldn't type, so the various personnel offices I went to showed no interest at all. (In those precomputer days, typing was seen as women's work, and there was not much else to be had, in an office, anyway. For a woman my age or older, perhaps the most astonishing progress wrought by the computer revolution has been that it forced men to learn to type.)

I filled out an application at CBS. When I got to the question asking, "Who do you know at CBS?" I put down William S. Paley. Mr. Paley, CEO of the company, had married my Aunt Babe, who previously had been married to my uncle, Stanley Mortimer. A slim connection, I was afraid, but it succeeded. The very next day, I began a temporary job at low wages tabulating Arthur Godfrey's fan mail.

The summer was hot, the apartment stifling, and the work, once I got past the rush of being employed, wasn't very interesting. But it introduced me to a world that I had known nothing of. Arthur Godfrey hosted *Arthur Godfrey Time*, a long-running daytime show that received stacks of mail. Every single morning he received a letter from a woman named Stella, seven or eight pages at least, written in cursive handwriting on the stationery of a hotel whose logo featured a crude lightning bolt at the top of each sheet. "Arthur, is there something wrong? You looked a little tired today," she would write. "Do you need anything?" Of course, Arthur Godfrey never knew about Stella, just as he never knew about me. I realized then that there were thousands of lonely people—fans who followed every move of a star they would never meet, even an old, grumpy man as Godfrey was by then, because they had so little in their own lives. Stella in that hotel became real to me—I imagined an old woman with thick, swollen ankles and a crinkly perm in her brown-gray hair, whose grown children lived far away, watching TV in her tiny, dark hotel room. Perhaps she worked at the switchboard there. I still wonder what became of her.

Other aspects of the job made me realize how atypical my life had been. No other girl in my office was hired because of a family connection with Mr. Paley, or had gone foxhunting, or come out, or had a grandmother with a butler named England. I had conflicting feelings: with my privileged upbringing, I had seen and done a far wider range of things than the two high school girls from Long Island with whom I worked. But, while I felt more sophisticated and worldly than they were, I was eager to fit in, be liked, and prove myself to our supervisor, a schoolteacher earning extra money with this summer job. I worked hard, sorting through the letters and putting them into their categories, but I didn't become friends with the others. When the Godfrey survey was done, everyone was dismissed but me. I was thrilled, then, to be offered another short-term project, listening to audiotapes and checking over transcripts that were at issue in a libel suit.

For the first time in my life, I lived without servants. Getting used to cooking and cleaning was easy, but it was far more difficult to get used to the new emotions that seemed to dominate my life. I was angry and resentful of my mother. Lewie was angry because I had upset Mummy and gone off to work in New York. I don't remember seeing Clarry at all. I was upset with Laddie, who had a summer job with a Philadelphia law firm. I saw him from time to time, and despite our troubles, I still wanted him to propose to me; but he wouldn't. In misery, I phoned Dr. Smith, who suggested that I come down from New York on the train on Wednesday nights for sessions with him. It was a terrible commute, and if I missed my train back, as I often did, I didn't get to the apartment until one or two in the morning, utterly exhausted for work the next day. I remember running from the doctor's office after each hour, through the green curtains that framed his door, out of the building to the subway, then dashing to the train station platform, miserable and frustrated to find my train gone, with an hour to kill before the next one. Still, I continued the therapy sessions because there was some relief in expressing the pent-up anger and hurt I had hidden for so many years. On that couch, I could start to figure out if I was ever going to be happy with the life I had been born into, and, if not, what I might do instead.

It was a wretched time. The two roommates, who had at first said I didn't have to pay any rent because my predecessor had paid through the time I was there, demanded money. I felt betrayed by them, and by everyone but CBS. The people there wanted me back again next summer. I had achieved a small success at a time when I was feeling especially low. Elated, I promised them I would work on the typing.

When the summer and the temporary work ended, I asked a Bryn Mawr dean if I could have a scholarship; that way I wouldn't take money from my mother and I would be independent of her. The dean said No, because scholarships were for the truly needy, which I was not. So, despite my earlier threats never to go back, I succumbed, returning home for a few unhappy weeks before the start of classes. I was disappointed in myself for still depending on my family for my tuition and for lacking the fortitude to give up college and find a job. Mummy and Lewie were aloof and distant but, I think, relieved.

I began my junior year a different girl than the freshman who had glided in two years before. Two or three times that year, Mummy made the forty-five-minute drive from the farm to Bryn Mawr to take me shopping for clothes and for lunch. On those days, I stood anxiously at the window of my college room, watching for her station wagon to appear. We exchanged tense greetings as I got in, the submerged hostility and hurt hanging in the air as we decided where to get a hamburger and where to shop. I still remember the discomfort that characterized those outings and the sweep of her eyes over my body as I walked down the sidewalk to the car. She signaled her emotions by observations about my appearance: "You know, Tops, that skirt might be a little shorter, and I wouldn't wear those shoes with it." That, said in a sharp and critical tone, meant that she was angry with me. "You look wonderful, dear, that skirt is just the right length," meant she was not. (That year I cut my hair very short, in part to annoy her, in part to try a new look.)

Once at Bonwit Teller or Saks, I could provoke her by trying on a garish dress I knew she wouldn't like, or please her by trying on one that she would. If I picked out a ballerina-length frock, she would frown. It was NOCD (Not Our Class Dear). Similarly, she disapproved of ruffles or anything remotely ethnic. I realized that I could change her mood with the flick of a hanger—and, since she was putting herself out to make peace between us, she had to moderate her usually caustic comments. Unfortunately, I was not quite confident enough to relish this new-found power. Torn between deciding to be polite or candid during our stiff conversations, I opted for a sullen middle ground. Although her visits indicated awareness that something was wrong between us, she chose never to bring up the topic of our relationship. These few meetings notwithstanding, I tried to stay away from home as much as possible, my usual strategy, and I didn't bring Laddie there any more.

He and I continued to go to the races over fall and spring weekends, but sex made things more complicated. I continued to hope that he would propose and tried to sleep with him as often as circumstances permitted.

My mother, who must have at least suspected what was going on, did take me aside one afternoon and warned nervously, "You know, girls who shack up get into trouble." That was it—no asking what I was doing, or whether we used birth control, or how I was doing, or whether I was even in love. Nothing. I just stood there, still as a stone, while she spoke.

But sometime during that junior year, I grew so tired of feeling inadequate and subservient to Laddie that I broke up with him. I continued to see the psychiatrist, and I continued to be both furious with my mother and frightened of her. Herb McLaughlin got in touch with me. He was a Yale architecture school student whom I had met a few years before at a coming-out party, gone out with a few times, and then ditched for Laddie.

We began to see each other again. While Herb billed himself as a Mick from an immigrant family, the truth was that his Irish great-grandfather had been a university graduate, and his great-grandmother owned large amounts of land in Illinois. Their descendants made a fortune with McLaughlin's Manor House Coffee, one of the oldest family businesses in Chicago, and were Catholics, both of which triggered my family's prejudices. One of my relatives, long ago, had been forbidden to go out with one of his because, it was said, an early McLaughlin "had delivered groceries to the back door." But one of Herb's rich great-uncles had owned the Chicago Black Hawks hockey team, married the famed dancer Irene Castle, and played polo, so while my snobbish family did not consider the McLaughlins quite their social equals, they lived in a big house, summered on Martha's Vineyard, and were part of Chicago society.

Tall and wickedly funny, Herb prided himself on his nonconformity. Instead of occupying his bedroom in the family section of his house, he moved into an empty maid's room in the servant's wing. He truly lived his religion, attending Mass almost every day, praying regularly, and worrying about the poor. Critical of his family's comfort with their social position and their country club values, he leaned on his rich relatives to send money to orphanages for black children in the South, and he denounced the elitism of Lake Forest, the swank suburb where he grew up. At a town meeting called to protest a new, modernistic building, he spoke out against the conservatives. "Who do we think we are, Athens rising out of the surrounding swamps?" he asked. That made the front page of the Lake Forest paper, to the great embarrassment of his mother and father.

Herb's ability to speak up for his beliefs was like catnip to me. And yet, given his background, he fit closely enough into my parents' environment that I felt I had the best of both worlds. I went to Yale for weekends, where he was in his last year of graduate school, or he came down to Bryn Mawr. There was no pressure about sex: by his lights, sex before marriage was sinful. After all the conflict and worry with Laddie, Herb's attitude came as a welcome relief. He loved to dance, had a great capacity for fun and spur of the moment excursions, and for considering what was the right thing to do. He worried about French kissing and discussed it with the Yale priest after a weekend when we had done that. "In the matter of putting my tongue in your mouth, it ought not to be done," he wrote in a letter. "I think there ought to be a little less flicking around even." He wrote long, sweet, stream of consciousness letters, like this one describing a dreadful drive back to New Haven after visiting me.

> Car was using a lot of gas, pulled into service station, had never checked the oil. . . . Absolutely no oil whatever in car, took five quarts. No damage done, proceeded merrily, nearing New York. Thinking, better not have flat as utensils are not too great. Played old game of get to post before car coming in opposite direction. Won. Felt good. Had flat two miles later. Got out, trucks whooshing by shaking car like birch every time, no jack, changed tire for crummy looking spare, drove on. Two miles more, spare goes flat, end of world.

And so on, through two more flats, until he got back to Yale.

We became inseparable.

Like Laddie, Herb held liberal beliefs, but he was more openly critical of my parents and the luxurious way they lived. Herb felt that people with so much money should be contributing more to society, and he disapproved of foxhunting, fur coats, and expensive jewelry. With his encouragement, I became more critical of them, too, at least in certain ways. I could find fault with the social hierarchy involved in foxhunting, for instance, but I could see nothing wrong with loving horses. As with Laddie, I was leaning on a boyfriend as I tried to break away from the influence of my parents. Having Herb's approval made me feel safer when—even just in my own mind—I challenged their values. I didn't realize then that I was trading in one kind of domination for another—that only came much later—but this man was certainly a lot more fun than Laddie had been, and very loving.

"There was a sudden emptiness inside me when I got onto the train and there I was, without you," he wrote, after we separated during a vacation and he went to Chicago to see his parents. "It was not good, and there was an almost sick feeling, very surprising in its strength. And then I saw you, on your train back to Bryn Mawr, and I was smiling at you and not really feeling it inside. I was feeling, I want you, I love you, I'm leaving you and that's bad. Trains going away from each other are two very separate things, and two people inside are alone." No one had ever been so rawly affectionate with me.

He was smart and a bit eccentric: Some Yalies accused him of ripping holes in new Brooks Brothers sweaters in order to look sufficiently ratty as he launched into his condemnations of wealth. I liked it that my mother was not fond of him.

As Herb and I were falling in love, my father and Cotty were falling out. She phoned me one day at Bryn Mawr to say that after fifteen years of marriage, she and Clarry were separating. She had rented a small studio in the East Seventies in New York some months before, supposedly to facilitate her successful career as an interior designer. She would be living full time in New York, she told me, and she hoped that we would stay in touch.

In June 1958, without any interest in European history, my college major, or any career plan, I graduated from Bryn Mawr cum laude and with honors. My mother, now forty, and Lewie came to commencement, where she drew considerable attention by being the only mother who was eight months pregnant.

Lewie was aghast when he saw my classmates. Had he known that I was spending months and years in the company of repulsive girls with greasy hair, he said, he would have removed me from college at once. My father came too, driving down from New York in a new blue Volkswagen, a graduation present to me from him, my Pell grandparents, and his sister, my Aunt Tinkie.

My mother wanted me to stay home that summer to help during the final weeks of her pregnancy. But that was the last thing I wanted to do. After a few tense conversations, I promised her that I would come home if anything went wrong and she really needed me. Then I drove out west in the bug with Sandy Colt, a college friend who had also gone to Garrison. We ate at places like Merl's Eat Your Fill for a Dollar Bill, stayed at Iowa motels that cost $6 a night, and visited our friends' opulent ranches and summer homes in Wyoming, Montana, and Lake Tahoe.

When we finally crossed over the Bay Bridge to San Francisco, we were disappointed to find the famous city hidden in a fog bank. Soon afterward, Mummy gave uneventful birth to my baby brother, John Livingston Ledyard. I stayed on in San Francisco, where I discovered one of the major advantages of growing up upper-class. Without lifting a finger, I had friends—dinner invitations, lunch parties, swimming, and gin and tonics—generously offered by girls I'd gone to Garrison with. A whole social network looked after Sandy and me.

After a week or so, as planned, Sandy and another friend drove my car back east, and I moved into an apartment on Telegraph Hill with two young women I had met at a party. The Tuesday Downtown Operators and Observers Club, a group of well-off young bachelor stockbrokers and professionals, invited me to lunch, and the social network saw that I had things to do on weekends. On weekdays, I went to Speedwriting school on Market Street, learning shorthand and typing so that I could get a secretarial job in the fall.

Apart from the brave women like my Bryn Mawr classmates who headed for advanced degrees or law school or medical school, it seemed that there were three options for women fresh out of college in 1958—nursing (too close to being a maid), teaching, or secretarial work. It did not occur to me then to question why young men who had just graduated from men's colleges such as Yale and Harvard and Princeton were not struggling to learn typing and shorthand. Instead, they were given work as trainees, with secretaries to look after them while they began their climb up various corporate ladders.

I, on the other hand, sat in a dingy room, listening to a disembodied voice say things like, "Dear Mr. Jones: Please find enclosed our latest inventory report. I will need two hundred copies delivered to our headquarters by March 19, 1959. . . ." And, like the other women hunched over desks in rows alongside me, I would try to get the words down exactly as dictated and then type them up in a letter. I had seen the ads promising that in six weeks: "u k ri 120 wpm" and though 120 words per minute seemed like more than one would ever need, I took the course. Actually, I would come to use Speedwriting in my work as a reporter. But I never approached the promised 120 wpm.

While I was transcribing the words of the disembodied voice, Herb, who had just graduated from architecture school, joined the Air Force as a hospital architect. After basic training in Alabama, where he distinguished himself by fainting during a graphic, bloody movie about treating injuries, he was stationed in Washington, D.C. (In those cold war days, between Korea and Vietnam, young men had to join the military once their education deferments had expired.) He asked me to move to Washington, too, so our courtship could continue, and I agreed. We did the standard thing for young people starting out there: four young women friends and I rented a house in Georgetown, and he moved into a huge house several blocks away with four or five young men. I found a job working for the manager of a television station, a man who always had two secretaries. The first, an older woman, had been there for many years and could have done the whole job herself. But he liked having a young one around, too, so he hired me, despite my pitiful typing and stenography.

Ever religious, Herb considered joining a monastery but decided to marry me instead. Not that it was a decision easily reached. He had to overcome his worries about marrying a non-Catholic woman from a much-divorced family, which he did, finally proposing in January 1959. My mother didn't like the idea; she thought Herb was selfish, had bad manners, and wasn't kind enough.

This was the kind of thing that offended her: One fall weekend when he was visiting in Pennsylvania, my mother was riding in a ladies' race. While the rest of the family and other spectators watched the prerace saddling in the paddock, Herb ostentatiously stood to one side and read a book. And after my mother's horse fell during the race—she wasn't hurt—he told her how thoughtful she was to have a crash in front of the stands where all could see.

The more I knew she was opposed, of course, the more I wanted to marry him. So when we went to the farm to tell Mummy and Lewie our news, they reacted rather coolly. "When would you like the wedding to be?" asked my mother.

"The first weekend in April," Herb answered.

"That's not possible," she announced. "We have a horse running that Saturday in a race. In fact, we have a horse running every Saturday in April."

Surprised, perhaps, by her priorities, Herb continued gamely. "Well, how about the first Saturday in May?"

"Out of the question! There's a big cockfight that day," she replied. So our wedding was set for the second weekend in May.

We visited Herb's parents in Lake Forest and drove in to his Aunt Harriet's apartment in Chicago. A tall, imposing, no-nonsense spinster, Aunt Harriet greeted us warmly and got right to the point. "I suppose you'll be needing an engagement ring," she said. She walked over to a closet, opened the door and took out an old cigar box. "You can choose one of these," she told us. In the cigar box, rattling around, were three immense diamond rings. One was in the form of a four-leaf clover, a good-sized diamond for each of the four leaves, one was a single immense rock in an ugly setting, and the third consisted of seven diamonds, one row of three on top of a lower row of four. It wasn't the biggest or most spectacular, but that was the one I liked best. Herb, for all his scorn for wealth, did not protest.

But his other self showed up a short while later. My grandmother Mortimer offered to give me linens and bedding as a wedding present, and my mother drove up from Pennsylvania to New York so we could shop together. Herb, a budding modern architect, had strong opinions about the way things looked and decided that he would come along. My mother and Gargy regarded this excursion as strictly female but felt they could not shut him out. I was caught in between, and dreading the whole thing.

Mummy, Herb, and I met at Leron, a small, very expensive and traditional linen shop on Madison Avenue staffed by polite, gray-haired ladies. My grandmother was a good customer of theirs, and they were all smiles at our arrival, bringing out sheets and towels and blanket covers for our approval. But the genteel atmosphere was fleeting. At the first pale blue, lace-trimmed, and monogrammed blanket cover, Herb wrinkled his face and announced, "I'm not having anything like *that* in my house." His tone startled the elderly lady who stiffened, then trotted off and came back with some lovely flowered sheets to show us. "Those are very nice," said my mother, trying to set a different tone.

"I'm not having anything like *that*, either!" barked Herb.

"Well, Mr. McLaughlin, what style of monogram do you think you would like on your linens," asked the saleslady, still determinedly cheerful.

"Monograms! I don't need any monograms. I don't have to look down at the sheets in the morning to know who I am!" he exclaimed. I wanted to be anywhere else in the world but there.

"I don't think this is working out," said my mother through gritted teeth. "Perhaps we'd better try another time." To the immense relief of the gray-haired ladies, we left. At tea, she and I told Gargy what had happened. "I think Herb is a little confused," said Gargy gently. "He designs the closet, not the things that go in it." I couldn't stand the prospect of any further shopping, and I imagine my mother couldn't, either. I never did get the linen from Gargy; as I recall, Herb and I later bought our own unornamented sheets and towels.

We were married the second Saturday in May. It was a lovely country wedding, the pastures sparkling green into the distance, my mother's flower gardens in full bloom, a tent built out over the lawn behind the house. In the basement there were 425 wedding presents, most of which Herb and I later took back and exchanged, turning in antique dessert plates and china tea sets for modern crockery or furniture.

Before the ceremony, which was at four in the afternoon, Mummy and I had a sandwich lunch together by the swimming pool. Even then, she had not given up; she still thought Herb would not make a good husband. "You know, we can just send all the presents back," she offered. "If you'd like to change your mind, it would be no problem; we'll just have a big party." But, though now I appreciate her concern for my happiness (and her own), her poolside offer only made me more determined than ever to become Mrs. McLaughlin.

As we stood in church at the altar during the ceremony, Herb fixed his attention on the priest and never once looked at me.

CHAPTER NINE

Marriage

Our failures only marry.

—Alternate version of Bryn Mawr's unofficial motto

Afin our wedding and a honeymoon in the Bahamas, Herb and I rented a small apartment in Washington, D.C. I dutifully wrote 425 thank you notes. Despite our families' wealth, we did not have our own trust funds and were determined to live simply in order to maintain independence from our parents. I made pathetic attempts at learning to cook and sew curtains, things my mother never did and for which I had no training or aptitude. I quit the TV station and, now that I had found a husband, poured my energies into finding a more meaningful job. Although I had gone to college not expecting to put my education to use, now, being a wife no longer felt like enough.

Most of our new Washington friends were upper and upper-middle-class graduates of Ivy League or Seven Sisters colleges drawn to the center of American political power to begin careers in law or politics. They referred to pending legislation by bill numbers—SB1437 or HR32—and, at our frequent dinner parties, argued over the most effective ways to structure taxation, manage foreign policy, or win elections. Many had influential relatives who helped them.

My cousin Robert Pell, known to all as Robin, lived and worked in Washington. Robin knew Pennsylvania Senator Joseph S. Clark and his family—he (and the ever-useful Speedwriting) helped me get a job working for Clark, a liberal Democrat. I was still typing, but at least I was composing some of the letters myself, and I had a window seat on the operations of one of the world's most exclusive clubs, the U.S. Senate.

Although Clark came from an upper-class family, he favored civil rights, better education, and world peace through international law. And even though his fortune stemmed from holdings in oil companies, he opposed giving them tax breaks. He believed that human beings could build a better society, one that gave opportunity to minorities and the poor, and he dedicated his life to that end. Having spent a lot of my life, privileged though it was, feeling cowed and stifled by harsh parents, I rooted for underdogs and those who would protect them. In Clark's office, I absorbed the hope that in the 1960s, with the Eisenhower years a thing of the past, our nation would make progress toward equality and justice.

Perhaps emboldened by this same spirit, my cousin Claiborne Pell, who was quietly active in Democratic politics, decided to plunge into public life. I was visiting in his Georgetown house one morning when he walked downstairs in his bathrobe, some papers in his hand. "Topsy, I'm thinking of running for the Senate. Would you have a look at my CV?" he asked. Since I had dismissed him as a nice but family-obsessed fellow too rich to need a job, his ambition took me by surprise. But, once I read his resume and learned that he had been arrested three times by both Nazis and Communists during years of work on behalf of refugees and other humanitarian causes, I developed a new respect for him. Besides, as I knew from spending time with them in Washington, his was the kindly, public-spirited branch of the family, utterly different from the rigid, critical style of my father. I wished I had grown up with them.

In Senator Clark's office, I fell equally in love with politics and John F. Kennedy. As a young man, JFK had been friends with my Aunt Goody, and my mother had had a few clandestine trips to the races with his older brother, Joe, the one who was shot down in the war. Gargy and Grandpa Mortimer disapproved of the Kennedys, lace curtain Irish and bootleggers besides.

But that didn't matter to me, and times had certainly changed. The charismatic Massachusetts senator was a rising star in the Democratic Party, and his name was floated as a presidential candidate. His charm, wit and looks gave him tremendous sex appeal, and his marriage to Jackie Bouvier brought him into our social class, or just about. War hero, ladies man, fighter for the underprivileged—a dazzling combination. Senator Clark's staff knew of my crush and, since Clark and Kennedy often sponsored the same legislation, often sent me as a messenger bringing documents to Senator Kennedy's office in the hope that I might encounter him. His receptionist, whom I knew through a childhood friend, introduced us, or maybe it was Jackie's half-sister Nina Auchincloss, a friend from Bryn Mawr. At any rate, when I met JFK, I explained that I was Goody's niece. He smiled broadly, either at memories of her or at my starstruck eagerness to talk to him, and we chatted a little about her and my family and Senator Clark. Afterward, he would nod in my direction when we passed in the halls of Congress and say "Hello." I left those encounters giddy, thrilled, and hoping he would win the White House.

I was remarkably ignorant, having majored in European history at Bryn Mawr and snobbishly ignored anything to do with the United States. But I quickly learned the ropes and, schooled by Senator Clark's kindly staff, received a crash course in government and high-level gossip. Kennedy had affairs, Russell Long drank, and LBJ humiliated people by making them confer with him while he sat on the toilet.

But my adventure was cut short. Herb's goal, when he finished his two years of military service, was to strike out on his own, far from both our families. So he arranged a transfer from his Air Force job designing military hospitals in Washington to one based in San Francisco supervising military hospital construction.

I wanted to stay on in the Senate, but in those days, women didn't question their husband's career decisions; we simply followed along. So, much as I hated to leave, I sadly said goodbye to the senator's staff, and the two of us headed west in my little blue Volkswagen. Once there, we found a roomy flat on top of San Francisco's Nob Hill for $135 a month, and I promptly became pregnant.

Still seething with Potomac Fever and annoyed at being exiled to a political backwater, I grumpily kept in touch with politics by subscribing to the *Washington Post* and the *Congressional Record*. Though I had no qualifications or experience, a friend who taught at a girls' private school arranged part-time work for me there as a substitute teacher. I learned to keep order in the classroom at Miss Hamlin's, which was all that anyone expected and, in the late spring, Herb and I took a sight-seeing trip to Japan.

Herb and I traced the baby's development from month to month, thrilled that a little person was growing inside me. The worst difficulty I had was to remain upright while walking belly-first down the steep hills of San Francisco.

On August 12, 1960, Daniel McLaughlin was born, a dark little fellow with snapping eyes and fine black hair. While I was still in the hospital, the school where I had substituted telephoned—they suddenly needed a half-time English teacher for the ninth grade, would I do it? Overwhelmed with new motherhood, I refused. But Herb overruled me. "If you just stay home, you will be boring," he declared. Fearful of displeasing him, I took the job.

It was a terrible decision: I had no idea how to care for a baby and no idea how to teach English, yet I had to do both at once, immediately. The few times I had substituted at school the year before did not prepare me for making lesson plans, keeping two classes a day occupied five days a week, or explaining Shakespeare. So I struggled. I hired a series of incompetent babysitters. In class, when I forgot how to diagram a sentence, I called on the brainy student who knew more about it than I did. My milk dried up, Daniel cried, I made mistakes with my students and with my baby. I felt a failure at everything, and I wept through every weekend. Senator Clark's office seemed a million miles away, and my once-burgeoning sense of self was fast evaporating.

In the middle of this ordeal, Herb, who was nearing the end of his service, did the unthinkable. He announced that, since he still could travel free on military planes, he would take a six-week vacation to see more of Asia. "Since you have a baby and a job, you can't go," he said airily, and off he went. Though he missed Daniel and me so much that he came home two weeks early, I never forgot his abandoning me while I was desperate.

Now, I can't believe what a doormat I was. But, just as I didn't feel entitled to protest our move to California, I didn't dare refuse him his trip. In hindsight, I could have hired a good nanny for Daniel or I could have quit the job—I earned such a tiny salary that we could have survived just fine without it. But those options never occurred to me. Herb was determined to save every cent, he was determined that I would work, and so I plugged away. Eventually, I figured out a little more about child raising and teaching, and he returned.

After Herb finished his stint at the Air Force, he went to work for a leading San Francisco architecture firm, Skidmore, Owings and Merrill, and

I became pregnant again. Since we wanted more space and a garden for our growing family, we decided to stop paying rent and buy a house. But the place we bought was nothing I ever would have contemplated living in.

3072 Jackson Street was an ugly, run-down rooming house located in Pacific Heights, one of the best neighborhoods of the city. The four-story building, which had about twenty-five rooms, was extraordinarily cheap because it had been cited for violating city regulations. After taking out the mortgage (which was embarrassing to me—I had never imagined myself in the position of owing money to a bank—certainly my parents had never had any mortgages) I remember the panic I felt signing the papers—whatever would we do with this repulsive, enormous, place? But Herb, showing his business acumen, understood that, once remodeled into apartments and cleaned up, the building would bring in a substantial income, as indeed it did. He was not afraid to take the grim, dilapidated structure, or to stray from the young-married norm of a single-family house.

The building was filled with lodgers, many of whom had lived there for decades. We cleared out the first floor, which would become our flat, shuffling people around as best we could so as to keep the agreeable ones and get rid of the others. Suddenly, I was dealing with a kind of person I had never expected to know—those who had so little money that they lived alone in rented rooms, sharing kitchens and bathrooms with strangers.

Among those was white-haired Miss Jamieson, the matriarch, message taker, and mail sorter of the establishment. She somehow managed not to look shabby padding down the dim corridor to the bathroom wearing a camel hair coat and sneakers. She ardently supported the United Nations, and she had twelve photographs of Dag Hammarskjold on her walls. She didn't want to leave. But though she threatened that moving would kill her, one day a Yellow Cab carried her and her possessions away. There were marks on her walls where the photographs had been, and no one to sort the mail.

Mr. Macaulay, the roomer with the most seniority, stayed on. He told us of the time, twenty years before, when the building had been a residence club with green hedges in front, where genial businessmen sat in a real parlor and ate in a pleasant dining room. He moved upstairs, to a small, quiet room at the back. On his last trip up the steps, he carried a wooden hanger from which dangled an aged tail coat, its plastic cover filmed with a heavy coat of dust.

As we kept discovering, the rooms on our floor were loaded with reminders of former occupants—thirteen poison oak cures in one astonishing drawer, dandruff shampoo in a rusty medicine cabinet, even a blue plastic arrow pointing out the location of the newly removed coin telephone. But most of all there was the smell—equal parts old bacon, dust, and neglect. It was everywhere, and nothing on the Safeway shelf would erase it.

We were intruders. The tenants eyed us with suspicion and rightly so; who knew where we would strike next? We were amateurs at this business, utterly unlike the former owners, and they had as little idea how to deal with us as we did to deal with them. Mr. Capp, from whom we had bought the place, had squeezed as much rent money out of it as he could and put back as little as possible. He specialized in running hotels for old people and knew where to buy seconds in toilet paper, how to make a light fixture from a coffee can, and what to do if people didn't pay their rent. He was not a believer in cleanliness or building codes, so the walls were riddled with bootlegged plumbing and uncertain wiring, all of which we had to repair. But Capp was so terrified of officialdom that a few notices from municipal inspectors had frightened him into selling out, quick and cheap, to the first people who made him an offer—us. So there we were, the young architect and his family, owners of real property, with the pregnant wife aghast at the entire project.

I felt guilty all the time. Making old people move out, raising rents, arguing with building inspectors—just for some money. This was not what I had been raised to do—Pells were lords of the manor, not landlords of rooming houses. I so dreaded face-to-face encounters with tenants that I slipped notes under their doors when communication was required, and if the doorbell rang I hid.

In October 1962, although the remodeling was not finished and we were still camping in a couple of newly painted rooms, Peter was born. Because I had not been happy with the old-fashioned doctor who delivered Daniel, I had changed obstetricians to a practice that encouraged natural childbirth techniques and urged fathers to be present in the delivery room—at that time, a scandalous innovation. Herb at first refused to come into the delivery room, then relented. I huffed and puffed through labor and, after the intense discomfort of pushing out his head, I still recall the delicious feeling in my body when Peter's little shoulders slipped on through.

I wanted only to be a mom, as my mother had not been to me. But, remembering Herb's threat that I would be "boring" if I did that, I continued along with his ambitions. He left Skidmore and, with a partner, founded an architecture firm. We two wives, of course, dedicated ourselves to its success and did the bookkeeping. I entertained potential clients at dinner parties, ran the rooming house, sat with other young mothers as the boys played at nearby parks, and continued part-time at Hamlin School. We hired an au pair girl to help in the house.

Our building was just a few blocks from the Presidio, an old Army base set in acres of woods and meadows. On weekends, businessmen and lawyers who lived nearby sweated, passed, and dribbled on the basketball court at Julius Kahn Playground, a lovely spot tucked into a corner of the Presidio, or they served, volleyed, and grunted on the tennis courts. There, Herb and I engaged in the form of marital torture called mixed doubles, where husbands scored points by slamming shots at the stomachs of the opposing wives. On the court with him, I was locked into a state of anxiety, overpowered by memories of the father-daughter tennis tournaments of my childhood. It didn't occur to me to stop playing mixed doubles, or even to confess how much I hated it—that was what one did on weekends, and I was well schooled in hiding what I felt.

A way of life that marked us as up-and-coming members of the upper class accompanied our Pacific Heights address, a routine that defined who we were and pointed us toward the city's power elite. Despite my still-pitiful backhand, I played ladies doubles on Thursday mornings with three other wives. (Without the men, I could enjoy the game.) One was married to an insurance executive, one to an investment banker, the third to a developer. We sent Daniel to the Town School for Boys and Peter to St. Luke's Nursery School. I was invited to join a top-drawer social group that raised money for Children's Hospital.

Though my family looked down their noses at Herb's midwestern, new money (relative to ours), and Catholic origins, in San Francisco those things were not social strikes against him. While at Garrison in the early 1950s, I met a few California girls. The United States seemed very wide in those days of slow, propeller-driven airplanes, the West Coast exceedingly remote. These girls were sent far from home to pick up polish and refinement along with an education, and as a condescending Easterner, I considered them exotic, imagining them not far removed from gold miners and prostitutes. Their own sense of slightly inferior social status, I surmised, combined with a warm-hearted, Western hospitality, led them to shower Herb and me with invitations to Tahoe weekends, parties in the city, their spacious houses in Hillsborough, and the Burlingame Club.

Herb and I were welcomed into San Francisco society not because of anything we had done but because of the social class we were born into. As Topsy Pell, I had a maiden name that people recognized as well as a cutesy nickname. My accent bore a hint of "Locust Valley lockjaw"—Locust Valley on Long Island is a suburban haven for New York's rich and well-born—marked by difficulty with the letter "r". My mother pronounced my husband's name "Heuh-bie," and at college I had had to take a remedial speech class, repeating phrases such as "the stwawbewwies on the woof" until I learned to er-roll my "r's." These things, and the manners my parents had drummed into me, stamped me as the genuine article. And though it wasn't the same as cantering across the Pennsylvania foxhunting country where I grew up, one afternoon each week I pulled on my old riding boots, drove to the stables, and did a friend of mine a favor by exercising her horse in Golden Gate Park.

Herb and I were part of a particular social scene, young marrieds who dined at each others' houses, danced at the Bachelors Ball and the Gaieties, and professed to despise the cocktail parties they attended so often. After those cocktail parties, we had what our set blithely referred to as "TV dinners"—not the frozen meals heated up by ordinary people, but tasty feasts at Trader Vic's pricey restaurant—where of course the headwaiter knew us and seated us in the tastefully spare Captain's Cabin with the Crockers and Bradleys, far removed from the Polynesian rooms stuffed with tropical kitsch and tourists.

But we maintained connections with our East Coast roots. While the San Francisco couples summered in Tahoe or Woodside, Herb and I were drawn back to his parents' small compound in Lambert's Cove on Martha's Vineyard, waving as we drove in to the guard who was posted at the entrance to keep the public out. There, our boys spent time with their Grammy McLaughlin, their McLaughlin aunts and uncles and cousins, swimming on the private beach and visiting favorite spots on the island. Besides the Vineyard pilgrimage, I took the boys to visit my mother on the farm in Pennsylvania, my father at his summer place in Narragansett, Rhode Island.

In my mind, at least, Herb and I were a popular couple, invited to mix with Interesting People. I was long-legged, energetic, and thin, with good bones from my mother and dark eyes from my father. He was tall, with a receding hairline, hazel eyes, and a crooked smile. If he was sometimes tactless, he made up for it by being quick with a quip. I wasn't as amusing, but I was nice, as I had been trained to be.

There were things I had to put up with. He routinely ate all the chocolate icing off the top of Sara Lee cakes and left the rest of it, stripped, in the fridge for us. While I knew Herb basically liked my slender figure, I was a bit self-conscious about having small breasts. In that era when Jacqueline Bisset's busty wet T-shirt look was all the rage, he gave me a white plastic exercise gizmo designed to give a woman bigger tits. A joke, but I was not amused. Though he gave me nice things over the years, that gift stuck in my mind

I rarely challenged him. My repertoire was long on smiling and deference, short on candor and confrontation. I was struggling with the burden of having been raised a young lady in the Silent Generation of the 1950s. Girls deferred to boys; a smart girl would never be popular; and wives did not contradict their husbands. Accordingly, Herb made the decisions about everything from where we would live to furniture arrangement and whether I would work or stay home. He explained to me that I had no taste, and I accepted his opinion. He liked it that I was bright and competent, but he left me no room to be myself.

One summer afternoon, he brought home an abstract painting. It was mostly red, punctuated with jagged black lines. It looked nasty; I suggested that he hang it in his office downtown. He refused. Summoning up the grit to argue with him, I insisted that he respect my wishes—after all this was my front hall, too. Angry at my opposition, he went ahead and hung it anyway—bashing in the nail with strokes of his hammer as I begged him to stop. Plainly, my feelings about that painting did not matter to him. I swallowed my hurt, but the incident festered.

What I had first experienced as Herb's decisiveness was beginning to feel like domineering. When I took the boys to the park, I talked with other mothers sitting on benches by the sandbox. Some of them, too, were tired of deferring to their husbands and were reading a new book called *The Feminine Mystique.*

Another episode with a painting showed Herb in this new light. We were at a party in Washington given by John Varick Tunney, son of the legendary prizefighter. Varick, a classmate of Herb's from Yale, was then a California congressman. (The congressman, whom we always called by his childhood name of Varick, had had to give up using that name in public and instead become "John." A poll taken before he ran for office showed that voters found "Varick" to be "subversive and/or Communist.") Varick/John was tall and handsome despite his prominent front teeth and awkward air.

I remembered him from cotillions in New York years before—but now he was recast in a Kennedyesque role as socialite-turned-liberal-politician.

We were sitting around the fireplace in the living room after an elegant dinner, sipping brandy and green mint. Varick, who knew that Herb collected art, eagerly showed us a painting he'd recently bought. Clearly, he wanted Herb to praise the work. But Herb didn't like it, and he wouldn't give his approval. "How about the composition?" asked Varick, breaking an embarrassing silence as Herb stood before the picture, hand raised to his chin and obviously not impressed. "Nice composition, don't you think?" he persisted. It seemed to me that Varick was gently pleading for a compliment, which Herb stubbornly withheld. "It's not exactly my taste," said Herb, or something like that, and the two moved away from each other to strike up conversations with other guests. I felt sorry for Varick, who had been so hospitable to us, and irritated with Herb for being so mean.

I fixed on this seemingly innocuous incident probably because I couldn't allow myself to acknowledge the way Herb put me down—I was used to that from my parents, and besides, such a realization would have been too threatening to my marriage. But my anger surged when I saw him do it to someone else.

Times were changing. I learned to smoke marijuana—which by then was being passed around at some upscale dinner parties—and, at a suburban party one summer evening, I shed my clothes and joined some friends in a hot tub under the stars. Herb stayed clothed, pursed his lips, and disapproved, but it was certainly more fun being naked in the hot tub than having tennis balls drilled into my stomach.

But political expression in the expanding counterculture was not my cup of tea. Mario Savio and the long-haired Berkeley radicals of the 1964 Free Speech Movement struck me as unmannerly, unkempt, and unattractive. I opposed the Vietnam War, but I hadn't yet joined a march. I was in favor of civil rights, but I'd never sat in or been arrested.

To our delight, I became pregnant again, and soon after John was born on New Years Day in January 1967, Herb and I decided to take a family walk in Golden Gate Park. He heard that a good soccer game was taking place there so we set off to find it. But as we drove through the park, we were surprised to see crowds of hippies drifting toward the polo field where we were heading. We walked along surrounded by young people blowing bubbles, pounding drums, and dancing. In the distance, rock bands were playing. Someone parachuted from a plane. Long-haired, free-spirited men and women were everywhere, smiling and laughing on that lovely winter day as the bubbles sailed skyward. Struck by their joyful freedom of movement and dress, I was curious. They seemed happy, involved in something evidently wonderful that I didn't then understand—gleefully showing off their liberation. The scene was a long, long way from gated compounds like Piping Rock and the etiquette of dancing class, but, though I felt out of place, I liked being in the middle of it.

Later, I learned that we had accidentally stumbled into the Human Be-In, a landmark in San Francisco history where a huge "gathering of the tribes" took place and the counterculture celebrated itself. Timothy Leary, the Grateful Dead, and Jerry Rubin entertained the crowd. But we didn't see them, and we never found the soccer game.

While Herb and I occasionally smoked dope and sometimes went to the Fillmore Auditorium, my life continued to revolve around husband, kids, and social life. Perhaps because I had been raised so much by Zellie and Nursie, I stayed close to my children. My station wagon packed with kids, I drove car pools to Marin Country Day School and cheered as Daniel and Peter raced across the field in soccer games. Tears of pride and love ran down my cheeks at their Christmas pageants. I scheduled visits to check out nursery schools for my youngest one, John; I got up in morning darkness to ferry them to orthodontist appointments as Peter, who was always cold, huddled in a blanket on the car floor next to the heater. My engagement book for that period shows dates for tea with women friends, committee meetings, parties, and lists of people Herb and I invited to dinner.

Eleven years into marriage with Herb, I was ensconced in what should have been a perfect life. He had become a successful architect. With our three sons, Daniel, Peter, and John, we moved out of the rooming house into an elegant Victorian on Broadway Street. From our library and bedroom windows we looked out over the Golden Gate Bridge, Alcatraz, and sailboats dotting the bay. Herb designed an extensive remodeling of our house, tearing down old walls to make a living room so long that the boys could play indoor hockey there; through French doors at the back, you could see a lawn ringed with shrubs and flowers. The dark floors were covered with thick rugs in the entrance hall, a deep red flecked with yellow. He reserved for himself the right to choose and arrange the paintings and prints that would grow into a notable art collection. When it came to books, forget the Dewey Decimal system. Because he thought it looked better, he grouped the blue ones together, the red ones, and so on. To find the book you wanted, you had to remember not the author, not the topic, but what color it was.

I only lived there for nine months.

CHAPTER TEN

2500 Filbert Street

Wommen, of kynde, desiren libertee,
And nat to been constreyned as a thral;
And so doon men, if I sooth seyen shal.

—Geoffrey Chaucer

My first step toward a double life began late in 1967 with a nervous knock on the door of 2500 Filbert Street in San Francisco. I had an appointment to meet with the writer Paul Jacobs, then in search of a part-time researcher for a new book. His office, on the ground floor of his big house, was just a few blocks down the hill toward the bay from mine; I didn't have to go far. But despite its similarly posh address and comfortable furnishings, as I would soon learn, the atmosphere in that house was worlds apart from anything I had ever known.

I heard about the job from Fred and Greta Mitchell. Fred, a wealthy Yale classmate of Herb's, had adopted radical political views and invested most of his inheritance in a New Leftist magazine, *Ramparts*, founded by Jacobs and several others. Having taught and tutored girls in middy blouses and navy blue skirts at Miss Hamlin's School for the last several years, I had had my fill of young ladies, grammar and *Julius Caesar*. The new job sounded interesting, but Jacobs had a reputation as something of a boor so I approached the interview with trepidation.

A few years before, I had met Paul, a short, jug-eared dynamo who shaved his head. As a young man, he left a career in New York's diamond business, where his Jewish family was prominent, to become a labor organizer, beginning as a Trotskyite orating from soapboxes in New York City during the Depression. An author and activist, he moved to San Francisco, where he became known for his leftist views and studied lack of inhibition. To illustrate the daily life of the very poor, Jacobs shocked television viewers by eating dog food from a can on a news show. He talked loudly and graphically about sex; he kept a stash of marijuana in his library tucked jauntily behind J. Edgar Hoover's *Masters of Deceit*.

I had seen him at parties and had been offended by his behavior. At a party in a Nob Hill mansion, the hostess served a luscious chocolate cake. "I need milk wit' dat," he demanded in his Brooklyn accent. "You can't have chawklit cake widout milk!" After she dutifully went to her refrigerator and handed him a glass, he finished his cake, downed the milk, and beamed with pleasure. "Just like a good fuck!" he chortled.

Now, as I waited nervously at his house for someone to answer the bell, I wondered. What would he ask? What would I answer?

Jacobs, wearing a rumpled sweat suit, opened the door and invited me into his cluttered office. Books were piled everywhere, file folders piled on top of the books. He sat behind his large desk and tipped back in his chair. I handed him my neatly typed resume. But he didn't conduct the sort of job interview I was used to; he didn't inquire about my education or my past employment or my qualifications as a researcher. Instead, he was charming. He asked about my husband and children, where I lived and who my friends were. He listened with apparent interest to my answers. That was it. Then he explained the idea behind the book, which would show how blacks, Indians, Chicanos, Asians, and other people of color had been treated in North America from Columbus to the Ku Klux Klan, and how they responded to the racism imposed by whites. A short chapter on each group would sum up its history, followed by a section of documents detailing their experiences. No one had yet put all this history together, he said. Together with his co-author, filmmaker and activist Saul Landau—another Jewish Socialist from New York—we would be pioneers.

That was good enough for me. So what if I knew little about American history and even less about anything that happened after 1900? So what if Jacobs wasn't a gentleman by Pell standards and said "Fuck" in public? Because I spent so much of my childhood immersed in books, I loved the idea of working on one—I would have an apprenticeship. And, for the first time since my forced departure from Senator Clark's office, I saw this as a chance to become involved with something that mattered. Besides, Jacobs was funny and irreverent. At the very least, this would be a big change. Excited at the prospect, I agreed to the small salary and went home to tell Herb. He seemed pleased at the idea his wife was working on an interesting research project.

Although histories of racial groups in the United States are plentiful now, in 1967 this kind of study was unorthodox. The Jacobs household was, too. Paul got up around 5 a.m. and worked until lunch, which he sometimes cooked for Saul, the secretary, and me. A fabulous chef who delighted in exotic foods, he awakened my palate, (which was used to lamb chops, BLTs and green peas) with hummus, kim chee, roast peppers, lox, and persimmon pudding. I was embarrassed when he said that he liked roasted red peppers because they reminded him of vaginas (not the word he used). I was astonished and shocked by the house rule: everyone must be out by two o'clock because one or another of his lovers arrived at that time for the afternoon. I'd heard about open marriages but I'd never encountered one before. His wife, Ruth, had affairs, too.

Who were these people? Not only did they talk about sex, they did it as they pleased. In fact, they seemed to delight in trampling the rules of decorum instilled in me from birth.

But although I was put off by Paul's crass and crude comments, his down-to-earth vitality and quick-witted humor drew me in, as did the idealism embodied in his life. He sided with the oppressed; he'd been jailed in civil rights marches, his writings exposed the cruelty that the powerful inflicted on the powerless. Moreover, he and Saul believed that life could be more fair, more just, and more humane than the society in which we were living.

And that wasn't all. Paul and Saul joked about all kinds of people, including the "goyim"—my people—and particularly WASPs, with their uptight demeanor, their sense of entitlement and their narrow Protestant minds. Make fun of such Brahmins as Averell Harriman? Henry Cabot Lodge? I hadn't seen anything like this before, but I was more curious than offended. Now that I think of it, their disrespect gave me permission to recognize my own gripes against the privileged, overbearing men in my life. Doors in my mind were quietly opening.

But mostly, I worked. I trotted off to libraries and unearthed the books and documents they sent me to fetch. I found powerful writings by ex-slaves and Indian chiefs, contemporary newsletters from black and Native American organizations, and outrageous long-ago court decisions that, contrary to principles of justice and fairness, arrogated power and land to white people. I read them and wrote up memos; I tracked down old handbills and speeches.

The two were highly amused when I came in on Thursdays in my short white tennis outfit and little socks with colored pompoms at the heel, dressed for my ladies doubles, and they howled upon hearing that I still wore white gloves when I visited New York.

As months went by, I began to feel a split between my life at work and my life at home. The work took on more importance; I felt more alive and involved when I was searching for the information we needed, which often was heartbreaking. There were anguished letters written by Japanese-Americans interned in desert camps during World War II telling of homes and businesses lost, dreams shattered, families split apart. There was Richard Wright's poignant description of exhilarated blacks in Chicago rushing into the streets in 1935 to celebrate vicariously after Joe Louis punched out Max Baer. There was Logan, the Mingo chief, telling a British lord in 1774 how the very white men whom he had sheltered murdered his family and stole his pelts; the agony of Frederick Douglass watching his wife tied to a stake and beaten.

I was appalled by the white supremacy preached by the Tuxedo resident Madison Grant, whose books railed against the "darker, lesser peoples" that were "mongrelizing the white race in America." I began to see my people, the governing class celebrated in my school textbooks for spreading democracy across the continent, less as heroes and more as villains.

In fact, people who would be seen as villains by my family turned up at Paul's. One morning, alone at my desk in the back office typing up a memo, I became aware that someone was watching. Turning my head, I saw a tall, well-built black man, sleek body naked to the waist, posing in the doorway with his back against the wall, thumbs hooked over his belt. "Is this the research department?" he asked, in a low voice with a sexy smile. "Yes," I stammered, taken aback. "It is." I knew this face. The man was Eldridge Cleaver, author of the acclaimed and controversial *Soul on Ice*, Minister of Information for the Black Panther Party. Cleaver, who would shortly go underground because he was wanted by police in the wake of an Oakland shootout, was visiting Jacobs for a few days. He flirted with me a few minutes longer and disappeared.

I was partly aghast, partly thrilled. The Panthers were making big waves in California politics at the time by appearing armed, in black-jacketed formation, on the steps of the Capitol in Sacramento, and by carrying law books on Oakland city streets to insist on their rights and fend off police harassment. One or another was constantly being sought for shooting people. Revolutionaries? Fighters for civil rights? Thugs? I didn't exactly know, and Cleaver made me uncomfortable, particularly since he had written about raping white women. Was I racist, I wondered, or was there something sinister about him? But he certainly seemed to be on the front lines of rebellion, and after he fled underground, I didn't want the police to catch him.

New Left politics, open marriage, iconoclastic jokes, casual talk of sex, Black Panther houseguests, revolutionary politics, battles against injustice, defiance of authority—these things flouted everything I was brought up to revere. But I was liking this new culture and moved by its ideals. I admired the heroism shown by historical figures such as W. E. B. DuBois, Chief Joseph of the Nez Perce, and Queen Liliuokalani, and also by the unknown students, writers, and organizers who spoke out against the subjugation of their peoples, whose manifestos and pleas we put into our book. They said what they felt, and they rebelled—the very things that had been so forbidden behind the walls separating me and my family from the outside world. Maybe it was possible to bring about a better society.

Maybe individuals—even female individuals—could count for something.

Uncomfortable questions began popping up in my head. Why were men always in charge? Did the upper-crust status of my family actually make us any better than anyone else? Could you believe what our government said? What if there were big changes in society? Was there more to life than I had thought? I took the children to the park less often, worked furiously, and was less patient at ladies' committee meetings.

This is how I remember one of them. We gathered at the museum near the Opera House and City Hall, a dozen or so Ladies Who Lunch, doing our civic duty by nibbling at salad and planning a fundraising event. I didn't feel as if I belonged. My mother never played Lady Bountiful, being far too occupied in her flower garden, riding horses, or seeing her friends at the races at Belmont. Though her family was rich and prominent, she didn't bother with symphonies or operas or hospitals.

But I was a city person now, married to an ambitious architect on his way up, and besides, these were good people—women like Orian Taylor who died young of cancer, and Margie Boyd, a supporter of art and culture in San Francisco. Months earlier, I had been vaguely pleased to have been invited to join their committee, but now I was irritated.

"Don't you think that blue tablecloths would be the best?" asked Anne Whitmore, leaning forward over the table. Her tone made it perfectly clear that anyone with taste would take her side. Anne, whose fashion-model poses, fabulous clothes, and striking, dark looks made her a star of the local social scene, was a perennial name in Frances Moffatt's society column in the San Francisco *Chronicle*. She came from a very old family in the city, and her husband's company produced clever ad copy. Mr. Lee did her hair; she had facials at Elizabeth Arden.

"But I liked the very pale peach," countered Marian Kahn, whose husband had made a fortune in retail. Marian wore an artfully cut, Chanel-style jacket trimmed with braid; her brownish hair shone with just the right touch of highlighting. Like the rest of the committee members, she wore pumps with a medium stacked heel and a bright scarf knotted at the throat. "The peach is so much more striking," she continued. "Think what we could do with the flower arrangements." And so the discussion went: tablecloths of blue or pale peach, flowers in baskets or small vases, menus of squab or shrimp.

My polite smile was tired. I mumbled an excuse about a car pool, fled to the library on the other side of City Hall, and went to work. Paul had asked me to write up a section on Filipino farm workers in the Central Valley and their fierce, doomed, attempts to form a union.

Recognizing my diligence, Paul and Saul announced that my name would go with theirs on the cover of our book, *To Serve the Devil*.

But despite my promotion, I was less patient at the office. One day when Paul asked me to get him a pen, I snapped, "Get it yourself! What am I, your slave?" My outburst surprised us both. I was appalled at my behavior, but somehow exhilarated. He got the pen. Saul tactfully suggested that I go to a women's consciousness-raising group at Glide Memorial Church.

Not knowing what to expect, but eager to explore this curious experience of speaking out, I went. I found dozens of women of all colors, ages, and shapes sitting around on huge cushions in the dim church basement. The group leader divided us into small clusters and told us to talk about our lives. My group included an open lesbian (the first open one I had ever met), and the wife of San Francisco's sheriff. We traded stories: parents favoring our brothers, mothers kow-towing to fathers, husbands expecting wives to wait on them. Energized by the discovery of similar histories despite our varied backgrounds, we decided to meet again.

Herb didn't like that one bit. As I walked out the front door of our house to the next meeting, he was standing part way up the stairway. He turned and called out angrily, "Where are your boots? You forgot your whip!"

Later, I brought him to a Black Panther rally at an Oakland theatre. Stone-faced, arrogant black men in black leather jackets searched everyone at the door before allowing anyone inside. Long-winded speakers exhorted us to rise up against fascism, join the coming revolution, and support Huey P. Newton. Tentatively, I added my quiet voice to the crowd's chant of "All power to the people!" while Herb remained grimly silent. I hadn't felt comfortable or much liked the evening, but he had hated it.

Our marriage grew shakier. We battled more often. I was torn between loyalties to East and West, past and future: to Herb, my parents, and the life I was brought up to lead, or to the glimmering hints of freedom I was discovering and the possibility of a more exciting and fulfilling existence.

Perhaps it's not surprising that I fell in love with a friend of Paul's. I'd interviewed him for our book; he began inviting me for breakfast—pork buns in a Chinatown coffee shop—and he spoke of racism, politics, and socialism. (In hindsight, how could that have been sexy? But it was.)

Paul, of course, sensed an affair brewing and encouraged it. One rainy afternoon when he was out of town, the friend came over to his office where I was working. We made love. "Just look at your face in the mirror," he said afterward. I could see that it was glowing.

Predictably, when I confessed to Herb, he was hurt and furious. Predictably, I was anxious and guilty, but also thrilled at the discovery of passion. The affair was short-lived but its effects were not. There was no going back.

CHAPTER ELEVEN

Breaking Out

The vilest deeds like poison weeds,
Bloom well in prison-air;
It is only what is good in Man
That wastes and withers there:
Pale Anguish keeps the heavy gate,
And the Warder is Despair.

—Oscar Wilde, The Ballad of Reading Gaol

In 1970, *To Serve the Devil* and my apprenticeship were finished. My co-authors pronounced me a free-lance writer, ready to sally forth and use her typewriter to fight injustice. Saul introduced me to a charismatic Berkeley lawyer named Fay Stender, who had a long history of defending civil rights activists, Black Panthers, and draft resisters.

When I went to meet her, she told me about her current case: three black inmates were accused of killing a white guard at Soledad Prison—in fact, she said, they were being railroaded to the gas chamber. One of them, the alleged leader, was known for protesting racial discrimination in the prison system. As part of the plan, Saul also introduced me to the people who ran *Good Times,* an underground weekly that championed revolution, rock and roll, drugs, and sex. They would publish articles about the prison case if I wrote well enough, and perhaps we could make it into a *cause celebre.*

I had never done anything to help victims of the racism I had so recently discovered, and here was an opportunity. I gladly took on the new assignment, accepting as Gospel everything Fay told me. I didn't think through how that commitment might mesh with my young-matron life, but covering a murder trial was bound to be more absorbing than tennis matches or dinner parties.

Pretrial proceedings were already taking place in Salinas, a dusty cowtown near the prison, a hundred miles south of San Francisco. Fay suggested I check that out, and the *Good Times* people agreed that it might make a good article. I soon found myself again headed off to do something for which—like teaching school—I had no qualifications. Anxious about my ability to carry out this new assignment, I drove down with Fay in her tiny blue MG.

I had never seen anything like the scene at the Salinas courthouse: The three accused prisoners were led in like slaves, dressed in rumpled uniforms and hung with chains that clanked as they shuffled along in leg irons, their hands shackled to their waists. They acknowledged the smiles and waves from the spectators—their families, and what were then called "movement" people, antiwar and civil rights activists, Black Panther supporters, and leftists—with nods and smiles of their own, raising their fists as high as the chains would permit. The three accused sat quietly beside their lawyers; armed guards were posted along the courtroom walls.

The hearing was marked by confrontation and rancor. The defense lawyers argued that they needed to inspect prison records and interview inmate witnesses in order to prepare their cases. But the judge denied all their requests, siding with the prison officials who opposed release of the documents. How, I wondered, could the prisoner defendants get a fair hearing if their lawyers could not obtain official reports? The judge seemed to give the prosecutor whatever he asked for and sometimes even suggested what motion he should make next. Moreover, the judge showed his disdain for the antiestablishment crowd—long-haired law students, hippies in beads and granny dresses, Chicano activists, fat black women and small black children with big eyes and hair in pigtails sprouting all over their heads. Before the hearing began, he warned the spectators not to act as if they were at a barbecue or a pool hall.

That courtroom scene in Salinas scared me; in truth, I found almost any confrontation with authority frightening. But I filled a pad with notes, struggling to recall my Speedwriting as I scribbled down the judge's comments, details about the setting, and as much of the lawyers' arguments as I understood.

Afterward, I raced home to San Francisco in time to get ready for a dinner party Herb and I were having. Harriet, the ethereal strawberry blonde who was then our au pair, had fed the children and peeled the vegetables. I needed to pick up something for hors d'oeuvres, time the cooking of the roast, see that the flowers were nicely fixed in their silver bowls and the house tidied up. Herb really cared how things looked.

That evening, I dressed in a silk blouse with velvet pants and fastened the lustrous Pell pearls around my neck. My aunt Tinkie had given them to me when I came out. I welcomed the guests, saw that they had drinks, chatted brightly of things I no longer cared about, and tried to ignore the hostile undercurrents that now flowed increasingly between Herb and me. "Topsy, I hear you've been working on the most *interesting* book, *do* tell me what it's about," said my tennis friend Barbara Sedgwick, gin and tonic in hand. As I began to explain, her expression went blank and her eyes wandered over my shoulder.

"Hanging around with those lefty agitators again?" teased Herb's friend Joe Patterson, a rumpled man with curly hair who had put together a profitable real estate empire. "Dinner's ready," I told the guests, cutting short the political discussion he was hoping to start. Joe was amusing, but I wasn't in the mood and I knew he'd get the better of me in an argument even if I knew I was right. "Let's go in. Get a plate and help yourself—everything's on the sideboard." I escaped into the kitchen to get out the silver serving spoons as the guests drifted into the dining room. Tomorrow, I would write my article and take it in.

My Pacific Heights set read *Town and Country* and *Time*—certainly not a voice of the counterculture like the *Good Times*. Again, as seemed to be happening to me so often these days, I found myself in strange surroundings. A haze of marijuana smoke and incense hung over the dingy Bush Street commune that published the paper. Dust piled up in the corners, the sagging sofas would have been rejected by Goodwill, and an air of decay suffused the whole building.

Harry the Corpse, nicknamed because of his tall, bony body and pale, sallow complexion framed in lank locks of dirty hair, was in charge. He edited the paper and, with his partner, Ruby, presided over the resident commune. They had gotten a baby girl from somewhere and were raising her in what, to my mind, was squalor, though she seemed to do just fine.

The *New York Times* it wasn't. A weekly column by "stone grower" covered the city's drug scene: "Pounds of hashish $750-$800, all kinds of ounces, about what you'd expect. Good purple acid is being liberated around and about. Clear yellow acid with big A on it, same batch as JuJuBes," he reported in the Valentine's Day issue of 1970, whose front page featured a naked couple lying on their backs, arms entwined, the young man plainly not circumcised. Inside were articles headlined "Free Huey," about the Black Panther founder then in jail for killing a policeman; "Army Sentenced to Death," about a People's trial that found the military guilty of genocide in Vietnam; and "Teasing the Tenants," about slum landlords in Berkeley and a rent strike. Political activists falsely accused of crimes were a perennial topic: Black Panthers, Los Siete, Native Americans. My favorite section of the paper was the "comix": the Furry Freak Brothers, Mr. Natural, and those bomb-breasted, jack-booted wimmen straight from the demented brain of cartoonist Robert Crumb. Among the *Good Times* reporters were "windcatcher," "benhari," and my favorite person, "batman." A pale, mustachioed hippie in his thirties, he had gone to Harvard, drove a motorcycle, and wrote fastidious prose—beneath the long-haired, leather-jacketed, stoned-out getup lived a strict grammarian.

My Pacific Heights mansion was only eight blocks uphill from Bush Street, but those eight blocks spanned social and cultural light-years. I felt as out of place walking into the commune as I must have looked—my neatly done hair washed and set by a hairdresser; immaculate in my preppie Shetland sweater and tartan kilt. Women at the paper sported jeans and boots, or long, flowing tie-dyed garments, and their cascading tresses went untouched by stylist's scissors. Harry and Ruby, who actually liked my reporting, did their friendly best to move me along toward liberation, showering me with hospitable, sometimes pushy, offers of wine, joints, and sex.

I didn't dare write for an underground newspaper under my own name, so I signed my articles "harriet," taking our au pair girl's name as my nom de plume, and beginning it with a small letter as the other *Good Times* reporters did. A few weeks before, I had seen the real Harriet go off on a date at night with a man I had met, a bright, rebellious, and sexy hippie. She rode off behind him on his motorcycle, her arms clasped around his waist, his long beard whipping in the wind. I knew he was taking her to his studio on Telegraph Hill where the walls were lined in shining Mylar and the drugs and wine flowed freely. Watching Harriet speed away up Broadway Street in the moonlight, I felt a rush of envy.

It was an impossible stretch, the span from J.K. park to the *Good Times* office, from "Topsy" to "harriet." Sometimes, as I headed back up the hill to cook supper after dropping off a story at the paper, I wondered how I'd gotten into such a bizarre situation.

Several weeks later, after covering three or four court proceedings, and experiencing the thrill of seeing, if not my name in print, my articles in the *Good Times*, I walked south down Fillmore Street with Herb to get ice cream cones. At the counter, also buying ice cream, stood none other than Harry the Corpse and Ruby. Nervously, I introduced them to Herb, one pole of my life meeting the other. I felt schizophrenic—how could Topsy and harriet be in the same place at the same time? How could I please both sides? We parted awkwardly.

As the pull of my new life as harriet grew stronger and stronger, the fights with Herb multiplied. I was miserable. I didn't see how I could get the sense of myself that I wanted so much and still stay married to him. And I couldn't see breaking up the home of our three young boys because I knew firsthand what divorce did to children.

However, when the galley proofs of *To Serve the Devil* arrived at Paul's from Random House with our names on the cover: "Paul Jacobs and Saul Landau with Eve Pell McLaughlin," an impulse swept over me. As the page lay on Paul's big desk, I grabbed a pencil, reached over, and drew a circle around "McLaughlin," adding the little squiggle that means "delete." That was my first step toward becoming "Pell" again, and when Herb and I were divorced later on, I formally took back my family name—to the distinct annoyance of my father. As a Pell, I could be identified as his daughter, and he could be publicly shamed by his daughter's behavior.

I continued writing about prisons, and after my first article as Eve Pell was published in a national magazine—the radical publication *Ramparts*—Clarry was mortified. He sent a clipping of it to our cousin Claiborne, the senator from Rhode Island, with a note attached: "Terribly sorry about this."

For years afterward I told that story for laughs and to ingratiate myself with whomever I was talking to, but I never dwelt long on its meaning. "Express your own opinions," it seemed to say, "and I disclaim you." Clarry didn't want any blots on the family escutcheon, and now I had become a blot.

But I'm getting ahead of myself.

My engagement book for 1970 still showed the same planning for dinner parties, car pools and orthodontist appointments as before. But new notations crept in: "Women's lib" meetings, "beds for two marchers" on a day of an antiwar demonstration, the Marxism class I was auditing at U.C. Berkeley, appointments with the therapist I had begun to see, and the couples counseling sessions Herb and I were attending.

Instead of bringing us together, however, the counseling sharpened my desire to leave. As I look back on it now, the process—and the times— were not fair to Herb. I was the oppressed woman struggling to free herself from the emotionally rigid, chauvinist husband; in that period of burgeoning liberation, we were heroine and villain. The therapist mostly sided with me, so Herb couldn't get much of a hearing. Encouraged by those dynamics, I felt more and more entitled to speak out against a system—and people—that made me feel hemmed in and inadequate.

All through this unhappy period, one image haunted me. The year before, Herb and I had gone to Bermuda on a trip with my father and my Pell half-brothers, Peter and Haven. One sunny day, we went on a moped excursion, riding the motorized bicycles that tourists on that car-free island delight in renting. On the way home, I was riding a little ahead of the group, jauntily tooling along and enjoying the balmy air, the tropical beauty. For fun, I speeded up a bit as we neared our rented house. But, as I was turning in the gate, Herb accelerated his moped so he could pass me and beat me home. But, misjudging the distance as he went by, he crashed his bike sideways into mine. I fell, with the moped on top of me, its burning hot engine seared into my leg.

I tried not to make too much of the injury, but it became seriously infected. I developed a fever, and, after I showed the ugly wound to my horrified doctor at home, was confined to bed. My leg healed, but in my mind the image of Herb racing to defeat me remained raw. Whenever I was operating independently, I feared, he would feel compelled to do the same thing.

One morning, after months of counseling, as we were seated side by side on our immense king-size bed with the fantastic view of San Francisco Bay, I told Herb I felt that we had to separate. If I stayed with him, I said, I would have to sacrifice my newfound sense of self; at some level, I felt I would die. Sadly, he consented, but he refused to move from our Broadway Street house, the usual form for husbands in that situation. "I just can't do it," he told me.

"But I can," I answered, and I did—taking the boys with me to a rented flat about ten blocks away on Divisadero Street. We agreed to let a year of separation pass before beginning divorce proceedings. He promised to woo and win me back.

"Since you have ruined my life," he continued sadly, "the least you can do is let me have the boys half time." I felt so guilty about leaving that I agreed, against my better judgment. We had had a very conventional marriage in which the children were my responsibility. Herb hadn't been closely involved with their day-to-day care and didn't know, for example, what they liked for lunch. I wondered how sensitive he would be to their needs. But he loved them and was not willing to settle for the then-usual visitation schedule where children of divorced parents lived most of the time with their mother and saw their father a couple of times a month.

As another concession to his feelings, I agreed to use one of our social friends as my lawyer, a man plainly on Herb's side with whom Herb would be comfortable; he was also a close friend of Herb's lawyer. Not surprisingly, feeling overpowered by these three men, I signed onto an unfavorable agreement that gave me my freedom, but too little money and too little time with the boys.

They were with Herb every Friday afternoon until Monday morning and during half their vacations. I dreaded coming home to my empty apartment whenever they were gone, and sometimes I lay on the rug in front of the fireplace and wept for my broken family. At their Christmas pageant, the first time I appeared at a school function after leaving Herb, I felt like a scarlet woman, embarrassed to be walking alone into that auditorium filled with married couples.

But I had decided to live a different life, and the divided child care schedule left me free for radical politics and my new lover, a Marxist philosophy professor.

One Saturday morning, a month or so after I moved into my new place, the professor and I had just undressed and gotten into my bed when I heard heavy footsteps walking in the alley beside my building. "Eve!" someone was calling out angrily. "Eve!" It was Herb. Though I had every right to be where I was, I got scared and stayed silent. The professor's eyes widened in fright. The steps pounded around to the back, where my bedroom was. Our passion vanished; we slipped out of bed and fled down the hall into the bathroom. We locked the door. The angry calling continued; the back door to my bedroom banged open and the heavy feet stomped inside, past the bathroom, and down the hall to the front door. The professor and I, cowering on the tile floor, wrapped towels around ourselves for warmth. The footsteps stomped back again, the back door slammed shut, and the footsteps faded away down the alley.

Shaken, we went back to the bedroom and put on our clothes. Once dressed, he started looking around anxiously, riffling through his pockets and searching beneath the chair where he had hung his clothes. He looked bewildered. "Eve," he announced after a few minutes. "He stole my wallet!"

I was stunned, then furious. Herb had just scared me to death, violated my privacy, and now this! I stormed out of my flat and over to the park nearby, where I thought I might find him with the boys. He was there. "You give that back to me *immediately*," I demanded. "And never come into my place again!" Herb smirked in a bad-boy kind of way, removed the wallet from his pocket, and handed it over. I took my gold wedding band from my finger and flung it at him, then headed back across the grass for my new home. If this was his way of wooing me back, it wasn't going to work.

In truth, there was no way Herb could compete with the lofty ideals (and the self-righteousness) of battling injustice, or the exhilaration of bursting from my uptight old self into someone who felt freer and more genuine. It's hard to explain, after so many years of Republican dominance and after so many idealistic movements have failed or become corrupted, how real our vision seemed back then. But the civil rights movement was changing lives, huge throngs were marching to stop the war in Vietnam, women were discovering that they had strengths, and freedom was in the air. I was determined to join forces with "the movement" and work toward an America where men and women of all colors and classes could be free and equal.

Forget being a Pell princess, I was off to the revolution.

CHAPTER TWELVE

The Comrade

The law, in its majestic equality, forbids rich and poor alike to sleep under bridges, beg in the streets or steal bread.

—Anatole France

In 1966, a federal judge described conditions in Soledad's maximum security unit:

Inmates being punished were confined in a bare concrete cell, naked and in darkness, with only a hole for a toilet and a stiff mat for a blanket. The cell walls were covered with excrement from previous occupants; each day the "toilet" was flushed once or twice; they were allowed only two cups of water and a disgusting mush of various foods mixed up together. They stayed filthy, and had to eat only a few feet away from the "toilet." Sometimes they became ill and vomited from the stench. Sleep on the cold concrete floor was painful and difficult. Twice a day, the cell door was opened for fifteen minutes.

Forcing people to live in such pain, wrote the judge, "results in a slow-burning fire of resentment on the part of the inmates until it finally explodes in open revolt, coupled with their violent and bizarre conduct."

He was right.

The more I learned about the prison system, the more I wanted to use my new skills to make people realize what was going on behind its walls. I was observing repression in action, and now I had a chance to do something about it. While I may have looked to an outsider like a silly neophyte rushing off to the latest fashion in political causes, it didn't feel that way at all. Involvement in Fay's case felt like the next step in a process that had begun a decade before in Senator Clark's office, hibernated during my young-married years, and taken root at 2500 Filbert Street with *To Serve the Devil*. The ironic image was that of barriers—those in Tuxedo insulating the upper crust from the rest of society, those of Soledad insulating the rest of society from prisoners. Contrary to the American ideal of upward mobility, I was breaking out of the enclave of the elite and, in a way, into the underworld.

I knew, as Cooky's older sister, the dangers that lurked in the world I was leaving. I hadn't tried to stop my brother's tormentors, but perhaps, together with Fay and other allies, I could help to challenge the wardens and guards who abused inmates. I didn't yet understand the dangers inside prisons, but I wanted to expose the abuses I was learning about and to see the cruel punishers brought to justice.

What I saw in subsequent court hearings, as the murder case against the three prisoners proceeded, confirmed my impressions of the first one. Unlike the judge who condemned the maximum security unit at Soledad, the trial judges in Salinas sided with the prosecutors so strongly that the defense could not get a fair hearing. For poor, black inmates, I believed, there was no justice.

The shocking facts about life behind bars reinforced the leftist creed I was absorbing. Among its tenets:

- Capitalism and private property beget injustice.

- Laws are made to protect the rich and powerful.

- "Common criminals" are actually political prisoners, guilty of being poor and nonwhite.

- Blacks and other colonized peoples have a duty to free themselves by any means necessary. When prisoners rise up against their jailers, for example, they are retaliating against unjust domination.

The choices were stark. Did you stand with the Ku Klux Klan, John D. Rockefeller, and U.S. imperialism? Or with Frederick Douglass, Joe Hill, and Fidel Castro?

In a study group, I read Marx and Engels, Franz Fanon, and Paolo Freire's *The Pedagogy of the Oppressed*. I endorsed their goals—or what I understood as their goals—with uncritical enthusiasm. Even so, however, I couldn't quite get with the "by any means necessary" part of the revolutionary program. I had been horrified by the wanton slaying of Fred Hampton, the Black Panther leader in Chicago who was riddled with police bullets in his bed during a December 1969, nighttime raid on his apartment, but "Off the pig!" rang harshly in my ears. Though I knew that for centuries in America, whites murdered people of color with impunity, the call for retaliatory violence made me queasy.

But, busy with the work at hand, I kept my reservations to myself. I helped to write press releases that Fay and a small group of volunteers mailed out, hoping to interest the media in the Soledad case and arouse public opinion. The situation certainly was newsworthy, we thought, but reporters usually did not pay much attention to prisons.

As Fay explained it, this was the story: Four years after that judge's decision about Soledad, things had not improved. In the prison's racially tense maximum security section, inmates remained in solitary confinement twenty-three hours a day. Black inmates in particular complained that white guards abused them. On January 13, 1970, guards released an explosive mix of hostile blacks and whites into a new exercise yard. When a melee broke out, a guard shot and killed three of the most politically active blacks. A few days later, Monterey County authorities ruled that the deaths were justifiable homicide.

This ruling incensed the black inmates, who were convinced that deliberate racial murder had been done. That night, a white guard on a prison tier was seized, beaten, and strangled, his body hurled over the railing to the floor below.

Three blacks were accused of killing the guard: George Jackson, John Clutchette, and Fleeta Drumgo. In an era that saw nicknames such as the "Chicago Seven" and "Los Siete," they became known as the "Soledad Brothers." Jackson, the powerhouse of the three, was serving a sentence for holding up a gas station eleven years before. A militant Black Panther with a long record of prison infractions, he was unlikely ever to be released by the parole board. He had become a hero to many black inmates, famous for his ability to do thousands of fingertip pushups, his vast knowledge of revolutionary literature, and his skill in martial arts. He had done seven of the eleven years in solitary; for one year, it was said, he was confined in a cell whose door was welded shut.

Because of his affiliation with the Panthers, Jackson's case came to the attention of Panther leader Huey P. Newton, then also in prison. Fay was one of Newton's defense lawyers, and it was at his request that she took on Jackson as a client.

A radical lawyer from Berkeley in her early forties, Fay Stender had a talent for organizing. She drew people to her, convinced them of the justice of her cause, then she enlisted their devotion, their money, and their time. Whatever she was engaged in, she made it seem vitally important. She played arpeggios on white liberal guilt.

Energy and passion, ideas and plans tumbled from her brain and her voice in a nonstop stream. But she was complicated, torn between the harsh morality of the New Left that denounced comfort, fashion, and wealth and her own desire for those very things. She was taken with the panache of her blue sports car and pleased by the gourmet dinners bought for her by a lawyer colleague. And there were troubling aspects of her personality that I didn't see until later.

Fay grew up in Chicago as a smart, awkward, Jewish girl trained to become a concert pianist. But for all her intelligence, she never quite knew how to act in a social situation. She walked into a party slightly wobbling on her high heels, one shoulder hunched a little lower than the other, springy black hair pulled back from her face. Her dark eyes scanning like radar, she singled out anyone present who might advance her cause. Ever the strategist, she wooed the entrepreneur who might give money or the reporter who could write an article or the campaign contributor who might be persuaded to lean on a politician. She arranged for a few vocal black California lawmakers to visit Soledad and hold a press conference, she got Lillian Hellman and other prominent people to make statements and be interviewed.

I had never seen anything like this before and I had no idea what I was getting into. In fact, by the time this adventure had run its course, many people—prisoners, guards, and others—would have lost their lives.

As a naive newcomer to political action, I made a perfect sidekick. Besides, I had good manners and I could write—two skills Fay needed in her campaign. She took me with her to prisons, to meetings with anyone who could help us. We explained how the defense of the Soledad Brothers would expose the evils of the prison system while acquitting three innocent black men. This worthy mission appealed to my new politics as well as to the ethic of service to the less fortunate that had been expounded at Garrison and Bryn Mawr. There may even have been a hint of influence from Lewie, who had served as a dollar-a-year public defender in New York's criminal courts. And there was excitement on all sides: risks from associating with desperate convicts as well as from prison authorities who powerfully resented any intruders into their walled-off domain.

Aware that she would have to organize support if she were to succeed in the prison defense, Fay pulled together a small group of old leftists, young radicals, and relatives of inmates. We organized meetings, mailings, and rallies. A few articles about the case began to appear in alternative publications—the underground press—including my stories in the *Good Times*—and the Socialist weekly, *People's World*. Fay was smart and tireless; the story was dramatic, more good lawyers joined the defense team; soon we were rolling.

Not surprisingly, my family looked askance at my new activities. My mother said it was all very well to work with poor black people, but I should work with young children, not prisoners who were too far gone to be rehabilitated. On a visit to New York, I stopped to see my Aunt Goody, my mother's sister. To my amazement, I saw on her coffee table a copy of *To Serve the Devil*, the book I had worked on with Paul and Saul. "Goody, I'm so pleased and surprised to see this in your house," I said, sipping sherry in her Upper East Side apartment.

"I'm loyal to my family, so I bought your book," she answered crisply. "And I'm loyal to my politics, so I'll never read it."

Though deep down, of course, I wanted their approval, I didn't expect my family to understand or support what I was doing. Neither of my parents seemed upset when I left Herb. I remember telephoning my mother with the news from a pay phone on the way to a court hearing in Salinas; she did not seem surprised, nor did she offer support or assistance. She did assume, however, that I would move back east where I belonged and make a more suitable second marriage.

I had told her and Clarry a little bit about my involvement in the prison case, leaving out of course anything about the *Good Times* and the Marxist professor. I downplayed my new-found politics, which Clarry did not like at all. When I was visiting his house, after he had had several drinks, he said, in a kindly, slurred voice, "You're all right, dear, but you're a little *pink*."

Every now and then, astonished at my new priorities and friends, I would stop and wonder how I had gotten myself into such an unlikely situation. And every now and then, some aspect of this new life would confuse and baffle me. Though I admired Fay, some of her behavior was upsetting and puzzling. One incident took place when I was still Mrs. McLaughlin in my Pacific Heights mansion. At her request, I hosted a meeting of some people involved in the Soledad Brothers' defense. About six of us sat in my library lined with the color-coordinated books, prepared to discuss press releases and assign tasks. Early in the meeting, however, Fay and a young woman she knew from the defense committee said they had to go upstairs for a moment. They went up, and they didn't come back. They didn't come back, and they didn't come back. The rest of us sat there, making conversation, even making a few plans, but essentially waiting. Without Fay we could decide nothing.

I couldn't imagine what was going on. What were they doing? Fay was our leader and I had been brought up never to be rude to leaders or to guests, for that matter. But the time was ticking away and the two women were still upstairs. After a while even sidekicks and hostesses get annoyed.

So I climbed the stairs and listened. Fay and the young woman were in Herb's and my bedroom giggling. Furious, I knocked on the door. I came up with a rather lame pretext for disturbing them, saying, "There is a pillow in there and I need it." The door opened and a pillow was thrown out. The giggling resumed. *What* were they doing? It didn't sound like a meeting to me, not at all. I stumped downstairs, bewildered, hurt, and resentful.

Finally they came down, clothing a little mussed, grins on their faces. Our meeting resumed for a few moments and then everyone left. No one said a word about their prolonged absence.

Although I had already met some lesbians at Glide Church, it took me awhile to figure out just what Fay and her young friend had been up to. Fay was a married woman with two children, and I was so naive that I couldn't readily jump to the right conclusion—that Fay was bisexual, and they were lovers.

I did realize that she had taken advantage of me. And on my bed—that was distasteful. But it wasn't the same-sex sex that troubled me—it was her violation of my hospitality. I had been proud to host a defense committee meeting, and now she had ruined it—I felt frustrated and powerless all over again. But I was so in awe of Fay and so caught up with the Soledad Brothers and the drama of our cause that I never questioned her about it, then or later. If I told her that her behavior had been outrageous, that she had hurt my feelings and abused my hospitality, she might drop me. Maybe I was just uptight. I was afraid to lose the excitement, the morally superior thrill of my revolutionary politics and my new friends. Even in this situation so far removed from Whitehackle Farm and Old Westbury, I didn't dare speak my mind.

Early in the organizing process, Fay gathered a meeting of activists from Monterey, a town near the prison. While most of them, like me, were mobilizing to prevent three innocent black prisoners from being railroaded, one pleasant-faced young man said he had come to the meeting because he thought they *had* killed the guard. He wanted to see such a brave, revolutionary act defended. I was surprised and troubled by the man's reasoning; by all accounts, the murdered guard had been rather a nice guy. But the young activist had been a radical for longer than I had so again, afraid to seem wishy-washy, I kept my concerns to myself.

I was troubled by a split between our public posture—defend the innocent blacks while exposing the evil prison system—and a secret, private agenda—use the case as a means of organizing support for a revolutionary movement. Tell the truth about the prison system—but play down anything that would hurt our cause.

More and more, as I saw how corrupt the legal system was, my sense of moral outrage trumped my personal misgivings. In the legal maneuvering before the Soledad Brothers went to trial, their defense lawyers needed to interview potential prisoner witnesses to the killing of the guard. But correctional officials swiftly transferred these witnesses to many other prisons in the system, then made it extraordinarily difficult for the defense lawyers to find and interview them. We heard of authorities threatening inmates with longer terms if they talked, while offering early release for those inmates who refused to be interviewed.

The Soledad Brothers trial was transferred up from Salinas to San Francisco, and the three accused were moved to San Quentin, across the bay from the city. George Jackson and I corresponded in order to arrange a meeting. We pretended in our letters that we had known each other before he was arrested so that I could meet the conditions necessary to get on his list of approved visitors. I was approved.

The day came that I was to go through the gates of San Quentin, so many worlds away from the gates of Tuxedo Park. Upon arriving, I sat for several minutes in my car in the sun-baked parking lot. I was frightened, anxious about possible confrontations with prison officials, and exceedingly aware of my past. How would Topsy the Debutante be received by this revolutionary black convict? But I wasn't that Topsy any more, so I took a deep breath and walked up to the entrance gate.

I passed through the metal detector and the initial screening into the visiting room. But once there, I was summoned to the office of an associate warden. I knew this was not the usual routine. Terrified that George's and my little ruse that we were old friends had been discovered, and of what might happen to me, I went in quaking. But the kindly middle-aged man behind the desk spoke only of his concern for my safety. Jackson was dangerous, he warned, and I would be wise to have a special security officer standing nearby throughout our conversation in case the prisoner attacked. Wondering whether I was taking a terrible risk, I summoned enough presence of mind to refuse his offer and insist on a regular visit. Nonetheless, a strange mental gymnastic had taken place. The warden, the pillar of society, felt like the enemy; the prisoner, the outlaw I had yet to meet, like my ally.

I was escorted into a large, sunny room. Long tables ran across it, separating prisoners from their visitors. George, who had been seated, rose to greet me. He smiled, extended his hand, and began, like a good host, to put me at ease. "I know you. I have a picture of you in my cell," he said. Someone had sent him a photo of me at a rally. We talked about prisons, about the situation of blacks, about what he considered the existence of fascism in the United States. George punctuated his conversation by tapping my hand with his finger to emphasize a point. After a while, he took out a pair of spectacles, put them on, and studied my face.

I studied back. He was huge, with the most impressive physique I have ever seen. His biceps strained against his prison denim shirt. He was handsome, with a wide grin and lively eyes. Emotion followed emotion across his mobile features as he strained to communicate, to make me know some of what he knew so that I would leave San Quentin a changed person.

I didn't understand all that he was saying—literally. I had trouble making out the words spoken by black people who do not speak like whites, but I was too embarrassed at first to admit this and just nodded politely. He smoked nonstop, pulling the filters off the cigarettes I had brought him.

Other prisoners and their visitors occupied the tables around us. Most of them looked listless or desperate, their faces lined with worry. I imagined overdue rents, cars and houses about to be repossessed, kids in trouble, anxious mothers. George—who was called "The Comrade" by his allies—seemed different: vital, outgoing, purposeful. A few men greeted him; he responded, usually with a raised fist and a smile.

My nervousness, my fear of black men, my fear of prisoners—these began to fade as we talked. Along with his revolutionary intensity, the man was charming, asking me about my life and telling me about his. After an hour, a guard tapped him on the shoulder and said, "Time's up." George spoke a couple of minutes more and then rose to leave. We reached to shake hands across the table but fumbled hands instead—I was doing the ordinary grip and he was doing the revolutionary kind. Awkwardness hung between us. I watched as he walked out a metal door back toward his cell. "Walk on out, miss," a guard ordered. I obeyed.

Other visits followed. George asked about my experiences with black people. I told him that the only blacks I had seen much of were employed on my stepfather's farm or in my father's kitchen. "If I worked in your stable when you were growing up," he asked with a smile, "Would we have made love?" I was taken aback. "The closest you would have gotten to me would have been to hold my stirrup while I was mounting my horse."

He laughed at that, but he grew serious as I described the attitudes with which I was raised and my own prejudices. He was the first black person I had ever really talked to. At the end of that interview, he kissed me. "That's the first time I was ever kissed by a black man," I told him. Wide, wide grin. "It is! Well, I better do it right, then." He gave me an enormous bear hug, a longer kiss. Enveloped in his powerful arms, I relaxed my body into his. And quickly pulled back, aware that we were in a visiting room and watched by guards. But it had been a wonderful, intimate, moment.

Through the letters and visits, affection grew between us. George liked to touch my hand, to stroke my arm, and I liked it, too. It felt as though he were trying to take me into his skin. I savored the romance of being with a warrior, a man on the front lines delighting in the company of a woman while enlisting her in his cause. He was powerful, and he knew it. Once, he signed a letter "Milestiba." I asked him what it meant. He wrote,

Milestiba—I felt a deep thrill of milestiba at our last meeting. I learned 50 ways to say 'love' in 50 languages, that's just one way folks express it somewhere that escapes me now. I wander around that way often, terrible waste of time for a guerrilla, but perhaps I'm not all guerrilla. Or more properly, maybe guerrillas get to be guerrillas through such 'great feelings.' Che said that.

George wanted to know about my sons. On another trip to Bermuda with my father, my son Daniel, who was then ten, encountered a group of black boys who made him get off his bike while they rode it around for a while. While playing at the park in San Francisco, he had been frightened by run-ins with gangs of black boys. He told me that he was worried about becoming a racist. I suggested that he write George about it. He did, and the following correspondence ensued.

Dear Dan,

I advise you not to take the encounters that you will continue to have with Black boys personally. It will never be a case of personal dislike for Dan. It must be understood as a case of unconscious frustrations or anger for the general conditions of their day to day lives. They are too young to know that the enemy is really a system. And that it is the system that creates the contradictions.

I would try to explain myself if I were you. But you must learn to defend yourself from unreasonable attacks. At the end of the fight, if you are sincere, and whether you win or lose, if you are sincere there may be a better atmosphere for talk and explanations.

People must respect each other, and I'm afraid I'll have to be truthful and warn you that often you will find the flying side-thrust more of a peacemaker than words.

George

That letter, accompanied with a crudely drawn illustration of the flying karate attack, frightened Daniel. He wrote:

Dear George,

I am 4 feet 8 inches tall. I weigh 70 pounds. You expect me to fight against 5 guys who are bigger than me. I do not think it would improve communications, only get me beaten up. I have taken karate for four months. Getting beaten up is not worth a bicycle. I cannot take your advice. About my being scared of blacks, only blacks have attempted to mug me, never a white.

My mother says that my generation is the hope of the future. What do you think she means?

> Yours almost in the struggle,
> Daniel

George answered:

Dear Dan,

You're 4 feet 8 inches tall and weigh 70 pounds. I knew that. But consider this, what if you stopped growing right now? If my advice was bad, you would have to live the rest of your life buying new bikes.

I've been outnumbered 9 to 1 all my life. Now people have taken things from me. I've lost a very great deal—but they took it at some risk of losing what they had. I'm afraid it's not a very nice place that we live in. The new relationships your mother referred to have yet to be built. . . .

The Blacks figure that since they have been mugged and seen their parents mugged by big white men, it's all right to mug you—turn-about as fair play. You understand. When it happens to you, try to avoid violence by offering one a ride, or start a new conversation about China's new missiles, something elevating.

But again, if you met a bear somewhere, would you let him eat you?

Daniel never wrote to George again.

I had a scare myself. The Soledad Brothers Defense Committee, set up by Fay, raised some money and rented an office in Berkeley. The all-volunteer staff consisted of three white women, including me. I had not been aware how strongly the black families of the accused prisoners resented us, but on our second day there, three large black men in berets, black leather jackets, and gloves stormed in. In menacing tones, they told us to get out, they grabbed our paperwork and threw it around, and they ordered us to cease operations. Terrified, we fled to Fay's law office as the men took away the meager furnishings we had assembled. I was upset that our well-meant efforts provoked such a bitter response and at being the target of racial anger. We closed the office.

George apologized to me afterward, explaining that such misunderstandings were inevitable in a nation where blacks and whites grew up in an environment poisoned by racism. I accepted what he said but nonetheless resented the way that our black "brothers in the struggle" had driven us off.

Racism had dominated the life of his younger brother, Jonathan, a tall, intense seventeen-year-old with a light brown Afro who was obsessed with seeing George go free. As a high school student, Jonathan had played hooky to observe the workings of courts in Los Angeles where he lived, and he became convinced that blacks could never obtain justice.

I had been in my new apartment for a month when, one August Friday, word spread that Jonathan was involved in a kidnap attempt gone wrong, and several people had been killed at the Marin County courthouse just north of San Quentin. I was horrified to learn that Jonathan, the quiet, well-mannered teenager, might be among the dead.

In fact, he had set off the slaughter. Concealing several guns under a short raincoat and in a flight bag, he entered a courtroom where a San Quentin prisoner was on trial for stabbing a guard. Several other inmates were on hand to be called as witnesses. Rising to his feet as the court session began, Jonathan announced, "This is it, gentlemen. Everybody freeze." Demanding freedom for the Soledad Brothers and an airplane to take them to Cuba, he passed out guns to the inmates, took five hostages including the judge, and loaded them all into a yellow van. But as the van drove away, a group of San Quentin guards along the roadway opened fire; one of the hostages in the van grabbed a pistol and started shooting at the inmates inside. When it was over, Jonathan, the judge, and two inmates were dead. Three others were wounded.

I'm surprised now that I didn't pull out of prison work immediately, shocked by so much blood, death, and horror. The plan reeked of craziness in the name of revolution, the fruit of slogans like "off the pig" and "by any means possible." Was this what I was heading toward, being involved with George Jackson's defense? This was not what I had signed up for.

But I could see that the death and blood, as the federal judge had predicted years ago, followed, at least in part, from cruel and inhuman prison practices. Jonathan, "the man-child," as George called him, seemed to me like a desperate revolutionary downed in an attempt to ransom his doomed brother. It wasn't that I wished any evil to the judge or the other officials, but, as I saw it then, they were part of an oppressive system that deserved to be overthrown. I wanted to do my part in overthrowing that system by helping to empower the oppressed, but however carried away I might have been with revolutionary rhetoric, I wasn't going to get involved with things like this.

A few months later, Fay suddenly bowed out of George's defense, leaving her co-counsel in charge. Instead of working on behalf of one individual who was becoming celebrated, she said, she wanted to take on the California prison system and its abusive practices. So, together with a few young lawyers and me, she set up an organization we called the Prison Law Project. We were going to use the law and public education as a means of ending the terrible abuses we were seeing inside the prisons. I was mystified by her about-face and wondered if something was going on that I didn't know about, but soon accepted her rationale and was happy that she invited me to join the new venture. She was my leader, my ticket into this arena of political struggle between good and evil, so I followed along. When we went to make a fundraising pitch to foundations, I was usually part of the group. Because of my ruling-class background, as we called it then, Fay thought my presence would add to the Project's respectability. If it would help, I was happy to use my name and status. While I didn't exactly idolize her, I admired her courage, her smarts, and her commitment to fight for the oppressed. Put less elegantly, I wanted to be with someone who was standing up for the underdog.

As soon as word spread throughout the prisons that a predominantly female group was organizing to file lawsuits on behalf of inmates whose rights had allegedly been violated, letters started flooding in describing beatings, denials of visits, racial harassment, and censorship of books and letters.

Many were like this one from a convict in Folsom Prison who wrote us about a beating. Guards, who were searching the papers of a prisoner returning from a visit with his lawyer, illegally ordered him to leave one envelope behind. The prisoner refused.

> 'Thud, Thud, Thud.' I heard the Prisoner's first cry of pain, followed by his pleading for the officers to stop their attack, as blow after blow was struck, the sound of the club echoing down the tier, 'Thud, Thud, Thud.' . . . I could hear the other inmates helplessly crying out of their cells to 'Leave the man alone.' Over this I could hear also the jeering voice of one officer hissing: 'Had enough, Nigger? Had enough?'

I felt sorry for the prisoners and furious with the guards. While the lawyers in our group looked into individual cases—like that beating—I helped with correspondence and fundraising, writing articles, and selecting the most powerful letters—such as that one—for a book. Through selling such a book, we hoped to raise money for the Project and to expose to the world the abusive and inhumane conditions in California's maximum security units. If the public knew what was going on, we believed, people would surely be outraged and demand change. We found a publisher.

I had to visit the inmate authors, ask each writer's permission to publish, see whether he wanted his real name used, give him the bad news that he would receive no payment, and explain that the money we made would go to support the Project. On top of all this, I also had to ask him to violate a prison rule: to sign a release authorizing the publication of his letter. (Prison rules forbade inmates from signing anything in the visiting room.)

Quite a daunting agenda, particularly considering that I was a complete stranger to the prisoner-authors, who had nothing to gain but increased harassment by cooperating with me. The Project designated me a legal investigator, which allowed me to go inside and visit inmates. So I drove off to Soledad, San Quentin, and Folsom Prisons, terrified by my assignment but determined to succeed. In a way, I had lived with fears a lot of my life—of being sent to live somewhere else, of horses I could not control, of tongue-lashings from Mummy and Clarry—and I was used to winging it through situations for which I was ill-prepared. Despite being frightened, I had learned that I could get through things. And maybe find a certain pleasure in meeting the challenge. In these odd circumstances, my upper crust training proved useful.

Folsom then was the scariest prison: a gray, dark fortress of a place, which one entered through a creaky iron gate tended by a stooped, old prisoner. In my overheated imagination, he was like a dwarf guarding Bluebeard's castle, or a gnome from a horror movie. I always feared that, once inside that gate, I might never get out.

Almost all the prison letter writers graciously agreed to let their work be published and used their wiles to sign the release without being caught. But the transaction of our business was the least of the experience. No woman that I worked with in those years escaped the power of the visiting room and neither did I. I have never again felt the quality and power of the attention that radiated from those maximum security inmates. They lived in isolation twenty-three hours a day; they had to undergo a humiliating strip search upon leaving their cell blocks, and they had perhaps half an hour with me before guards hustled them back to their cells. For some, it might be years before a woman visited them again. Every atom in their bodies strained to connect with a female from the magic of the world outside.

The prisoner never relaxed his concentration, never deviated from his masculine, protective role. The pigs, he could handle them; the risk of punishment for signing the release, no problem. The only thing that mattered was his time with you. To my surprise, almost all of them acted like gentlemen. Not, of course, like graduates from Mr. de Rham's dancing class, but with a generosity of spirit and an appreciation for the work of the Project that made me feel like their valued ally. I'm sure they were manipulative, too, using their personalities to score a connection with the outside, but I was careful to maintain a businesslike distance.

We women at the Prison Law Project talked about the electric atmosphere of visiting rooms and joked that our theme song ought to be "Ladies Love Outlaws." Erlinda Castro, a colleague, remembers: "Every visit was like a first date, like a drug." A lawyer colleague married an inmate.

I was careful not to become personally involved with prisoners— George being something of an exception, and even there, I was on the outer periphery of what he called his "female army." Fay, his lawyer; Mary Clemmey, his literary agent; Angela Davis, Elaine Brown, and other women from the Black Panther Party, all were closer to him than I was. He needed some of them more than me—Fay and Mary; others were his political and revolutionary comrades, Angela and Elaine, in ways that I was not. Perhaps I was naïve but, so far as I knew, none of his "army" was involved with him sexually. (Somehow, however, despite prison procedures, apparently he did manage to have sex with a young woman named Lynn, who came to my apartment one evening and told me about it. I wasn't jealous; it sounded entirely too risky and complicated.)

Having been isolated so long from society, George was hungry for political discussion. He argued with me about the readiness of the United States for revolution. Steeped in leftist writings, he was convinced that America was on the verge of rebellion—if someone only had the courage to begin, thousands would join up. If he were to escape, for instance, he believed that people would throng to follow him.

Obsessed with Jonathan's failed kidnap attempt and death, George became even more desperate and depressed. He wanted me to bring him weapons, which I refused. I tried to tell him that, however many thousands marched against the Vietnam War, the world out there was not as he believed to it be. He got angry at being contradicted. "You just believe that a nigger can't think," he retorted one day in the late spring of 1971. Afterward, though, he seemed to relent. "Eve, I do need you," he wrote later, asking me to keep visiting him. "You stand out oasis-like in all this stupidity." But other visitors, perhaps trying to act just as revolutionary as he was and to look strong in his eyes, fed his delusion that revolution was just around the corner.

After his autobiography *Soledad Brother* was published, George became famous. He reported that guards tried to beat him more often. Once he bragged that he had killed a dozen people in prison, and this one—the Soledad guard—was the first they had pinned on him. In that strange atmosphere, I didn't know whether to believe him or not. I knew that he felt at total war with society. "The pig is ruthless, and for real," he wrote me. "How I want a chance at his iron ass. I have this diamond-tipped, razor-edged, flaming spear. . . . I *want* to see him squirm and writhe on the business end, bad." He sensed my fear and the confusion I felt when he went on like that. "You don't take my determination serious," he said in another letter. "Regretfully that seems to be the case with most of the people I've encountered over the last year. Then finally when they do, they recoil with a variety of different excuses." He mentioned my nervousness at meeting him and something else he saw: "Confusion. Yours. Are you still trying to decide which of me is the real me?" Of course I was. Charming writer of love letters, stone killer, revolutionary, common criminal—all those, and more. I was drawn to him and afraid of him. He wanted sex and weapons; I wasn't about to provide either one. I didn't want to see any more violence. I had my three children, and whatever else was going on, my loyalty to keep them and myself safe came first.

Over the next few weeks, it became difficult to see George. Sometimes, even with an appointment made and the red tape complied with, I had to wait for hours to see him. Instead of the open visiting room, we were confined in a closet-like space reserved for death row inmates, tiny, dirty rooms like bathrooms without fixtures. The visitor entered from one side and was locked in. Being enclosed in that tomb made me feel anxious, hemmed in, pessimistic.

While George remained locked down behind prison walls, I flew to Pennsylvania—to an environment as different from his as one could imagine. As I always had in the past, I brought the boys east to visit my parents. These visits were like trips back in time. Life at my mother's farm, except for things such as automobiles, electrical appliances, and a few changes in costume, could have been taken from a Jane Austen novel: farmers still tipped their hats to ladies and gentlemen foxhunters trotting by on their horses; afternoon tea was a daily ritual in which neighbors called on one another; and children were sent off to Episcopal boarding schools at the age of thirteen. In this English squire's world, servants "knew their place," though my mother perpetually complained how difficult it was these days to find good household help.

My visit to the horse farm that summer was fraught with more than the usual generational tension. Besides disapproving of the prison work, Mummy found my feminism both misguided and silly, and she hated the way I looked.

At thirty-four, I grew my brown hair long and parted it in the middle the way hippies did; sometimes I wore it in braids. I stopped wearing a bra and let the hair grow on my legs and underarms. Why should I conform to patriarchal standards of beauty? Did men shave *their* underarms? So I threw away my razor and leg wax, happy at being Ms. Natural.

But this small defiance of male standards didn't go over at all with my mother. On those visits, I stayed in my old bedroom downstairs, with its pretty chintz curtains and girlish twin beds. I was getting dressed for dinner one evening when my mother unexpectedly walked in. As I raised my arms to slide into my dress, her eyes flew to my bushy underarms. "You've *forgotten* something!" she said, aghast.

"No, I haven't," I answered. "I just don't shave any more. It's the way we were made."

She wasn't buying. "When we bring a maid to this country from Jamaica, that's the first thing we do, give them a razor and deodorant. It's *civilization!*" she declared, upset and angry. I continued dressing and she walked out.

I questioned whether it showed absence of true political commitment to keep in contact with my wealthy, reactionary parents. One prisoner criticized me roundly for going on a trip to Bermuda with my father. How could I indulge myself in bourgeois pleasures while others suffered? he scolded. I could see his point, but I was not willing to make such a sacrifice for a revolution that seemed far off and theoretical. I was conflicted: moved as I was by the ideals of the movement, at that point, at least, I was not going to give up my secure way of life or break completely from my family.

And besides, too young to care about ideology, my San Francisco sons found many pleasures at "Mam's ranch," as they called the farm. Our old

English Nursie, frail and stooped after thirty years of caring for my brothers and sister and me, kept closets filled with toys for them. She dispensed treats and read stories to the new generation, complaining only that her twisted hands were now so arthritic that she could no longer pick the children up. Tommy, a tiny, good-natured pony with a white mane, grazed in front of the house and graciously allowed the boys to pat him and sit on his back. Black and white sheepdogs trooped in and out of the house in the wake of their god, my stepfather; other dogs fetched sticks for the boys and romped with them. The cook baked them cookies, and an assortment of cousins came over to play.

For them, it was an idyllic vacation—unlike me, they were not split between two worlds and constantly evaluating when to speak out and when to be polite. I enjoyed seeing them so happy. But our vacation ended dramatically on August 21, 1971.

It started out as a benign and lazy summer day. My mother's brilliant green lawn stretched out to fenced-in pastures where sheep and horses grazed in the sun. Sprinklers swished under a leafy maple tree while a gardener trimmed the grass around the swimming pool. On one side of the lawn stood an old stone barn where the thoroughbred brood mares and their foals were stabled. On the other side of the lawn, to the left of a flagstone terrace just off the house, my mother's flower garden bloomed—a cloud of blue delphinium, pale yellow columbine and red Sweet William. From the terrace the view extended down across the pastures, past a large pond at the bottom of our hill, to rolling fields and woods stretching as far as the eye could see.

I was walking across the lawn when Mummy called out, "Phone for you." Hurrying through the French doors into the living room, I picked up the phone at her cluttered antique desk. It was Patti Roberts, a lawyer at the Prison Law Project. "There's bad news," Patti said. "I don't know any more, but something went wrong at Quentin and George is dead."

Time stopped.

While I was talking to Patti, hanging on her every word, the beauty and comfort of my mother's home turned instantly oppressive. I needed to go home. I didn't know it then, but a cellblock deep inside San Quentin was running in blood. Three inmates and three guards were slain in the worst violence ever to occur there. It was almost exactly a year after Jonathan's death.

I got on a plane as fast as I could, flying from my old life back to the new. My mother was appalled that I could be so disturbed by the death of a black convict, someone she would not have hired to groom horses in her barn. After I left, my mother told my sister, "She was so upset, you would think that one of *us* had died."

I went to George's funeral, standing in a long line to view him in his casket. But the face on the satin pillow wasn't George's: it was swollen, thick-featured, and waxen; the product of a mortician reconstructing the face of someone who had been shot in the head. He wore the uniform of a Black Panther field marshal: sky blue sweater, black leather jacket, black beret, and black trousers. Because it was a small church, I couldn't get in for the service so I stood outside, listening as the words and music blared over a loudspeaker. Huey Newton and other Panthers spoke, praising the "revolutionary fight against all oppressors" and George as a fallen leader.

Prison officials claimed that the deaths stemmed from an escape attempt set off by a young lawyer named Stephen Bingham who visited George and smuggled a gun to him. George supposedly hid the weapon in his Afro and walked back into his cell block. A bloody slaughter ensued, in which three guards and two trusties were killed. Three more guards survived despite having their throats cut by convicts wielding a razor embedded in the plastic handle of a toothbrush. Then, as other guards outside that cell block heard noises, they sounded an alarm. George and another prisoner fled through a door into a yard, where George was gunned down. The cell block they left behind was a charnel house.

Stunned and bewildered, with knee-jerk reflexes, we prisoner advocates stoutly defended the inmates. Using autopsy records, I worked with a wild-haired old lawyer named Ernie Graves on an article aimed at proving that prison authorities had executed George with a pistol shot to the head as he lay wounded in the prison yard. Parsing the prison spokesman's contradictory statements, we argued that it was impossible to smuggle a gun through San Quentin security, and that a guard must have brought the weapon in, planning to assassinate George. The guard's plot then went terribly wrong, resulting in the subsequent loss of life.

Bingham disappeared the afternoon Jackson died; we maintained that he fled not in guilt but in justifiable fear for his life because of the way prison officials blamed the violence on attorneys who represented prisoners. At the request of some friends, I secretly gave money to help him get away.

Several months later, I was horrified to find in some office files a copy of the surviving guards' grand jury testimony. In those pages, the men testified that Jackson had indeed pulled a gun from his hair and taken control of the unit. They told in excruciating detail how the convicts had murdered the guards, one by one, as they pleaded for mercy, then piled them on top of each other in a bloody heap. Maybe, I thought, it had happened like that. The testimony about prisoners sawing on jugular veins with nail clippers was as horrifying as it was explicit. Was this "killing the oppressor" and "rising up against the slave-master?"

I could not reflect deeply on the implications of these deaths. I thought then that this was the dark side of revolution; it was warfare, it was a code of behavior outside the mainstream, the brutalized exacting retribution.

I think about a passage from one of George's letters to me:

> I'll never be much different than I am now—amoral, starved, calculative, threatened, defensive sometimes.... In no sense of the society's mores would I be considered a nice person. I really don't try at all.... I love you, not so easy when you confessed to being racist. I'll have to die one day because of racism, it made me less than what I might have been. It killed at least one of my close friends per month, my brother. But you didn't come with the artificial lines so popular with the rest. I've tried real hard to train love out of my being/action, I failed. I forget who said it, but he was Black, 'I have always loved, I will always love.' Tenderness is my favorite side; it's the only one you will ever see.

George's madness, his propensity to violence, his manipulations and pleas for weapons were real. He inhabited a psychopathic world of murder, betrayal, and brutality behind the walls, and he could be very scary. He lusted for freedom and for revenge.

But I loved George's tender side, his expressions of affection across the bounds of color and class, his interest in who I was and who I was becoming. I was open to his masculinity—the muscular body, the force of will and the easy charm. He made me feel like a real woman—not the lady I had been trained to be, but a female comrade in the struggle against oppression. It was heady stuff, this closeness with a man so vastly different from the other men in my life. If he could value me, as I believed he did, then maybe I was more of a person than I had previously suspected.

CHAPTER THIRTEEN

Complications

In the middle of the road of my life
I awoke in the dark wood
where the true way was wholly lost

—Dante, Divine Comedy

The first copy of my prison letters book and my final divorce decree arrived in the very same mail. Out with the old, in with the new, I thought, feeling pleased with myself. But the new was more complicated than I had expected.

From the beginning, I believed that what prisoners said about guards was basically true. Though I didn't think of myself as a propagandist, I focused my writing on the cruelty of the guards and the prison system while minimizing the sins of the prisoners. This would come back to bite me later.

I didn't fully understand that I was living in a treacherous environment. For example, in the world of prison gangs, informants, plots, and vengeance in which I now found myself, information could be a lethal commodity. We in "the Movement" believed that FBI and state agents listened in on our phone conversations and infiltrated our groups. As it turned out, those suspicions were more truth than paranoia: years later, Congressional hearings revealed that the FBI ran a program called COINTELPRO set up to fracture leftist political organizations. Agents planted informants and provocateurs as they devised strategies to turn one group of activists against another, sometimes with murderous consequences.

A few politically active people who knew too much turned up dead. In 1975, a bookkeeper who worked for the Black Panthers was found in San Francisco Bay. A kindly, well-intentioned woman, Betty Van Patter used her skills to help the Panthers achieve the social goals they said they were seeking. But she was killed, most likely because she discovered financial dealings that the party wanted to keep hidden.

The burned body of Fred Bennett, a Panther I had seen at rallies and court hearings, was found in the Santa Cruz Mountains. And, of course, the violence behind bars continued, with both prisoners and guards as victims.

In this highly charged atmosphere, some activists lost their heads. With women, perhaps it was the vulnerability of caged and shackled men, perhaps the sexual energy of the visiting room, perhaps the convicts' revolutionary rhetorical heroics that combined so strangely with their loneliness and suffering. Or maybe it was the intoxication of trying to topple class and racial divides in the struggle for a better society that uprooted them from their better judgment. A divorced mother from an East Coast background like mine fell in love with a black ex-con and put up her house for his bail. When he fled after trying to knock over a 7/Eleven, she lost her house and custody of her kids. Having left a marriage that felt like a prison, I was not about to risk my children or my newfound freedom by falling for an inmate.

I saw Fay let her sexuality loose again. We drove together one morning to Folsom. I had letter writers to visit for my book; she had a client to interview. We were assigned adjoining visiting rooms just off the captain's office. The lower wall sections of these rooms were built of wood just to a height of three or four feet, the higher sections were made of glass. Fay was meeting with Earl Satcher, a hard-line black revolutionary with a bodybuilder's physique. From where I sat, I could see him and Fay talking.

But, as I glanced over a few moments later, things got weird. Fay and Satcher moved their chairs closer and closer together, slumping lower and lower. After a while, she was necking with him, their contorted bodies as close as they could get, huddled down to avoid being seen. I couldn't believe it. If I could see them, so could the captain. Fay and Satcher continued their necking for several minutes.

Bolting from his office, the irate captain threw open the door to their interview room and reprimanded Fay. "Unprofessional . . . disorderly . . . bad for inmates," he scolded, forcefully escorting her from the room. She patted her hair down with her hands, looking frazzled. Satcher was hustled back to his cell.

As we drove back, I was still too unsure of myself to ask her what the hell she had been doing; I sat tense and silent. Much as I hated to be on the side of the authorities, I didn't like her behavior at all. By that behavior, she was jeopardizing the work we were doing, casting doubt on our motivations, and perhaps falling under the influence of the inmate. But she was still the authority figure whose approval I needed, and at that point, feeling quite new to politics and activism, I remained her compliant sidekick.

Eventually, however, I had to stand up to Fay. After George Jackson was shot trying to escape from San Quentin, all of us at the Prison Law Project except Fay wanted to support and defend the six prisoners who had been charged with murdering the three guards and two trusties who also were killed that day. This issue crystallized what had been a growing issue. Although our group had been organized as a collective, with group decision making the rule, Fay had been making all the decisions herself. All along, she dictated what cases we would take, who would be hired, and what lawyers we would work with. A young lawyer named Patti Roberts turned into Fay's harshest critic, accusing her of violating our pact by failing to consult with the rest of us.

As the dissension grew, Fay became even more authoritarian. Patti was banned from the office literally, Fay told her to work from home. In some ways, Fay reminded me of my mother: arbitrary, take-charge, energetic, and self-absorbed. She made me feel secure as she took me under her wing, but as time went on I got the swing of this new collective ethos and grew closer to my co-workers. Fay's behavior in the office struck me as duplicitous, giving lip service to the "revolutionary" way of working while still acting as a boss. The group divided into pro- and anti-Fay factions. I had to decide where my loyalties lay. As weeks went by, I crossed the mother figure and went with the "anti's."

The problem was, Fay had raised all the money for the Prison Law Project, she wasn't about to give us any, and we had exactly nothing. How, if we separated from her, could we continue our work? The answer, we decided, was larceny.

One Sunday morning, we borrowed an old truck. We would liberate the necessary equipment and set up shop in my large, unused basement on Divisadero Street. It was a Keystone Kops operation—the rickety truck we borrowed boiled over, so our heist got off to a late start. Then, as we packed up and loaded more and more of the Project's furniture and typewriters and phones, I became queasier and queasier. The idea had been to take half of everything, rather like California's community property law in the case of divorce; but it seemed to me that we were taking too much. "Shouldn't we leave them some stuff?" I inquired, feeling like a mushy liberal. "Don't be such a chickenshit," scolded one of my partners in crime. I shut up.

Finally, the truck piled high, we drove to my house and unloaded the spoils. I was thrilled with what we had done but petrified of what would ensue; I had never defied authority in such a flagrant way in all my life. We had stolen thousands of dollars worth of equipment! But, given the shared attitude among radicals that the police were "pigs" and agents of the evil ruling class, we did not expect Fay would call in the law. Nor did she. The next day, one of Fay's assistants left a wry message on my answering machine. "Thanks for leaving us the mail," he said.

In an effort to negotiate a settlement, Fay and I began a conversation about the rift. But the discussion ended in recriminations, and we were never again on speaking terms. Later, a sort of divorce and property division was worked out between the two factions, and we were able to raise some money to go on. We named our group the Prison Law Collective in recognition of our everyone-is-equal form of organization.

What was never discussed in this drama was the daunting issue of the violence that had erupted in the prisons and outside, violence that essentially had led to the splintering of our group. We didn't confront the issue of prisoners' killing guards; we went along with the "revolution by any means necessary" rhetoric, blinding ourselves to the moral concerns or dismissing these concerns as "bourgeois." In the San Quentin escape attempt, for example, whether or not the authorities had correctly singled out the Six for prosecution, someone had hacked away at the victims' throats in a barbaric slaughter and someone had turned a gun on the guards. Did we really think that was the right thing to do? Yet as a group, the Prison Law Project split, not over the morality of violence, but over the abstract political principles of collective versus hierarchical decision making.

Our new group continued to investigate complaints and file lawsuits on behalf of prisoners who claimed that guards did things such as beat them up, subject them to arbitrary punishment, or deny needed health care. My book of letters, *Maximum Security*, was banned from the prisons, which meant that the inmate writers were forbidden to read their own works.

The Collective didn't stay long in my basement. My son John, who was then four, became terribly ill with encephalitis: the disease destroyed his sense of balance and impaired some of his brain function. He was hospitalized and suffered through painful spinal taps. Those were awful days: the doctors were helpless; they could only wait to see the disease run its course. Panicked that he would not recover fully, and superstitious that his illness was God's punishment to me for leaving Herb, I was frantic. Despite her sermonizing on the importance of "family," my mother did not come to help.

After several days in the hospital, John came home. He had to wear a football helmet padded with Kotex so that if he fell, he would not injure his head. He hated having the Collective staff in the basement, and, for a few days, he walked from desk to desk, a tiny figure topped by the enormous helmet, ordering the Collective members, "Go away! Go somewhere else." Understanding my predicament, the staff found office space and moved out. Slowly, John recovered, and when he was better, I went back to work.

This is a peculiar place to bring in a Victorian children's book, but it helps to explain what was going on in my head. I had read *Editha and the Burglar* when I was small. In the story, a little girl from a rich family, Editha, hears a noise downstairs in her house at night, when everyone else is asleep. Padding downstairs in her white nightie, blonde ringlets down around her shoulders, she encounters a burglar stuffing things into his sack. She sits on the stair and asks what he is doing there. The two of them get to talking and somehow, entranced by her purity, virtue, and trusting nature, the burglar, instead of bopping her over the head or stuffing her into the sack, decides to reform and live a good life forevermore. As the book ends, Editha goes safely back upstairs to bed while he climbs out the window, determined now to follow the straight and narrow path. This rather silly story had somehow taken root in my psyche and made me believe that criminals wouldn't hurt me.

That feeling must have been in full force one Saturday evening when my doorbell rang. It was late, the boys were at Herb's, and I was home alone. I went to the door and looked out. There stood Sugar, a convict I knew who had been recently paroled from prison and whom we had helped with some legal problems. A relatively young guy with a cute face and a reputation as a punk (a slight man who is used by stronger prisoners for sex, and who, in exchange, is protected from being raped by others) Sugar had been out for several weeks and was living in San Francisco. Somewhat anxiously, I let him in. He wanted to spend the night at my house. He showed me his gun.

I am not sure what a normal person would have done in those circumstances, but a normal person would probably not have been affected by the story of Editha and the burglar. Like Editha, I didn't think Sugar would hurt me. I gave him some dinner. I said he could spend the night in one of the boy's bunk beds, but only if he gave me the gun. He handed it over, cold, metallic, and heavier than I expected. I never asked if it was loaded. After dinner, he lay down on Daniel's lower bunk bed, hands folded on his chest like a laid-out corpse, fully dressed and on top of the blanket. So far as I knew, he never moved all night long.

I hid the gun in the kitchen cupboard, up behind the Cheerios, and went to bed myself, though I don't think I slept a wink. In the morning, I gave him some of the Cheerios for breakfast and returned his gun. He thanked me politely and went off, never to appear on my doorstep again.

But scarier experiences began to show us the true nature of some of our prisoner allies. Soon after his release, Earl Satcher, the black bodybuilder who had necked with Fay under the captain's nose at Folsom, went on a rampage of extortion and thuggery in San Francisco. He shot and killed a black ex-con named Popeye Jackson, who was organizing a union of prisoners, and Popeye's schoolteacher companion. Shortly after that, Satcher himself was killed in a shootout.

A white convict client of ours escaped from Folsom. After he was captured, he lied to prison officials about our work, accusing us of preaching violence and stirring up trouble inside. Whether he was a plant from the start or just trying to get brownie points from his captors after he was caught, we never knew.

Given his behavior, as well as Satcher's, I began to wonder how well we in the prison movement understood the people we were working with. A jailhouse lawyer whom we helped to get paroled and had taken into our group turned out to be a junkie. I felt disappointed, defrauded, and naïve. Fay wasn't all that she had seemed to be, and these "revolutionary" prisoners weren't, either.

Around this time, I heard disquieting rumors about Fay's puzzling and abrupt resignation from the Soledad Brothers defense. One: Carried away by the spirit of the times, she had once said something that led George to think that she might help him escape. But when he asked for tangible assistance, she refused. Two: George had demanded that royalties from his book go for the arming of ex-convict guerrillas who were hiding out in the Santa Cruz Mountains. Again, Fay refused. Well aware of both his reputation for violence and the fierce loyalty some black prisoners felt for him, she quit, terrified that, like the bookkeeper who wound up in San Francisco Bay, she might be marked for retaliation. I didn't like either version.

As the disappointments continued, frightening revelations grew, and funding dried up, I resigned from the Prison Law Collective. Taking on the prison system was uphill work at best, even with my illusions intact. It was worse when so many of those we helped turned out to be genuinely bad guys or so damaged that they could not function outside prison walls. Contrary to revolutionary rhetoric, oppression did not necessarily transform the downtrodden into capable leaders of the revolution.

In the midst of these confusing experiences, my personal life took a happy turn. I met Mark Dowie, a tall, handsome fellow who ran an outfit that found jobs for ex-prisoners. ("Hire a man with convictions," quipped a friend.) An outdoorsman who climbed mountains and backpacked, he had left a promising career at the Bank of America to join the prison movement. He even liked the idea of a ready-made family with me and my three boys. Besides, he was funny and sexy, with a delicious ability to enjoy life.

After the Marxist professor, I had had a few relationships, and I was getting better at defining my wants and needs. He seemed perfect.

I thought he was the un-Herb: easygoing, politically left, and not chauvinist. He seemed to respect my work as activist and writer, and the journey I was making to become my own person. He didn't expect me to become his sidekick. We moved into an apartment directly across the street from Herb's house on Broadway that Mark's sister was moving out of. The place was huge and airy, and it was easy for the boys to go back and forth between parents.

But such proximity to my ex-husband and ex-house became too weird; we bought a house in Mill Valley, across the Golden Gate Bridge. The new place was in a good public school district for John, and it was near the private school Daniel and Peter attended. Mark quit working with prisoners; I set out to become a real reporter and work for my own goals—not those of my mother or Clarry, or Herbie, or even Paul or Saul or Fay. Paul promised to find work for me at a new magazine he was involved with, *Mother Jones,* but, though I applied, I never even got an interview. I was downcast, and it didn't help our marriage when the magazine offered Mark a job as business manager. In 1977, I turned forty.

I had some success as a free-lancer. I was writing articles about Wendy Yoshimura, the Japanese-American woman arrested with Patty Hearst in 1975, after Hearst, who had been kidnapped by the Symbionese Liberation Army, became a member and helped the group hold up a bank. The SLA was on the run, hiding from the law. Wendy was on the run from the law herself, having fled after police found explosives in the Berkeley garage that she and her radical activist boyfriend rented. At the request of some sympathizers who had helped her get away, Wendy befriended Hearst and lived with her.

The radical boyfriend, who had been convicted and done his time, wanted to manage Wendy's defense even though she now wanted nothing to do with him. Angry at me because he thought I was prejudicing her against him, he drove to Marin and hurled a brick through a window of my house. The brick landed on John's bed, covering it with shards of glass. John wasn't hurt because he was in school at the time, but I was terrified. This man was huge and furious, and who knew what he would do next?

Because of my political beliefs—that the police were enemies—I couldn't very well go to them to ask for help or to turn him in. My friend from the Prison Law Collective, Erlinda Castro, came up with an idea. The brick thrower was white and, as a professed revolutionary, shared the notion that black and brown people possessed an advanced consciousness because of the discrimination they suffered in a racist society. In this particular hierarchy, where bourgeois whites ranked toward the bottom, black and brown ex-prisoners with revolutionary politics carried immense moral authority, perhaps the highest of all.

Erlinda, as a brown woman and the daughter of farm workers, was similarly imbued with political cachet. She called together a meeting to resolve the issue. She summoned Willie Tate, who was black, and Luis Talamantez, who was brown, two of the San Quentin Six. Both had been acquitted after a long trial and released from prison. They had formidable reputations for the firmness of their political principles as well as their dexterity in navigating the fearsome world of prison gangs.

We sat around a table: Erlinda, Willie Tate, Luis at the head of the table, the brick thrower and one of his friends looking like miscreant schoolboys, and me. Luis spoke softly. Looking the culprit in the eye, he said, "Eve is our very good friend. If anything should happen to her, we would be upset. And we would have to come to her defense." The brick thrower hung his head, acknowledged that he had done wrong and apologized. The whole thing took about a minute.

After that, I had no further trouble.

My life at that time was far removed, it seemed, from the violence that had marked the early '70s. I had mixed feelings as I looked back at the prison activism: although the work on behalf of the Soledad Brothers and the Prison Law groups raised public awareness of terrible abuses and helped to ease conditions in a few situations, it seemed to have had no lasting positive effect. The revolution, which had seemed so possible in the late '60s, was plainly not going to happen, and our rhetoric back then seemed to me to have been overblown, pompous, and divorced from reality. I was all too aware that the American Friends Service Committee, the Quakers, had been trying to bring about prison reform decades before Fay and the rest of us came on the scene. Although we disparaged them as "liberals" instead of "radicals" like us in the "vanguard" when we came on the scene, they were hard at work when we left, and they are still there today. While prisons cried out for reform, I concluded, our tactics had failed. We had the right target but our approach was based on faulty premises. It was embarrassing to remember slogans like "The black prisoner is the vanguard of the revolution!" that we had so blindly accepted. In hindsight, I still believe that most everything that prisoners say about guards is true. But, after those experiences of the '70s, I have come to believe that most everything the guards say about prisoners is true, too.

I felt a little like Goldilocks: the upper crust was too cold, and the far Left too hot. I couldn't find a comfortable spot or a voice that felt genuine in either situation. I took refuge in marriage and family.

As my boys grew, I continued writing on other topics. Mark and I took up running and I planted a vegetable garden. Most of our friends were activists and reporters, and I continued to meet with my women's group who became—and still are—my closest friends.

Also, I became active in the American Civil Liberties Union and Delancey Street, an organization that rehabilitates ex-cons and addicts. In my former, more extreme period, I regarded both of these groups as "soft" and "liberal," too-willing compromisers with bourgeois society. Now, I saw them as effective groups working for social justice, and I was glad to pitch in.

My personal life felt more calm and content than ever before. But in the midst of this tranquility, violence struck again, horribly. Late on a May night in 1979, a black man shoved his way into Fay Stender's Berkeley home. Holding a gun, he forced her son to take him upstairs to her bedroom, where

Fay, long separated from her husband by this time, was sleeping with her lover. "Have you ever betrayed anyone?" he asked her.

"No," she replied.

"Don't you feel you betrayed George Jackson?"

Another "No." The man then made her sign a "confession" saying that she had betrayed George Jackson and the prison movement "when they needed me most." He demanded money, then tied up her son and her lover. He took Fay downstairs to the kitchen and shot her five times in a cross-shaped pattern: twice in the body, once in each arm and once in the head. He fled into the night.

Upon first hearing about this, I panicked. If some ex-con thought Fay had betrayed George Jackson, maybe he would think I had, too—after all, I had been her sidekick all that time. Bricks through a window were one thing, being shot five times entirely another. I called the police, told them what had happened, and of my fears that I could be next. Forget that cops are "pigs," and the enemy. I didn't want to get shot, and those principles flew out the window.

The cruelty of her assailant was chilling, the extent of her wounds horrible. Her desire to relieve suffering and change the brutality of life behind bars—and her romanticism about prisoners—had earned her perpetual torment. And now she lay in a hospital fighting for her life.

She survived, only to endure excruciating, constant pain and paralysis from the chest down. She committed suicide in 1980.

A year later, a journalist named David Horowitz who had been a big Black Panther supporter and former editor of the radical magazine *Ramparts*, called. He was writing an article about Fay and the prison movement and asked if I would talk with him. Thinking he was still on "our" side, I agreed. We met at a nice restaurant. I ordered white wine and crab salad, he took out his tape recorder, and, as its wheels spun around, I wandered fecklessly into a trap.

Horowitz got me reminiscing about George Jackson and Fay Stender. Making sure he understood that it was off the record and never to be repeated, I told him about George's violent side, the free-flowing sexuality of some women, the careful editing of information I made public, my subsequent fears for my own safety, and my fear of seeming like a reactionary in the eyes of my comrades if I spoke out critically.

What I had not known when I spoke with Horowitz was that he had done a political about-face and renounced his previous beliefs. Now a staunch conservative, he was intent on exposing the prison activists instead of criticizing prison conditions. When his article appeared, I was mortified. True to his bargain, he did not reveal me as the source of the most damaging material. But he painted Fay and the rest of us as misguided ideologues—silly, oversexed women awed and bamboozled by slick, violent con men, indulging our fantasies while imperiling ourselves and others. Much of his information had come from me, and it was true.

Upset, embarrassed, and offended, I fired off an angry letter to the magazine, *New West*. It was published, and there matters would have stood, but for a lawyer friend who asked me to go after Horowitz one more time. I was then an officer of Media Alliance, an association of journalists. The lawyer asked me to write an article in the Media Alliance newspaper criticizing Horowitz at greater length and in more detail. Still angry at my own stupidity and what felt like Horowitz's duplicity, I agreed.

Big mistake. Without saying a word, the Media Alliance newspaper editor betrayed me. He phoned Horowitz, told him of my article, showed it to him and invited his response, to appear in the same issue—all without telling me. When the newspaper came out, I was aghast to see that Horowitz had broken his pledge to keep my off-the-record conversation with him secret. He named me as his main source and said I had told him that George Jackson had killed twelve people. He called me a propagandist and excoriated me for not telling the full truth of what I had known about the prisoners.

Apart from feeling humiliated at having spoken so irresponsibly, I was terrified. By breaking his pledge of confidentiality, Horowitz had possibly placed me at risk. For all I knew, a psychopathic ex-prisoner dedicated to the memory of George Jackson could have me and my family in his sights. I worried when John was late from school, worried if I heard little noises at night.

In this feud, I was no match for Horowitz. Journalist friends came to my defense, criticizing him for revealing off-the-record information and for putting me in jeopardy. Others blamed me for being a reckless reporter who failed to expose the violence I knew about. There was a huge and very public blow-up. I was sick at heart and depressed.

After all the changes I had been through, striving to make a more fulfilling life for myself and my kids, separating myself from the values I had been raised with, becoming involved in causes I believed in, learning to become a reporter, developing strength as a woman—I was an utter failure.

Not long afterward, Mark Dowie abruptly left me. Our relationship had for some time become fractious and competitive. He had become a skilled investigative reporter at *Mother Jones*, breaking an award-winning story about the Ford Pinto, the infamous automobile that burst into flames when struck from behind. The magazine, co-founded by Paul Jacobs, had developed a reputation in its early days for treating women badly, and its editors later turned on Jacobs, forcing him to resign. So Mark was allied with people who had, in my view, treated Paul and me very badly.

To make things worse, my writing career was going nowhere. While Mark's star was rising, mine was falling. Articles were rejected, a book project failed. Moreover, he didn't like living in Mill Valley, a comfortable suburb, and I was reluctant to move. "The real people live in the Mission!" he snapped, citing a predominantly Hispanic part of San Francisco. Counseling did us no good. As we were having an argument one day, he snapped, "I'm leaving. I haven't been happy for some time." He flung a flowerpot across the deck, hopped into his green Saab, and sped off. He never came back.

Oddly enough, it was my father who best described my situation, though at the time he was talking about a woman he knew: "With the first husband, she became Maggie Ives. After she got divorced and remarried she was Maggie Lewis. Then she got divorced again and now she's Maggie Nobody." Divorced women, he continued, were "on the beach." Topsy Nobody, that was how I felt.

It was a double whammy that struck in 1981: Mark Dowie moved out of our home, and Ronald Reagan moved into the White House. With his presidency, the New Left, which had provided me with causes to believe in, broke down. No longer a wife, no longer an activist—who was I? Where was I? That was easy: on the beach, and in despair.

Soon after Mark left me, my sister Wendy separated from her husband. When I was visiting at the Pennsylvania farm, she picked me up at my mother's house, and we went out to dinner together. "There go the two rejects," Lewie remarked, as the two of us walked out the door. Mummy said rather smugly that she had always known Mark was a three dollar bill. Clarry was not much help either: he told me to sell my jewels, take flying lessons, and get a dog.

CHAPTER FOURTEEN

On the Beach and Making It Anyway

Whatever you can do, or dream you can do, begin it. Boldness has genius, power and magic in it.

—Goethe

N ow, dear reader, let me fast-forward seventeen years. You left me in a ditch, personally and professionally crushed. Though I slowly bounced back, there were more troubles in store.

Over a long period, I had angered my tribe. So it might not come as a surprise to learn that in 1998 my tribe whacked me back. But by that time I had managed to get some control over my life, to make better decisions, and, as you will see, to cope more effectively with reverses.

But first, here's how the whacking came about.

Clarry and I were estranged for many years. Long troubled by my politics and my writing, he didn't like it that in 1987, doing research for this book, I had gone to see Cotty at her home in Italy to ask what she remembered about the kidnapping of Cooky and me, and about her years as Clarry's wife. He exacted a silent retribution: That year, without a word, his annual Christmas checks stopped coming. Though I wrote asking for an explanation, none came.

Things between us worsened a year later when *Women's Sports* magazine asked me to write a magazine article about men's clubs that exclude women. I told him about the assignment and asked if he would be interviewed. His response: I should refuse the assignment. He had my Pell half-brothers ask me to refuse. Stung by their disapproval and anxious about challenging my father so directly, I went ahead anyway.

In the lengthy article, I mentioned the all-male Racquet Club and Clarry's role in denying permission for a woman court tennis player to practice for a few weeks on its courts. He stopped speaking to me. After the issue was published, his wife Frankie told me later, he haunted the local library, terrified that *Readers' Digest* or some other publication might print it again. He felt humiliated.

I hadn't exactly schemed to infuriate and embarrass him—I was just carrying out my writing assignment, or so I told myself at the time. Looking back, though, I see that, with the sure aim of the aggrieved child, I had hit him in his most vulnerable place.

Six years later, in 1994, he called me to propose a truce. We could be on civil terms, he said, if I promised never to write about him and the family either during his lifetime or after his death. "And your promise has to be an unconditional surrender," he snapped.

"I can't do that," I said, and hung up, feeling offended and righteous. This book mattered too deeply to me, more than any other project I had ever undertaken.

Shortly after that, Frankie phoned, begging me to give up the idea. "It's not worth it, Tops," she urged. "No book is worth dividing a family like this!" She explained that my father had written me out of his will, and if I had any hopes of an inheritance, I had better give in. That was a shock, his willingness to reject me so totally, and I didn't like losing the money, but his threat stiffened my determination to proceed.

Two years later, however, Clarry softened. I didn't know it then, but my mother had called him and chided him for being mean to me. Since he had never stopped being in love with her, he did as she asked. He called and asked me to come see him next time I was east. I did. We had a tense visit, then another, easier one a year later.

On that second visit, he even seemed to accept the idea that I was writing about our family. After breakfast, he descended into a storage room and slowly climbed back up the stairs, lugging a dusty leather valise. "Here," he said. "You might like to look at this." The valise was filled with family photos, documents, and clippings. Though he didn't say so—but then, he never brought up emotionally charged subjects—the offering appeared to indicate a belated approval of my book project. I thought he was providing me with material I might want to use, and I spent a happy afternoon going through the yellowed papers as he looked on. He let me take some old photos home, and I thought that meant we were reconciled.

I did notice that he was forgetting things and driving a bit erratically. He seemed confused at times and oddly passive. Sure enough, after I was back in California, he phoned. "Dear, I have something to tell you and I want you to hear it from me. I've been to the doctor and he tells me that I have . . . I have . . . um . . . it's Alz . . . Alz . . ."

"Alzheimer's?" I filled in.

"Yes . . . that's it." In fact, Clarry could track his deterioration by his trouble with the *New York Times* crossword puzzles, which begin with easy ones on Mondays and progress to hard ones on Saturdays. First, he couldn't finish the Saturday puzzles, then he couldn't do the Fridays, then the Thursdays stumped him, and so on.

The thaw continued: in October, he asked me to come to his birthday dinner—he was having only his children and Frankie. I went.

So it seemed only natural that, when he was hospitalized with heart trouble a few months later, he asked me to come see him. Immediately, I jumped on a plane. He was pleased that I came, and, despite all the conflicts we had had over the years, I was happy to be at peace with him and glad that I could show him I cared. His condition improved; I flew back to California. But, a few days later, he died. Deeply saddened despite our feuds, I flew back again for the funeral, and at the request of my half-brother Haven wrote a splendid obituary. I touted all the things he loved: colonial ancestry, clubs, Harvard. The *New York Times* ran its own obit, and the Racquet Club flag flew at half staff over Park Avenue.

My sons arrived, and we all helped with preparations, meeting planes and making beds as the family gathered.

The day before the funeral service, I was taking a walk with my half-brother Peter and his wife Christine when Haven drove up. He had been meeting with Clarry's lawyer to learn the details of the will. "Am I in or out?" I asked jokingly as he drove by, quite sure I was in.

But, as I learned later that day when the family gathered for cocktails, I was wrong. The last section of the will said, "For my daughter, Eve Pell, I make no provision."

Clarry had disinherited me.

It felt as though he had slapped my face, hard. I was hurt, furious, punished, confused. I didn't like losing the money, but I felt my father's rejection more keenly and it stung, it stung. Even though he had once hinted about his intentions, this still felt awful. How could he have wanted me at his last birthday dinner? How could he have asked me to fly to his bedside, knowing what he had done in his will?

I was completely shaken, and told Daniel, Peter, and John. I told some other relatives. A little while later, my sons came up to me. "Come with us," Daniel said. We walked outside onto the lawn for a private conversation. "We love you," they said. "We respect you. And you never need to worry; we will take care of you. Whatever you want to do about this is okay with us."

Overcome by their love and loyalty, I wept. And I even felt lucky. I knew who had real riches that evening, and that was me. So, though I hated what my father had done to me, and it would bother me for a long time, my sons in five minutes had more than made up for it.

I griped to my cousins and to Frankie's daughters about Clarry; I cried. But I was damned if I was going to cave in. The next morning I took my place with the family in church, stood before the assembled relatives and friends, and gave the eulogy I'd written.

On the morning after, I sat at the breakfast table with my brother Peter. He was not happy about the way I had been treated, but he had made his own accommodation to our father's ways. "Clarry lived his life between two very narrow lines," Peter said, looking out the window. "I've lived my life the same way, and I'll go on doing that."

My father had even left a letter saying that, out of loyalty to him, his sons were to observe the terms of his will. As they did.

Upset and angry as I was, I did not go to pieces or fall into a depression as I had after the green Saab went down the road. In the years between Mark Dowie's abrupt departure and my father's disinheritance, I had managed to construct a better life and a stronger sense of myself.

It was a long and sometimes tedious undertaking. But, compressed and cut to essentials, here is how I did it. Although the process may sound like an organized step-by-step campaign as I tell it now, it really wasn't. At the time it felt like a series of lurches and happenstance, like trial and error—heavy on the error.

To start with, after Mark left, I was unemployed—worse than unemployed, I was disgraced. Besides that, I had been unceremoniously dumped, and I felt very alone. I didn't have much money. So, following one part of Clarry's advice, I sold my jewelry, including my family heritage, the Pell pearls. I was very sad to send the necklace in its shiny, round, velvet-lined box off to Sotheby's, but it bought me some freedom. I had a little income from a grandparent's trust and from my mother.

Work played a big role in my deliverance. At the time, I didn't see any pattern. But I realize now that I managed to find my way into jobs through which I could indirectly address my own internal conflicts and fears, a process that had begun with Paul and Saul so many years before.

When I went to 2500 Filbert, I had started to feel oppressed by my parents and my husband. Apparently by happenstance, I fell into a job that taught me both about the oppression of racial minorities and how brave people challenged authority to help themselves and their communities.

As I saw more of the outside world, I felt constrained by the emotional walls behind which my social class lived its lives; I found work—or the work found me—on behalf of prisoners confined behind three-dimensional walls of concrete and barbed wire.

Of course there was no comparison between the hardship minorities and prisoners suffered and my own privileged white woman status: I am not silly enough to imply that there was. But it was satisfying to be drawing attention to their struggles, and I felt that I was in some way helping myself at the same time. I felt a meaning and commitment to that work far beyond what I'd felt as a teacher at Hamlin School. Besides a salary, these jobs provided an arena where, without being conscious of what was happening, I could symbolically confront old terrors. And I could channel my stifled rage at my parents into exposing and criticizing brutal prison conditions or rapacious white settlers. Through the people I met and the feedback I received from working hard, the jobs contributed to my growing sense of myself.

My journalism career and this newfound sense of meaning developed, like some graph charting the stock market, in gradual ascents and sharp declines. Working my way back after the post-Dowie crash, I had some success as a reporter for the local weekly newspaper, was awarded a fellowship to Yale Law School, and proudly went off for a year in New Haven. But I couldn't hack living alone, which I was doing for the very first time. My youngest child went off to college. My love life was a complicated mess: a California boyfriend whom I had left behind quite rightly broke up with me, and I was devastated all over again. After a couple of miserable months at Yale, I quit and slunk home, depressed and defeated. A private investigator friend offered me a job, and, having nothing else going on, I took it. "Why did you hire me?" I asked him recently.

"You were Eve Pell," he said. "A fine writer and a natural interviewer. I took advantage of your weak moment." As if I had been somebody, even then. He too was part of this accidentally-with-a-purpose progression. As a child, I had felt baffled by family secrets and threatened by the prospect of unjust punishment, so what should he provide but a job as an investigator defending poor people accused of crimes?

It went on. Both when I was growing up and as Mrs. McLaughlin, I didn't dare say what I thought. Fittingly, as a reporter in the early 1980s I happened upon a phenomenon whereby activists were being sued for speaking out on issues of public policy; I wrote about them and was commissioned to write a book on free speech and censorship.

The Center for Investigative Reporting fit this pattern, too. I hated the arbitrary fashion in which my moneyed parents rode roughshod over those around them; in 1988 I was hired by CIR, an organization devoted to exposing and rooting out abuses of power.

In a strange, slow-brewing alchemy of emotions, dealing with my fears in these oblique ways helped to heal my own wounds. In addition, the work both served my goal of being socially useful and led to new opportunities and new friends. At the time, it seemed that those opportunities just popped up, and the only choices I had to make were whether to let a door remain closed or whether to open it and explore whatever lay beyond. But now I suspect that something else was going on—without knowing it, I must have been seeking, and something in the universe was providing what I needed.

My reporting won a few awards and, through a bit of serendipity, the approval of my mother. As a true member of the Establishment, she naturally regarded muckraking as a rather unworthy enterprise. She didn't pay much attention to the articles I wrote or the Frontline documentaries I worked on at CIR. I can thank the now-retired journalist Anthony Lewis for helping to reconcile my mother to my work.

Mummy liked it when her children succeeded, so in 1989 she went to a journalism award presentation in Washington where I won a minor prize. As it happened, the major honoree at the event was Lewis, then still at the *New York Times*. She listened to his acceptance speech—but far more important to her than what he said about journalism was the man himself, his background and his style. Lewis, a Harvard graduate, dressed in tweeds and spoke in a cultured voice. He was modest, witty, and nice-looking, three other qualities that endeared him to her, and of course, anyone who had gone to Harvard had to be all right. If I was on the same podium as Anthony Lewis, she decided, my work must be well regarded.

But throughout the 1980s and '90s, my relationship with my mother and Lewie remained complicated. When I was east on visits, I sometimes got into arguments with them over political issues—women's liberation, the criminal justice system, welfare. But the curious and interesting aspect of these trips for me was the decline in anxiety that I felt, year by year. Where once I dreaded my mother's appraisal of my hair and clothes, I could amuse myself by speculating what thing she might find to criticize this time. Her disapproval was losing its sting. Perhaps softened by age, my Ledyard family became more comfortable with the idea that I was different from them, and they kidded me about my politics. At one point, my mother owned a Cadillac, which I was borrowing for an errand. When Lewie saw me at the wheel, he smiled, threatening to take my picture and send it to Angela Davis.

Everything was not perfect. Basically, they stuck to their Republican politics, and we disagreed about a lot of things. But they saw that I was a loyal mother and that my sons were turning out all right. They saw that I didn't abandon them. Despite being "pink," I was okay. In addition to charting my own progress by testing myself with these visits—(how candid could I be? How much could I disagree with them?) I had an odd nostalgia for the good parts of my childhood. Besides, to cut off all my relatives would have felt like an amputation.

I wondered whether this behavior made me a coward, whether holding on to my economic privilege implied political backsliding or an absence of moral fiber or both. I helped some people out from time to time, but I didn't give all my money away and I lived comfortably in a Marin County suburb. Being insufficiently committed to live like a revolutionary—and being wary of self-described revolutionaries after my prison experiences—I kept a foot in both worlds.

Speaking less metaphorically, I used both feet to make a place in a very different world, adding another element to my sense of self. Toward the end of my marriage to Mark, we had begun to run, and my son Peter became a high school cross-country star. Our Mill Valley house was near mountain trails, and I enjoyed being out among wildflowers, hawks, and deer. We entered a few local races, and to my surprise, I did quite well in the over-forty age group. What a change: in third grade, I had been embarrassed at being the slowest kid in my class. My friend Natalie, a fast runner, would take me by the hand, pulling me behind her across the playground hoping by force of will to make my legs go faster. Didn't work.

But training and persistence did. I joined a local running club

I didn't expect what came next, a passion for the sport. Instead of galloping on thoroughbred horses as I had when young, as a runner I *became* a horse. I ran the Dipsea, the second-oldest race in the United States. It's a cross-country scramble that begins with a stiff climb up 676 steps and continues over a steep, rutted, rocky trail from Mill Valley up the slopes of Mt. Tamalpais, then plunges down across a creek, makes another killer climb, and, in a final, crazy descent, skitters down to end at the small town of Stinson Beach.

It was as exciting to race over that trail on my feet, pushing up the steep mountain, slipping through short cuts, and leaping down from banks, as it had been to foxhunt over the East Coast fields and fences. Besides, I had a chance to do well there: Dipsea rules include a handicap system that enables an entrant of any age to win, and as a middle-aged woman, I had a good handicap.

There were different workouts for each day, hill repeats up and down steep slopes till I could barely stand; speed drills on the track for fast leg turnover; two-hour runs in the hills for endurance, and weight training for strength. When race day came each year, I was skinny, fit, and ready. In 1989, I won—and over the years compiled a record that put me into the Dipsea Hall of Fame. I joined the all-women Impala Racing Team, known for its tough coaching, camaraderie, and focus on winning.

I've raced hundred of times, and my middle-to-old-age racing career continues to this day. The year I turned sixty, 1997, was my best ever: after finishing first in my age group at the Boston Marathon and other races, I traveled to the World Masters Games, a sort of Olympics for over-thirty-five athletes held that year in Durban, South Africa. (Among the events at those remarkable games: the 100-yard dash for men over ninety, the pole vault for women over seventy-five.) There, I had the honor of carrying the American flag at the opening ceremonies and won gold medals in two events. (If my old antiwar buddies could see me now! I thought. But it was thrilling to represent my country, no matter how much I disagreed with its policies.) At year's end, I was ranked the top United States woman road racer in the 60-69 division.

Actually, one of the effects of my peculiar upbringing is that I have never *not* known how to compete. Those years of schooling for horse shows by my mother and tennis tournaments by my father, plus the genes I inherited from a family of athletes, equipped me well. Unlike most girls raised in the '50s, I had been forced to push my body into all-out efforts. When I raced head-to-head against a rival, I didn't defer or back off—I tried harder. And I had enough sense of perspective to be a decent loser, especially if I had run well in the attempt. As they say in racing, there is always someone slower than you, and there's always someone faster.

When I win a race, I'm relieved—it (whatever "it" is) didn't catch me, and I'll live to run another day. And there's the primitive sense that, at this small moment in this very particular situation, I am somebody.

Probably, to get metaphorical, I have been running away from where I started out toward where I want to be, from Topsy the poor-little-rich-girl, the class snail, to Eve the Dipsea winner. Along the way, I've learned from racing that ego itself isn't the terrible thing I was led to believe—in fact, it's necessary. Over my desk is the passage Nelson Mandela read at his inauguration:

> Your playing small does not serve the world. There is nothing enlightened about shrinking so that other people won't feel insecure around you. We were born to make manifest the glory of God within us. It is not just in some; it is in everyone. And, as we let our light shine, we consciously give other people permission to do the same. As we are liberated from our fear, our presence automatically liberates others.

The problem is to get the ego, the anger-energy and the competitiveness into the right spot. Not, for example, in battles with a husband or lover over who is right or who is more deserving, as I've done all too often. But racing another granny to the finish line—Yes!

Besides running and journalism, I had other work to do of a very different kind. Having been brought up in a family that not only didn't show affection but also rebuffed those who showed a need for it, I had absorbed hard, bad lessons. "We are not the huggy-kissy type," my mother used to say, and indeed we were not. If you think of affection and kindness as a kind of lymph system that lubricates family relationships and allows for trust to grow, my family's levels were very, very low. Instead, we grew up in a rigid and unforgiving pecking order, where status and gender determined if you were favored or not.

While growing up, I saw my parents be charming and jocular with their friends, polite and dismissive to the professionals they dealt with—doctors, their children's teachers—unpredictable and harsh to lesser beings such as children and servants. So long as people treated them with respect, my parents could be courtly and pleasant. But when their authority was questioned in any way, they acted like dragons, like scorpions—and if anyone displeased or challenged them, they struck.

Why did they strike? Why did they mock people who needed and wanted to be loved? Why did they farm out their children to servants and boarding schools? Surely, the answers went back to the way they were raised, and so on back from one generation to another in a long chain of privilege and entitlement, coldness, hurt, and distance. For many years, I went to therapists—old-fashioned on-the-couch ones and new agers, good ones and bad ones. Overall, they helped me to understand the forces that shaped me, and to learn that there were other ways of seeing the world.

For all my complaining about the bad parts, however, I did pick up a few useful things during my childhood.

The capacity to endure—that's one. I get miserable and depressed, I fail, I make mistakes, I alienate those who love me, I misjudge situations and people. But I can usually stick things out. This capacity, learned in childhood as a way to survive (inspired by *Lassie Come Home*, *Black Beauty*, the child protagonists of Charles Dickens and Robert Louis Stevenson, where doggedness and pluck eventually won the happy ending) has kept me going. I was never the smartest, not the prettiest, certainly not the kindest of women, but I could stand a lot and plug along. I survived the terrifying horses that ran off with me, my mother's anger, my father's sarcasm, the putdowns from my first husband. It's not a pretty thing, and it can ricochet badly on those around you, but a strong will can get you through a lot.

Another thing that helped, oddly enough, was good manners. My friends tell me that I know the right thing to do or say in most situations. My mother taught me to make conversation and draw people out—like the time at Whitehackle Farm when she and Lewie pretended to be the Russian ambassador and his wife, and we children had to pour tea for them and chat. She bribed me not to smoke partly for health, but partly so that I would learn to talk with people directly, without asking for a match or falling back on the other conversational rituals connected with cigarettes. Having been trained to draw people out and to connect with them, I feel that I can go pretty much anywhere and manage.

But these attributes, while useful in the outside world, are not much help in the realm of human relations. There, I struggled. Like most children who grow up to become parents, I tried to do better with my own offspring—to be a more loving and humane mother than mine had been. I took care of them myself for the most part, and, determined to stay close to them when they went through their adolescent periods, I didn't send them away to boarding schools. But there were times when my private demons emerged, when I scolded them too hard, was blind to their needs, and demanded too much of them. I was sorry that they had to grow up split between divorced parents, going back and forth with their little suitcases from my house to their father's. Most of all, I wish that I had been able to show them more affection.

Fortunately, children are resilient and forgiving. I've apologized to my sons for my sins of omission and commission, and we have discussed the nasty family patterns that, despite good intentions, I imposed on them. I am grateful now that they live near me, so we are part of each other's lives. I baby-sit and play with my grandchildren—who love horses and whom, for some atavistic reason, I have taught to ride.

After Clarry disinherited me, unlike Peter and Haven, my Ledyard siblings came to my rescue. By that time, Mummy, too, had developed dementia, and they were managing her affairs. They upped my share of her trust fund income, which had been smaller than theirs because everyone expected I would get a nice chunk from my father. So, while the disinheritance cost me a lot, the financial blow was eased by their generosity and sense of fairness.

Perhaps to excuse his behavior, Frankie suggested that Clarry had simply forgotten about the disinheritance as his Alzheimer's progressed, which might explain his warmth to me in the last years of his life. (That left me in the uncomfortable position of thinking that while my father was in his right mind, he didn't like me. But when he lost his marbles, then he did.) Maybe Frankie was right. I know she felt badly about what Clarry did. When she died several years later, she left to me the cabochon emerald and diamond engagement ring that Clarry gave her. When I wear it, I wonder if somehow he knows, and I hope he is annoyed.

So I have ended up in a pretty sweet place. Like a traditional Pell, I am close to my family. But I've redefined family—dearly as I love my blood relatives on the Right Coast, the people whom I count on from day to day, and who count on me, in addition to my sons and my daughter-in-law, are my adopted family in California—friends, neighbors, runners, and reporters. Most of them are like me—people who left the places they were born in to come west and make a new life. We have known each other for decades and have seen each other through divorces, childbirth, sickness, and the other dramas of daily life. I know my friends' children and in some cases, their grandchildren—as they know mine.

And somehow, over the years, I began to feel something that I would not have expected: compassion for my mother.

CHAPTER FIFTEEN

My Demented Mother and I

Unlike the mother-son relationship, a daughter's relationship with her mother is something akin to bungee diving. She can stake her claim in the outside world in what looks like total autonomy—in some cases, even "divorce" her mother in a fiery exit from the family—but there is an invisible emotional cord that snaps her back.

—Victoria Secunda, *Women and Their Fathers*

As years went by, my mother needed a lot of care, and she didn't make it easy on those who helped. Dementia crept up on her as it had on Clarry. I first realized that something was wrong during a visit in the spring of 2000: she was standing in her pantry, staring fixedly at two small bottles of pills the vet had prescribed for Charley, the plump Corgi who followed her everywhere. Her gaze shifted uncertainly to the vet's sheet of instructions about dosages and number of pills per day. She turned to stare at Charley again. She stood there for ten long minutes, looking distractedly from the pills to the instructions to the dog, muttering to herself. From time to time, she picked up a bottle but quickly set it down. Ann, the housekeeper, happened along; she too saw what my mother was doing. We stepped in and gave the dog his pills.

There were more clues, like the day a relative named Carolyn came over for tea. An hour or so after Carolyn left, Michael's wife Cathie arrived, bringing dinner. "No one ever comes to see me!" my mother grumbled.

Cathie explained that Carolyn had just been there. "Well, I don't remember it," Mum retorted. "So it doesn't count."

Plainly, our mother had to be looked after. Even though I lived on the other side of the country and despite the years of bad mothering from her, I wanted to play some role in her care. Besides I had made a promise to Lewie years before while he lay on his deathbed, a promise he, or his ghost, reminded me that I had to keep.

Throughout the 1980s, Lewie suffered from heart disease, going steadily downhill but clinging to life far longer than any of his doctors expected. One winter day in 1990, the nurse who tended him called me at home, asking that I come quickly. I caught a plane as soon as I could. When I arrived at the house, she met me at the door and, after I had greeted my mother, she led me into the downstairs bedroom. Pale, with skin so white it was nearly gray, Lewie lay immobile on his back with oxygen tubes going into his nose. His eyes were closed, his long, emaciated body totally still. There was no sign of life but faint breathing. I had no idea what to do.

"Rub his feet, he likes that," she suggested as she left the room, closing the door behind her. Alone with the man who had been my stepfather for nearly fifty years, I felt helpless. I followed the nurse's advice and rubbed his cold feet for a while. There was no indication he knew I was there.

After a while I sat down on a chair and looked at him. And thought of how much sickness he had endured. An idea popped into my head. "You know," I said out loud. "If you are worried that we will not take care of our mother, if you are hanging on for that reason, you can let go. I promise you, we will take good care of her." I gave him a kiss, got up, and left the room.

The next morning I woke early; there was a hubbub in the house. Lewie had died. My mother and I stood together in our bathrobes in the living room, watching the sun rise over the pond, the fields, and the woods. I had my arm around her; she was desolate that she had been asleep upstairs and not by his side at his death. We reminisced about Lewie, what a benevolent and well-loved man he was, how his sense of humor eased all kinds of situations, how he had been her great love. We called my brothers and sisters, and soon they came over.

I was alone upstairs in Mummy and Lewie's bedroom, thinking about him, when it happened. Lewie's presence somehow suffused the room and I heard his voice, in the teasing tone I knew so well. "She's all yours!" it said with a laugh, and then it all disappeared. Despite the shock of hearing my dead stepfather speak, I had to smile. Just what he would do, I thought.

A moment later, my brother Michael walked up the stairs. I told him about my promise to his father the night before and the mysterious thing that had just happened. "Not to worry, Tops," he answered with a smile. "You haven't committed us to anything we weren't committed to anyhow."

Now, ten years after my promise to Lewie, it was time to deliver. As our mother's mind deteriorated, her doctor prescribed medicines to reduce anxiety and retard Alzheimer's. But she grew increasingly depressed, lonesome, forgetful, and terrified. Her demands for attention—to be invited for tea or dinner, to be taken to parties and horse races, or for someone pick up a dropped stitch in her knitting—multiplied. It was up to her children, she felt, to meet all her needs—never mind that she had never bothered particularly to meet ours.

I owed something to my siblings who lived near her, Michael and his wife Cathie, and Wendy. They had to figure out how to stop her from driving; they had to get her to doctors' offices and lab tests. Cass, who had retired and moved to Florida, managed her money. John, the youngest, was moving back to Pennsylvania from Montana, saying that he wanted to help. I went back to the farm more frequently.

There were more important dynamics at work besides what I owed to Lewie and my siblings. The more demented my mother became, the more she lost control, the easier it was to have compassion for her. Because of the changes I had gone through as I gained more control over my life, Mum couldn't hurt me very much any more. In echoes of that Bryn Mawr period when I realized I could manipulate her reactions by the kind of dress I tried on, I was no longer at her mercy. And I knew that I wanted to help with her care for two reasons: to comfort her and to know that I was doing the right thing. Even though Clarry had ended up by disinheriting me, I was glad to have made the effort to become reconciled with him. I knew that clinging to old hurts and angers, while perhaps justified, would only make me unhappy. Being part of a family mission to see our mother through her disease could be a rewarding experience.

We hired nursing aides to be with Mummy around the clock because she could no longer care for herself. She didn't like them because they were new to her and because most of them were African American. Unaccustomed to black servants, she tried, with a fair amount of success, to run them off. "Get your black hands off me!" she would scream at an aide who was trying to bathe her or change her diaper.

My mother hated seeing doctors. She was embarrassed when they asked her questions—"Who is President of the United States? What day is it today?"—that she knew she should be able to answer. She was often adroit in her responses.

"Can you name five cities?" a doctor asked her during an office visit.

"New York," she said right off the bat. A moment later, more tentatively, "Pittsburgh??" A long silence. She sat up straight. "Well, you know, I don't travel very much any more," she remarked, in a tone indicating that this part of the interview was now over.

She grew more paranoid, furious, and upset than ever. She mocked people by imitating them—wrinkling her nose and moving her shoulders from side to side and parroting what they said like a truculent five-year-old:

"Take your pills, they're good for you," said the aide.

"*Take your pills, they're good for you,*" mocked my mother.

"You look very nice this morning."

"*You look very nice this morning.*"

"It's time for your bath."

"*It's time for your bath.*"

It was hard to believe that this wild-haired harridan, with stains down the front of her wrinkled blouse and saliva dribbling from a corner of her mouth, hands trembling as she tried to feed herself and diapers rustling under her trousers, was once the toast of Tuxedo, the most beautiful debutante of her year, the nervy, elegant horsewoman with gold stock pin and shiny boots racing her hunter over big fences and, in black satin and tulle, charming the men at the ball afterward.

On one visit, I cooked scrambled eggs and toasted bagels for our supper. She got to reminiscing about the old days, happy that she remembered some things about Whitehackle Farm and Lewie and us as kids. But, for the first time, she asked for reassurance that I had had a happy childhood—over and over. She told how people had criticized her for putting me on wild ponies and taking me out of school to foxhunt. She seemed like a child eager to know she had been good.

Not seeing any point in berating her at this point for her lack of maternal compassion, or in telling her how terrified of her sharp tongue I had been most of my life, I just said how much I had liked the foxhunting and what fun I had had as a girl. She was hungry to hear this—which made me wonder why she worried, now that she was losing her mind, about having been a bad mother.

But such reflective moments were rare. Mum punched one aide in the stomach, stabbed another with a fork, and chased yet another with a rake. She even attacked her beloved Ann, jamming her into a closet.

The situation got crazier and crazier; finally, in a particularly anguished moment, she called her son John and told him, "Get me out of here!"

"I'll do it, Mum," he said, "I'll be right there." John phoned Cass, who was up visiting from his Florida home, and a family doctor, who arranged for Bryn Mawr Hospital to admit her. John and Cass got her into her wheelchair and into her van. But as they were driving, she had a change of mind. "You're kidnapping me!" she cried, and ordered them to take her home. They wouldn't. "I hope all you children die an early death!" she shrieked, struggling to unfasten her seat belt.

John told her to keep the seat belt on. She protested that it wasn't needed. "You have to keep it on," he said, "It's the law."

"You don't have yours on," she retorted.

"Yes I do, see?" He pulled the belt away from his body to show her.

"No, I can't see."

So he pulled it out even farther from his body. Swiftly, she struck. Lunging over, she grabbed John's belt and tried to strangle him with it. Cass reached over from the back and, after a short struggle, pulled her arm away.

Exhausted and anxious, they reached the hospital, where Mum was shot up with a powerful tranquilizer and admitted.

Aware that things were terrible, I had flown in from California, arriving that same night. The next morning, our mother was moved by ambulance to a psychiatric unit in a Philadelphia hospital where she was to be evaluated by specialists. We met with her newly assigned psychiatrist who said we had better find a nursing home spot for her. None of us were prepared for this. We had thought that she could stay at home if she had round-the-clock care. I volunteered to find her a suitable place, pronto.

The next day, when I went back to see her, the sedation had worn off. I had brought a huge bunch of fragrant freesia and a pottery vase that my grandson had made for her. When she saw me, her face lit up and her eyes widened. "How ever did you find me?" she asked. Then she looked dejected and said, "I have been waiting for you all day."

I explained that I had told the nurses I would be over in the afternoon. "There was a mistake," she said, "And there have been terrible consequences. Well, you are here now and I'll get my shoes and we'll go. Let's go to Gargy's." Gargy, her mother, had been dead for more than twenty-five years. I had to say that we were not going, that Mum had to remain there. She became angry. "No one has come to see me. Where is everyone?" she demanded.

"I've come from California," I answered.

"That's not very far," she scoffed. "You lying bitch! I never thought you would do this to me. This is a cruel place, go away!"

I put the flowers in the vase and left them on a table beside her. It was awful to see her so demented. But where once her fury would have terrified me, I could now write it off as a symptom of her disease.

The next day, I found her sitting in a TV room with the other patients, looking like the one person who did not belong in this picture. The others were slack-jawed, slumped old women with shapeless, colorless hair, bundled in colorless, shapeless clothing. Mum, by contrast, sat erect, wearing a fitted, bright yellow shirt, her iron-gray hair neatly brushed. There was rhythmic screaming from a woman in a room nearby and constant blare from a television set.

Mum looked astonished and happy when she saw me. "I thought I would never see you again!" she whispered. She was frightened and despairing and, for once, vulnerable. "I will never get out of here, no matter what I do, I can't win," she sighed. Again and again, she repeated what a terrible experience this was for her, how she suffered, how she longed to go home. "But I know you would never have done this to me if you hadn't had to," she said sweetly and earnestly. "I'm losing my mind, God help me!" and she sobbed.

"No one has come to see me," she said forlornly when she stopped crying.

"No, Mum, I was here yesterday," I said. "Who do you think brought you the flowers?" I cited those as incontrovertible evidence that I had been there.

"But I have no flowers," she answered, bereft. I went into her room and by God she was right, there were no flowers. I chased down a nurse and there in his office were the freesia and the vase! I said, "Those are *her* flowers that I left for her!"

The nurse argued, "But the vase is pottery and could break into pieces."

"Then let's find something we can use instead," I demanded, sending him off to find a plastic container. I was wild with sadness and rage—Mum so loved her flowers and they took them away, the one pretty thing in that godforsaken ward! Moreover, flowers have been one of the few links between us—I inherited her passion for gardening and creating flower arrangements—and leaving them for her had been a way of expressing my love that she could recognize. That nurse had snapped our tenuous connection.

It was a relief to arrange the flowers in the plastic jar and leave them again by her bed.

She cried with hopelessness. "They will never let you back in again to see me. I will never see you again!" I assured her that I would be back the next day.

I went down in the elevator, got in my car, and sobbed. While her fury of the day before had not much touched me, her vulnerability broke my heart.

I found her a nursing home where she could live in her own small apartment, furnished with things from her house. Her family visited often, as did Ann and the men who worked on the place. Our mother took to her new environment quickly and, to our great surprise, became the belle of the Alzheimer's unit. Several of the men courted her; she thrived on their attention and soon settled down into a sweet relationship with Bud, the most attractive one. For several months, they were inseparable—whenever I went to see her, she introduced him with a vague wave of the hand and said, "Tops, you remember . . ." She blanked out Bud's name, but she would say something like, "I don't think you've seen him since we all went to Florida." Plainly, she was having happy delusions. Her sense of class stayed with her, but it didn't seem to matter. When I sat with her alone in her parlor, she would say things like, "The people here are a little . . . *different.*" Or, "My friends might think that this is a *peculiar* hotel, but I like it here."

Alas, the honeymoon was not to last. Bud died—but, given the progress of her dementia, she seemed to get over the loss very quickly.

She had been in the nursing home for several months when she fell and became very ill. I flew back. When I arrived at the nursing home, she was better, sitting in the garden in her wheelchair with an aide. It was the first time she had not lit up on seeing me; in fact, she barely registered my presence and paid no attention to the flowers I brought. "Your daughter is here! See the pretty flowers," the aide fussed. But Mum was tense and uncomfortable. Clutching the edge of a picnic table with her knobby fingers, she held herself stiffly upright, an anxious expression on her knitted brow. I could not get her to relax.

When I went back the next day, I fed her dinner and sat with her after an aide put her to bed. I put my hand on hers.

Mum held my warm hand with her cold one, rubbing it with her thumb. She lay back with eyes closed, then a tremor passed through her body and she startled. She raised her head from the pillow, opened her eyes wide, looked at me blankly, then closed her eyes and lay down again. This happened again and again: She could not stay relaxed for more than a minute or two before startling. After about fifteen minutes, I let go of her hand and rose to leave. Immediately, like a tentacle rising from the ocean floor, her left arm rose from the covers, searching the air for contact. I took the hand and sat back down again. Every time I let go of her hand and got up to go, her left arm rose, seeking contact, so I grasped her hand again and stayed.

This scene contrasted sharply with one two years earlier. At that time, the dementia had set in but Mum was still at home. My son Daniel was visiting in Pennsylvania with me. After dinner, as the fire had died down and embers glowed in the hearth, she was half asleep in an armchair in the library. We sat with her. Afterward, Daniel, who, like all my sons was aware of my conflicted feelings about my parents, said he wished I had held her hand. I knew what he meant, and theoretically that would have been nice. But though I had considered it, I couldn't—touching her like that would have meant crossing a barrier between us that I had never dared to breach. Someone from a different family might have considered such handholding a simple expression of affection between mother and daughter, but it was foreign and frightening to me. I felt paralyzed by competing emotions: desire to be close with her and fear of the consequences.

Nonetheless, the possibility sat in my head all night and the next day. The next evening, prodded by Daniel's suggestion, I tried it. Pulling up an ottoman next to her chair as she dozed, I picked up her hand in mine. It didn't explode or slap me—in fact, it remained passive and she didn't stir. But I was uncomfortable and anxious, as though at any time she might snap to attention and ask, "What the hell are you doing!"

But now in the nursing home she wanted me hold her hand. This is progress, I thought to myself as time went by. I even gathered the nerve to stroke my mother's hair back from her forehead. It seemed to soothe her.

Then came the amazing stuff: A couple of times, my mother took my hand up to her lips and kissed it. "Sweet kisses," I said to her, when I could speak. After a few minutes, she raised her left arm up and put it on my shoulder. I put my head down close to her chest and we stayed that way for a while.

I was astonished at this expression of affection, by far the most intense Mum had ever shown me. I could feel how much she wanted the contact. It felt nearly surreal, like a drug experience.

There was no way for me to know if she knew it was me she was embracing, or whether she just needed someone, anyone, to be there. But it was enough that, whatever was going on in what was left of her mind, I was there, I felt her warmth, and I knew I was giving her some peace. It was satisfying to know that I love my mother, the dragon mother who had not been very good at loving me.

After a while, I raised my head and tried again to leave, but she kept raising that arm. Finally, I figured that she would keep me there forever if she could, and I needed to go. So I left the nursing home as night fell, after the most intimate experience I ever had with my mother.

Later, I learned that she was doing the same thing with all the people she liked who came to see her. At first I was disappointed not to be the most special; then I thought how nice it was that she could at last be sweetly expressive to those she cared about, then I thought, how sad for all of us that we had to wait so very long.

Epilogue

Dear reader, we are reaching the end. What follows is a sort of triptych that encompasses the story of my heritage, my family and me.

I.

In 2004, I went back for a weekend celebration commemorating the 350th anniversary of Thomas Pell buying that land in the Bronx and Westchester from the Native Americans. Now, three and half centuries later, we descendants of the buyer were to meet the descendants of the sellers, two members of the Lenape tribe who were coming from Oklahoma, where the tribe finally settled after years of being driven westward. The modern-day Lenapes had never before seen the homeland of their ancestors, and I was excited about meeting them—according to our family legends, they were distant relatives.

A committee of historians, local politicians, and Garden Club ladies organized the dinner on Saturday, June 26. There was a big tent, great food, a band playing old-timey music and a cheerful crowd gathered on the lawn in front of the Bartow-Pell mansion in Pelham Bay Park. Lili Pell Whitmer, a slim blonde dynamo of seventy who heads the Pell Family Association, and I were introduced to the Native Americans, Michael Pace and Bucky Buck. We shook hands in the very place where our forefathers had signed the treaty in 1654. Photographers lined us up, Lili and me with the two Lenape men, posing on the land that had been theirs from prehistory till 1654 and ours for about a century and a half after that.

After we had drunk our "Thomas Pell" punch, stuffed ourselves on corn bread and clams and barbecue, and danced a Virginia reel or two, Michael borrowed a drum from the band and took the stage. He, Bucky and their wives sang four Native American songs, then led the group in a traditional tribal dance. I got chills: For perhaps the first time in three hundred years, Lenape drumming and chants were ringing out over the woods and meadows where the tribe had lived for millennia before the white man came.

"Now, it's time for a blessing," he announced. Feeling the power of the moment as the drum and solemn chanting began, men in the audience took off their hats and people bowed their heads. The Native Americans' voices rose and fell, verse after verse, the drum sounded its rhythms, the chant worked its magic. "*Wanishi-Ta*," they said when it was over: Thank you, in Lenape. The old-timey band came back, fiddlers struck up a final waltz, and the party was over.

The next day, the actual to-the-day 350th anniversary of the treaty signing, the Lenape wore native dress—bright red tunics and white belts of bone and beads, with an otter skin coursing lengthwise down the back, long loose trousers, otter hats decorated with red cloth and beads, and brightly colored moccasins. Their faces were painted; Michael had orange lines radiating from his eyes.

While the crowd gathered around, the Lenape and a Pell cousin read the old treaty aloud. "We also," it concluded, "as loving neighbors and friends, do mutually agree to send two men off each year, one day in the Spring every year, to mark the bounds of the land so that a right knowledge may be kept, without injury to either side, so that a mutual peace and love may be maintained. . . . This writing was signed and witnessed before a great multitude of Indians and many English."

After the reading, Michael and Bucky went over to the old Pell graveyard for a rededication and blessing of the plot. In an iron pot, they had sage and red cedar shavings, burned down into coals which they fanned with an eagle feather to make smoke. Michael explained: The smoke goes up high as the eagle soars to the Great Spirit, who smells the sweet smoke, knows that he is needed, and comes down to Earth. The Native Americans walked around the group fanning the smoke over everyone there, inviting them to be purified. They chanted, sending out blessings over the land where their ancestors lived and from which their culture sprang. They blessed our family, too, who lived after them in this same place.

I couldn't help thinking back to other ceremonies here, so very different in feeling from this one. Then, I came like a black sheep in rebellion against my father and the upper-crust male cousins whose approval he craved. Then, I resented and feared my father and his cousins, so self-satisfied and quick to condemn—the ones who hired a private investigator to discredit Cousin Rodman the fishmonger after he first presented himself.

Now, I can see beyond their narrowness and be proud of the family's contributions to our nation: Pell grants, the most tangible expression of Claiborne's loyalty to his creed of noblesse oblige, have enabled millions of needy people to go to college—undoubtedly the best thing the family has done since our arrival in 1635. The brilliantly restored Fort Ticonderoga, overseen by my cousins and the wider circle of supporters they have recruited, dramatizes American history to thousands of visitors each year.

I've gotten to know and like the cousins of my generation—who seem to accept me, tease me gently about my radical past, and even helped me with research for this book.

Having finally made a truce with my past, I can now be the same person in New York that I am in California.

Better late than never.

II.

It's a strange thing to divide up your mother's belongings while she is still alive. But once we realized that Mum could never live in her house again and the place had to be sold, that's what we had to do. We obeyed the terms of her will, which specified that property was to follow blood.

This, of course, got complicated in a family where there had been several marriages and many children. In their legacies, Mum and Lew, like Clarry, treated the children of their first, brief, marriages differently from the later children they had together. We three: Jeep; Cooky's heir, his son Tom, then forty-one and living in Idaho; and I were not to share equally with the other four. The will made it clear that Tom and I were not to get any of the many paintings Lewie had made—probably the most prized items of all. Here we go again, I thought, with painful memories of having been disinherited by Clarry.

We were excluded from any money from the sale of the $4 million Pennsylvania farm, the proceeds of which were to be divided equally between Wendy, Cass, Michael, and John Ledyard. It didn't seem fair: The children of the later marriage didn't have to suffer through parental divorce; they didn't have to cope with stepparents; and they got the lion's share of the money.

It was all right with me not to get money from the sale of the place. But when it came to the furnishings, which were to be divided among my mother's children, I was shocked to learn that there had been a question as to who "her children" were. Cass and Michael initially considered that Cooky's son Tom and I, as Pells, were not entitled to anything at all because so many of the things on the place had been accumulated while she was married to Lewie. Upon reconsideration of the will, however, Cass and Michael decided that Tom and I should be included along with the Ledyards. They set a date for all of us to gather at the farm in order to divide up the household.

This business of Ledyard and Pell made me sad. While we were kids on Long Island, Cooky and I had always celebrated two Christmases, one with Mum and Lew in the morning, the other with Clarry and Cotty in the afternoon. But I would gladly have traded the second set of Christmas presents and much, much more to have been a real Ledyard and never to have had to go my father's.

As I thought about what we were about to do, questions arose in my mind: What of my family heritage did I want to keep? What would my sons want? How much of that way of life, of which I was so critical, did I want to have in my house? The answers surprised me: I wanted a lot.

I wanted the personal things that symbolize my mother to me: the white chaise longue from her bedroom and the mirror given to her by the father of her dead young lover Archie Smith. My mother had told me over and over about her teenaged romance and about the car crash. If Archie had not died so young, I reflected, my mother would never have given up on passion and settled for a marriage of convenience with Clarry. And so much misery might have been avoided.

In August 2002, I flew back to Pennsylvania for what we called the Divvy. Ann the housekeeper, Wendy, and I laid out all the silver on the long, polished dining room table. Lewie's forebears looked down from their gilt frames onto a huge, gleaming array: upright candlesticks and branching candelabra; round serving bowls and trays, trophies from long-ago horse shows and cockfights; monogrammed antique serving spoons; the covered silver dish in which the English muffins at teatime were served; the three-sided, engraved tankard that my mother's ancestor John Jay had given to a Livingston ancestor of Lewie's—or had the Livingston given it to John Jay? Wendy circled the table, briskly pointing out particular items. "That's Ledyard," she observed. "That's from Daddy's family," as if protecting them from Tom and me.

The next morning, we six gathered in the living room clutching our lists of the things we wanted, with our private agendas deep in our hearts and our sibling rivalries tamped down.

Among the things up for grabs: antique furniture and porcelain, fur coats, two tractors and a manure spreader, beds, saddles and bridles, linens, leatherbound volumes of Shakespeare, a Jeep station wagon, and chain saws, on down to sets of Pyrex custard cups, and four cartons labeled in our mother's rounded handwriting: "cheap wine glasses."

The Divvy went on for a day and a half. It was not all sweetness and light.

My mother's will caused hurt feelings that endure. Worse, I thought, than excluding Tom and me from Lewie's paintings, was what she did to Wendy.

Before the dementia set in, Mum had selected a few of her most valuable jewels and made a list assigning one piece to each of us children—all, that is, but one. Some weeks before the Divvy, Michael had shown Wendy the list—on which her name did not appear. The only one our mother had not singled out for a special gift, she had been devastated. As the child who had done the most errands, chores, and caretaking for our mother over the decades, she deserved something wonderful.

So, when it came time to hand out the rest of the jewelry, Wendy's tall, athletic body stiffened, her chin trembled, and her eyes filled with tears. Everyone knew she had been terribly hurt and now wanted one thing above all—our mother's pearl necklace. It was Mummy's signature piece, the one she most often wore. Lewie had given it to her, and it was stunning. Michael, who could have chosen it, deliberately took a bracelet instead. I too gave up my chance at it so it could go to her. She cried with relief and took the necklace. But I believe that no amount of pearls could ever make up for being left off our mother's list.

For me, the experience of the Divvy was healing, particularly by contrast with the miserable aftermath of Clarry's death. For one thing, Mummy was still alive, and we were not coping with death and loss. Although I was not quite on a par with the Ledyards, I was definitely included. More important, the two brothers in charge of the procedure, Cass and Michael, were open, friendly, and cooperative. They leaned over backward to minimize ill feeling and to make the process as fair as they could. I was one of the family.

Michael and Cathie bought my mother's place. Her condition improved enough that we could move her into a cottage on the farm where, tended by nurses, she lived nearly four years. She sat on her sunny porch looking at horses grazing in the fields, she received visitors, and she watched old movies, smiling when a favorite like Cary Grant came onscreen. Her memory deteriorated, but every now and then a sharp remark punctuated her bland responses, reminding those around her of the woman she had been.

I visited every few months, in the summer bringing my grandchildren along so they could ride and meet their East Coast family. Our relationship was uncomplicated and sweet.

Gradually, her condition deteriorated. By September 2007, she was barely eating or speaking. I flew east to see her. When I reached her cottage in the late afternoon, she had been asleep for a day—perhaps in a coma. I pulled up a chair to her bedside, spoke to her, and held her hand; she didn't wake, though every now and then she trembled. So I stayed there, sometimes stroking the wavy gray hair around her face. I wondered if she was close to the end, if she needed to be released. "Your children are all fine," I said in a quiet voice. "You can go any time you feel like it. Lewie and Cooky are waiting for you on the other side."

I'm not sure I fully believed that part about them on the other side, but I knew she believed in life after death and, if she was hearing anything, I thought she might be comforted.

I spent that night at Wendy's. About seven the next morning, my cell phone rang. It was Michael, and I knew what he was going to say: during the night, our mother had died. I sat down hard on the bed, tears stinging my eyes.

After the first shock of loss, I felt both sad and lucky—Mum was gone, but I had been at her bedside and I had sent her on her way. Did she really hear? Had she been waiting for me to come, as some of my friends suggested? I'll never know. But I knew that, in our final encounter, I was no longer afraid; I had developed the strength to be there, intimate and fully myself, in empathy with her.

We buried her ashes next to Lewie's on a wooded hillside. With her passing, an era in our family came to an end.

I'm left with mixed feelings. Mum was not a Mom. She did not provide comfort or nurturing; she did not see me off to school or listen to my woes or guide me into womanhood. I was sixty-eight when she told me that she loved me. But she was my mother, she loved me in her own way, and when, to my surprise, explosions of primal anguish seized me days later and I wept wildly, it was for her.

Now that I am home and going about my routine, I feel as though there is a pebble in my psyche—a steady discomfort that occasionally morphs into real pain, like a pebble in a shoe. That's the mourning, I guess. A month after her death, I'm still dreaming of her and I want to lie around a lot. Maybe that's part of the mourning, too. I'll see how it turns out.

I wish my mother had not caused so much pain, that she had been easier. But I am grateful that, over the years, the two of us managed to put our differences aside and become fond of each other.

Better late than never.

III.

I'm still working out some old issues. One failure in particular nagged at me for decades.

It was a hot, bright summer day on our farm, about 1955, and I was home on vacation from college. Maybe Lewie was bored. Every now and then when he had nothing special to do, he turned to his children for diversion. He liked teaching us odd things, like how to use a speed bag, the small punching bag that boxers practice on to sharpen their timing. (Hit it with one side of your fist, then the other, alternating left and right as fast as you can make it go, in rhythm: Ba-dada, Ba-dada, Ba-dada.)

So it wasn't unusual for him to suggest that I put on my bathing suit and we have a walk down to the pond. He would show me something new. Since, like all my brothers and sisters, I loved doing things with him, I agreed, and a few minutes later we were heading down across the pasture to the dock.

He was going to teach me to do a back flip. That sounded fine, but as soon as I was standing with my back to the water, toes clutching at the edge of the dock, my body froze. I was immobilized. "Come on," he encouraged me, "It's not hard. Just jump a little backward and swing your legs over your head. You'll go in feet first" He sat down, long legs extended in the sun.

Summoning up a feeble energy, I leaped backward into the water, but it was only a jump. Lewie looked disappointed. Next time I tried, I managed a clumsy, twisting back dive. I couldn't begin to figure out how to get the legs around over my head. He looked even more disappointed.

"You can do it; there's nothing to be afraid of," he said. "It's only water." I went silent, abashed and embarrassed. One of the worst things you could be in our family was chickenhearted. But, that afternoon, I was chickenhearted. Although Lewie stayed there with me for what seemed like an hour, trying to get me to somersault backward into the water, I never even made a good stab at a flip—only a series of awkward backward jumps and dives. Finally, he said that was enough and we retreated back up to the house. I went to my room, mortified.

That afternoon haunted me ever after. I wanted to please my stepfather, and I failed.

Fifty years later, I was reading Jane Fonda's autobiography, *My Life So Far*. I had met Jane when we were young, and we had some friends in common. We are the same age, and there are a few parallels in our lives: high status families, distant fathers, beautiful mothers who were sought after by men, and the suicide of a close relative. Raised to be debutantes and trained to be polite young ladies in society, we found escape from our cold parents and confusing environments by jumping horses over fences and going off to boarding school. After that, our paths diverged, to say the least, as she became *Barbarella*, *Klute*, and the workout queen.

So of course, when her autobiography came out, I read it. To my astonishment, I found another similarity in our lives. She had had terrible trouble learning to do a back flip for the movie *On Golden Pond*, and she had been determined to prove herself to her father, Henry, as aloof a parent as one could imagine. But she had mustered the courage to throw her body off a diving board again and again until she got the somersault right, ignoring the painful smacks when she hit the water wrong. Her book describes an agonizing, cold day when she had to do it one more time for the movie.

Though she could have used a double, she chose to do it herself, and she succeeded.

Jane's story reminded me yet again that I'd given in to fear, that I'd never managed to do that flip. At the time, I was a little stuck writing this memoir—and I thought, What the hell. I'll learn to do it. At worst, I'll stop feeling bad about failing Lewie, at best I'll unblock an old hangup and maybe my writing will gain strength.

So I phoned around to find a diving instructor. Not so easy—there aren't that many public pools with diving boards, and even fewer instructors willing to take on a sixty-eight-year-old client. But I was lucky enough to find an instructor who had coached college and Olympic divers. "It's easy," he said over the phone. "I'll have you doing it in half an hour. I'll bring a wetsuit for you."

The night before, I kept waking up and fretting for long periods. When I got up, I said to myself, "Don't be so silly. You're coordinated, you can do this." So, to prove to myself how flexible and athletic I still am, I did a front somersault on the carpet of my bedroom. Around I went like a kindergartner. But as soon as I was upright again, a wave of nausea struck and I nearly vomited. This was not going to be so simple.

I felt too sick for breakfast, downing only a little hot tea to settle my stomach before heading off to the pool.

The teacher showed up, though I was hoping perhaps he'd forgotten. I pulled on the wetsuit and we walked to the end of the pool where the diving boards were. A dozen or so women were serenely swimming laps as we went by. "Why aren't I doing that?" I wondered.

"We start with the back dive," he announced. "No problem," he said, leaning his utterly relaxed body backward until he fell over and plunged easily into the water head first. He showed me how to stand on the edge of the board and bend over as he had, craning my head back to see the water behind me. First he held me until I was in the right position, and I flopped in. Then I did it by myself. Okay so far, but I'd done back dives as a kid so this was nothing new.

Next step, surprisingly, was jumping off the board backward. Bob up and down, use the arms, bounce out. That wasn't hard. "Okay, you're ready now," he announced cheerfully. "Lean backward until you lose your balance a little bit, swing your arms up and around. Then jump, bend, and your body will turn over by itself," he said. Moment of truth. I stood at the edge of the board, rehearsing in my mind what he had said and hoping the instruction would get through to my muscles. Teetering at the edge of the board, I swung my arms, leaned back, gave a little bounce with my toes—and around I went! Splat! My legs slapped the water—feet first! Inelegant, but it was a flip. I swam triumphantly to the edge of the pool, climbed out, got on the board and did it again. "Grab your legs when you're in the air," he said. "Fold up your body. That first one, you landed as though you were sitting in a chair." I didn't care.

I did a few more. As the nervousness receded, I got a sense of where my body was in the air, what my arms and legs were doing, and how to fold up into a cannonball. It was even fun—a swift, short somersault in flight.

"We're finished," I said. "Thank you."

But I was feeling very queasy. As we walked back toward the locker room, I said, "I think I'm going to throw up." Stomach heaving, I headed into the locker room. Was it nerves? The unaccustomed spinning around in the air? It didn't matter, and I didn't get sick. I'd done it. After a hot shower, I felt better.

"Nice work," said the teacher, as I was saying goodbye, "You faced your fear. Most people don't."

Driving home, I wondered whether Lewie, who visited me after he died, could see me from wherever he was. But that didn't really matter either. Fifty years after that painful afternoon on the dock, I had done some back flips.

Better late than never.

One of the lessons I learned from running has been useful in ordinary life. When getting over back injuries that occurred while racing, I learned that healing often continues for a surprisingly long period of time; it goes on even after you are pretty well recovered, with your body getting stronger and stronger as weeks and months of training go by. The mind and the psyche are like that, too, I think. You figure something out, you get over an old wound, and that's good. But that isn't the end of the benefit—in unexpected ways, relationships improve, or difficult situations aren't as scary or confusing as they once seemed. Happiness grows; unevenly, and with setbacks, but it grows.

The other thing I have learned is that life is something like being in a batting cage. Whatever happens, the machine pitches you another ball. I've found that if you fail in a situation, it will come around again—and again—until finally you get the hang of it and learn to manage a little better.

I feel very lucky not to have died young. I am such a slow learner about how to live a good life that I've needed all seventy years of trial and (lots of) error to shape one that fits the person I have turned out to be. I even turned out to be lucky in love; at seventy, I became engaged to a fellow runner, a thoroughly kind, charming, and handsome widower to whom I am now happily married. (So much better late than never!)

The years of contorting myself to fit the rigid bed of Procrustes took their toll. But I broke away from the seductive and crippling environment of privilege and dread in which I grew up. I have connected with a world that feels alive and real, have failed and succeeded, had adventures, made mistakes, spoken my mind, loved and been loved—with more intensity and passion than I had any right to expect.

And I'm not done yet.